The **Big Book** *of*
Farm
Tractors

The Complete History of the
American Tractor 1855 to Present
. . . Plus Brochures and Collectibles

Text by Robert N. Pripps
Photography by Andrew Morland

Japonica Press

Edited by Michael Dregni
Designed by Andrea Rud
Printed in Hong Kong

ISBN 0 9533737 8 9

A catalogue record for this book is available from the British Library.

First published in the United Kingdom in 2001 by
Japonica Press
Low Green Farm
Hutton
Driffield
East Yorkshire
YO25 9PX

First published in the United States in 2001 by Voyageur Press, Inc., Stillwater, MN 55082 U.S.A.

On the endsheets: *A threshing crew poses proudly with its Rumely OilPull kerosene tractor and separator. (Glenbow Archives)*

On the title pages: *The VAO orchard version of the popular Case VA Series was built from 1942 to 1955; this is a 1947 model.*

Inset on the title pages: *A 1920s advertising painting of a Wallis Model K, sold by the J. I. Case Plow Works.*

Acknowledgements

This is primarily a picture book. My thanks to Andrew Morland for these excellent photos.

There were many who pushed, washed, started, moved, and struggled with their antiques so that Andrew Morland could get the photos that grace the following pages. They also provided reams of data and historical details. I won't list them here for fear of missing and offending someone.

I will list several, however, who went way out of their way to help us, often giving us a meal or two, as well as days out of their otherwise busy schedules: Les Abraham, Heritage Hall Museum, Owatonna, Minnesota; Tom Armstrong, N-Complete Remanufactured Ford Tractors; Glen Braun; Keith Bruder; Alan Buckert; Gary Burkey; Karen Chabal; Ed Claessen; Milan Duchaj; Great Dorset Steam Fair, Dorset, Great Britain; Carl Halverson; the Rich Holicky family; Bill Karl; Ken Kass; the Walter Kellor family; Larry and Ryan Maasdam; Midwest Old Threshers; Lennis Moore; the Eldon Oleson family; Ken and Dan Peterman; David Pruehs; Gary and Marlin Spitznogel; Frank Sticha; Mike Thorne; Wayne Timm; Steve Tolander; Billie Turley; and the Vouk family. My thanks to all.

Robert N. Pripps
Springstead, Wisconsin

1927 Huber 25/50
The 25/50 was a big tractor in any language, weighing 5 tons (4,500 kg). It was produced by the Huber Manufacturing Company of Marion, Ohio, from 1927 to 1941. After it was tested in 1927 by the University of Nebraska, subsequent production versions were labeled 40/62. The tractor featured a Sterns four-cylinder engine and two-speed transmission. Owner: the Timm family.

Contents

1907 Minneapolis 45

1919 Holt 10-Ton

1919 Wallis Model K

Introduction   9
Prologue   10

Chapter 1   The Steam Era, 1855–1920   13
    The Evolution of Steam Power   *14*
    The Romance of Steam   *24*

Chapter 2   The Genesis of the Gasoline Tractor, 1889–1920   29
    The Age of Invention   *30*
    The Age of Consolidation   *42*

Chapter 3   The Debut of the Lightweight Tractor, 1913–1935   61
    The Age of the Lightweights   *62*
    Doodlebugs, Jitterbugs, and Puddle Jumpers: Home-Brewed Iron Horses   *73*
    The Decade of the Fordson, 1918–1928   *76*
    The Minneapolis Ford Tractor and the Nebraska Tractor Tests   *84*
    The Great 1920s Tractor Price War   *86*
    Orphan Tractors: The First Industry Debacle   *88*
    Farewell to the Horse, Hello to the Farmall   *98*
    Those New-Fangled Rubber Tires   *104*

Chapter 4   Farm Crawlers, 1900–1960   109
    Caterpillars, Crawlers, and Tracklayers   *110*
    Holt, Best, and Caterpillar: The Industry Standard   *112*
    Cletrac-Oliver: "Geared to the Ground"   *120*
    Monarch and Allis-Chalmers: Persian Orange Crawlers   *124*
    Orphan Crawlers   *130*

1929 Minneapolis 27/42   *1938 Minneapolis-Moline UDLX*   *1999 Case-IH Steiger 9330*

Chapter 5   The Classic Years, 1935–1960   135

    The Best of Times and the Worst of Times   *136*

    Streamlined Styling Comes to the Farmyard   *146*

    Hydraulic Power: A Revolution in Utility   *154*

    Orchard Tractors: Streamlined Form and Function   *166*

    The Fuel Revolution: From Diesel to "Greased Air"   *168*

    Orphan Tractors: The Second Industry Debacle   *177*

    High-Clearance Tractors: Standing Tall   *180*

    The Evolution of Live PTO and Hydraulics   *184*

    Tractors of Many Colors   *191*

    Ford's World Tractor   *202*

    The End of the Reign of Johnny Popper   *204*

    Classic Tractor Replicas: A Labor of Love   *207*

    Hot-Rodded Farm Tractors   *208*

    The Development of Articulated Four-Wheel-Drive Tractors   *212*

Chapter 6   The Modern Era, 1960–Present   217

    Where Have All The Tractors Gone?   *218*

    The 100-Plus Horsepower Magic   *223*

    Factory Cabs: Comfort Comes to the Tractor   *228*

    Transmissions: The Ratio Race   *230*

    Technology Left Behind   *232*

    The Proliferation of Articulated Four-Wheel-Drive Tractors   *233*

    AGCO: A Proud Heritage   *240*

    CNH Global NV: A Conglomerate Rich With History   *246*

    Deere and Caterpillar: Steering the Straight Course   *249*

Index   253

Introduction

For three weeks in June 1999, we toured the American Midwest, getting words and pictures for *The Big Book of Farm Tractors*. We avoided freeways and chose the country roads—the blue highways on our map. Likewise, this book is not the usual straight history with chapters about each brand, but is instead a meander through the backroads of power farming from the early days to the modern era.

This journey begins with the great steam engines before the American Civil War. It then travels through the tentative beginnings of the internal-combustion era, through two world wars and the Great Depression, and on into the era of the diesel engine. There are peaks and valleys, ups and downs in the industry. We will see most of the big names disappear along the way. We will also see perseverance and ingenuity pay off in a big way for some.

This admittedly is history painted with a broad brush. It was our goal, however, to get into the personal side of the history of tractors and how the tractor fit into and influenced the life and times of the farm during the past 150 years. This is the story of people, both on the farms and in the great industries. Vignettes, quotes, timelines, and sidebars will help to fill in the gaps and indicate to the reader what else was going on in the country at the same time.

The practice of agriculture changed little from the beginning of time to the early nineteenth century. Then, changes came rapidly. Those of you who are, or were, farmers will probably see yourselves in the following pages. Hopefully, those readers with no connection to actual farming will gain a new perspective of the wrenching changes that have taken place on the farm over the years. In either case, we hope you'll enjoy this trip through power-farming history.

Robert N. Pripps
Andrew Morland

1934 Caterpillar Diesel Forty
The Diesel Forty was an upgraded version of the Diesel Thirty-Five, which was sold in 1933 and 1934. Tested by the University of Nebraska in 1935, the Diesel Forty tipped the scales at 15,642 pounds (7,039 kg). Owner: Alan Smith.

1938 Minneapolis-Moline UDLX
Only about 150 of the stylish, but not truly practical, Model U-Deluxe tractors were made by the Minneapolis-Moline Company of Minneapolis, in the years 1938 through 1941. Today they are among the most desirable and sought after of all vintage tractors.

Prologue

"It all began on a midsummer day in 1831 near Steel's Tavern, Virginia. The stillness of the countryside was about to be broken by a public demonstration that would mark the beginning of a new epoch in agricultural invention. The small crowd of bystanders was curious and skeptical, but as Cyrus H. McCormick's new creation moved down the field the wheat fell in a steady stream upon its platform. The whirling gears of the mechanical reaper soon would be a familiar sound in the American harvest field."
—Marvin McKinley,
Wheels of Farm Progress, 1980

Cyrus Hall McCormick had no idea of the changes he was unleashing on that midsummer day in 1831, either for himself or for agriculture. In fact, he thought of his "reaper" as a possible labor-saving device for his own farm only.

Prior to McCormick's reaper, the handheld cradle scythe was the tool for grain cutting. Scything was extremely difficult and skilled work, and five acres (2 hectares) of cut grain per person per day was the accepted rate. A cradler was a specialist, commanding as much as three times the daily pay rate of other farmhands. With McCormick's reaper, a farmer and a horse could harvest ten acres (4 hectares) per day, although separate farmhands to serve as rakers, bundlers, and shockers were still needed.

It wasn't until Obed Hussey of Baltimore, Maryland, applied for a patent on his own reaper invention in 1833 that McCormick recognized the implications and applied for his own patent. Citing prior art, McCormick challenged Hussey in the courts and in the fields of North America. McCormick's reaper was the first of a series of mechanical revolutions in the farm fields of the 1800s that led the way for the farm tractor, inventions that had a profound impact on not only agriculture but on our culture as a whole.

John F. Appleby's amazing Appleby Automatic Knotter of 1875 revolutionized the grain reaper, turning it into the labor-efficient binder and suddenly saving thousands of man-hours per harvest. The binder, cut the grain, sheaved it, and tied it with a cord still known today as "binder twine." The tied sheaves were deposited in the field, ready for shocking. The binder was the first mechanically complicated machine that confronted the farmer, who had to learn to use it, or else!

The rapid increase in acreage harvested per individual worker brought on by McCormick and

1860s Fearless thresher and power advertisement
Small firms throughout North America built a variety of separators, including the Fearless thresher made by the Empire Agricultural Works of Cobleskill, New York. Power, in the days before the widespread use of the steam engine, came from true horse power. The Fearless power unit was a tread machine for a two-horse team that fed power through a governor to a belt drive.

Appleby's inventions mothered the next big step—the threshing machine, or separator. Previously, threshing had been done with a flail, which was also skilled work similar to scything grain. A good flail thresher could only process about seven bushels of wheat in a long day. Now, the threshing process had to be mechanized to keep up with the harvesting work done by the binder.

The Jacob Pope's Groundhog thresher was the first on the North American scene, in 1802. Since it was invented before the reaper, its purpose was not necessarily to speed up the process, but to improve efficiency over the flail. Nevertheless, the hand-cranked Groundhog bore the elements of subsequent high-volume machines.

Pope's Groundhog only dehulled the grain, however. In 1837, Hiram A. Pitts created his Buffalo Pitts thresher and cleaner that included a fanning mill

McCormick harvester at work, 1831

Hat's were raised to the successful first demonstration of Cyrus Hall McCormick's harvester on a mid-summer day in 1831. The McCormick harvester became the foundation of the massive and supremely influential International Harvester Company of Chicago.

and walker to blow out chaff and carry out straw. The Buffalo Pitts machine required more power to operate, however. So, a horse tread was added to give one, two, or three "horsepower." When still more power was needed, horse sweeps came into being with as many as eighteen horses. With such a rig, a threshing rate of fifty to sixty bushels an hour was possible.

By the time of the American Civil War, the threshing machine had developed into mature technology. It was then made of wood, which required fine craftsmanship in its construction. It still lacked the feeders and straw stackers that would be added in the last half of the 1800s. What was needed now was steady, untiring power; the more power, the wider the threshing mechanism that could be accommodated.

And that's where the steam engine enters the North American farm scene.

1880s McCormick binder advertisement

The addition of the twine-binding mechanism as created by John F. Appleby suddenly revolutionized harvesting and reduced the amount of workers needed to cut wheat and other crops.

CHAPTER 1

The Steam Era, 1855–1920

"I foresee the successful application of steam power to farm work."
—Abraham Lincoln,
speech at the Wisconsin State Fair, 1859

1900s Nichols & Shepard 20/70

Main photo: *Running on full throttle, steam fills the air and the belt purrs on this Nichols & Shepard 20/70. Known as the famous Red River line, Nichols & Shepard's steam engines and threshers were made in Battle Creek, Michigan.*

Keck-Gonnerman trademark

Above: *The trademark on a Keck-Gonnerman steam engine shows the home of a prosperous thresherman. Keck-Gonnerman of Mt. Vernon, Indiana, began business in 1873, making steamers, threshers, and sawmills. The firm went into gas tractors in 1917 and went out of business after World War II.*

The Evolution of Steam Power

STILLWATER ENGINE.

1880s Stillwater engine

In the early days of steam, engines were typically known as "thresher engines" as they were designed simply to power threshing machines. The first steamers were basically stationary engines on wheels and were pulled into place by a horse team. This later Stillwater steamer was self propelled, with the front wheels steered by chain. It was built by the venerable Northwest Thresher Company of Stillwater, Minnesota.

Timeline

1850: California becomes a state

1851: The sewing machine is invented simultaneously by Singer, Howe, and Hunt

1852: The first successful airship is flown by Henri Giffard of France

1861: Abraham Lincoln becomes U.S. President

1861–1865: American Civil War

1862: The Homestead Act gives 160 acres to American frontier settlers

1863: Lincoln delivers the Gettysburg Address

1876: Alexander Graham Bell invents the telephone

1877: Thomas Alva Edison invents the phonograph

1879: Edison invents the incandescent light

1903: Ford Motor Company established

1914: World War I begins

1917: Communists take over Russia

1920: U.S. women win the right to vote

Confining the vapors of boiling water causes a dramatic buildup of pressure. Expanding these vapors through pistons and cylinders, turbines, or even jets results in the potential for useful work to be done.

Hero of Alexandria, Egypt, born about 130 B.C., was the first to recognize the ability of heated air or water to perform tasks. His "air engine" used air pressure generated by heating air in a closed container to force water from one jar into another. As the second jar filled and became heavier, it pulled open temple doors through a series of ropes and pulleys. When the fire went out, the water siphoned back, allowing a counterweight to close the doors. Naturally, the fire that activated the temple doors was the fire on the altar.

Hero's "Aeolipile" steam engine was also the first known reaction, or jet, engine. This steam engine did no practical work but was made to demonstrate a principle. It consisted of a sphere into which steam was fed through hollow support tubes. The steam escaped through two bent tubes on opposite sides of the sphere. Reaction to the escaping steam's force caused the sphere to rotate.

In the subsequent years, many attempts were made to harness the force of steam by means of a piston in a cylinder. Low-pressure steam was used because the materials available would not tolerate higher pressures. A pressure of only 1 pound per square inch (psi) above atmospheric was used by Englishman Thomas Newcomen in a steam-powered mine pump in 1712. The engine consisted of a vertical brass cylinder and piston, with the top of the cylinder open to the air. Steam from a boiler was fed into the cylinder under the piston and was then cooled and condensed back to liquid by injecting cold water into the cylinder. As the steam condensed, it occupied less space and a vacuum was created beneath the piston. Atmospheric pressure then acting on the piston forced the piston down on its power stroke. The piston was connected to a rocking beam; the beam's other end operated a mine-water lift pump. The pump mechanism's weight pulled the piston back to the top of the cylinder for another cycle. The engine, which had automatic control valves, could make eight or ten strokes per minute.

Scottish inventor James Watt developed the basic Newcomen engine into a more efficient concept. Patented in 1769, his engine employed a separate condensing chamber into which the steam was discharged and converted back to water. Rather than injecting cold water into the cylinder, the cooling was done in the remote condenser, saving three-fourths of fuel costs.

Watt later devised the first crankshaft and flywheel. This allowed the steam piston, with its linear motion, to produce continuous rotary motion. Watt's contributions also included valve gearing, double-acting pistons, throttle controls, and the governor. Watt is frequently referred to as the inventor of the steam engine because these elements made it a practical device.

While Watt's engines employed steam or flywheel power to return the piston for the next power stroke, the power was still applied by atmospheric pressure pushing the piston into a vacuum created by condensing steam. Engines with up to 76-inch-diameter (190-cm) pistons were common. Later, Watt used steam pressure, just above atmospheric pressure, for the power stroke; metallurgy of the mid-eighteenth century was not sufficiently advanced to handle much higher pressures with safety. Also, the building of accurate cylinders was a problem. In about 1762, pioneer iron foundryman John Wilkinson invented a boring machine capable of making the cylinders that Watt needed: Watt once commented that a Wilkinson cylinder was out of round by only 0.375 inches (9.375 mm).

Watt's associate, William Murdock, built a crude rail locomotive on the principles of Watt's patents in 1784, but the first practical rail locomotive was built in 1804 by Englishman Richard Trevithick. Trevithick was the first to employ high-pressure steam, using about twice atmospheric pressure at first. American inventor Oliver Evans collaborated with Trevithick in his experiments, eventually operating an engine at 200 psi. The Trevithick engine had four, smooth driving wheels running on smooth rails, proving that sufficient traction could thus be obtained. An important concept in the Trevithick engine was that the exhausted steam was not condensed, but was released into the smokestack, providing forced firebox draft. This design has been used in virtually all subsequent steam engines and provides the characteristic *chuff-chuff* or *choo-choo* sound.

Railroads were a boom industry in the mid-nineteenth century. The newly created Janney safety car coupling and Westinghouse air brake linked trains together and allowed them to brake. By 1848, there were 6,000 miles (9,600 km) of tracks in North America with 2,000 miles (3,200 km) added annually.

The farm steam engine was a result of progress made in railroad engines. With the development of the thresher, the horse became insufficient as a power source. Hence, it was mostly the thresher manufacturers that began building portable steam engines for the farm: A. M. Archambault & Company of Philadelphia in 1849; Hoard & Bradford of Watertown, New York, in 1850; Gaar, Scott & Company of Richmond, Indiana, in 1852; M. Rumely Company of La Porte, Indiana, in 1863; and J. I. Case Threshing Machine Company of Racine, Wisconsin, in 1869. Most of these companies either built threshers based on patent rights purchased from Pitts, or of their own design.

1912 Reeves Canadian Special 32/120
The Reeves Company was founded in Columbus, Indiana, in 1874. It was taken over by the Emerson-Brantingham Implement Company in 1912 and moved to Rockford, Illinois, shortly thereafter. The old Reeves plant in Columbus later became the home of diesel engine builder Cummins.

Russell steamer, 1890s
A custom threshing crew stands proudly before its Russell steam engine and separator on their way to thresh grain in Modoc County, California. The Russell was built by Russell & Company of Massillon, Ohio.

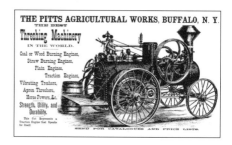

1880s Pitts steamer advertisement
The famed Pitts Agricultural Works of Buffalo, New York, offered a variety of steam engines that could be fueled by coal, wood, or straw.

In California, the Daniel Best Agricultural Works of San Leandro, California, built its traveling combined harvester powered by as many as forty horses, with ground wheels driving the threshing and separating mechanisms. Almost anything could spook such a menagerie into an uncontrollable runaway. The ground-wheel power would then drive the mechanisms to destruction. Best sold his first steam tractor in 1889. It was followed—literally—by a steam-powered combine that same year. Steam from the engine was piped back through a high-pressure hose to power the combine mechanisms.

With the advent of steam power on the farm, horse-powered treadmills and rotary sweeps began to disappear from the scene. Steam, the first non-animal farm power source, was taking over—although there was much resistance to the change at first on the part of the farmer.

Farms in the late 1800s were much smaller on average than what is now considered a normal size; some families subsisted on as few as ten acres (4 ha), cleared. In those days, farming was mostly a self-sufficient occupation. Besides staples like wheat, corn, potatoes, and hay, sheep were raised for meat and wool, cows for milk products and meat, chickens for eggs and meat. Most farms featured fruit trees and a large vegetable garden. In the north, maple trees were tapped for syrup and sugar. Hunting, fishing, and trapping provided food and skins. The women canned, spun, sewed, baked, churned, and made candles and soap. Excess crops were sold to get the few necessities of life not produced on the farm. Naturally, a farmer would not want to risk thousands of dollars on a machine that could only be used at threshing time. And if it failed, where would the horsepower come from?

1907 Minneapolis 45
Left, both photos: *The Minneapolis Threshing Machine Company of Minneapolis, made steam engines from 1890 through 1924 that were single-cylinder, single-tandem-compound, and double-tandem-compound. This 45-hp, single-tandem-compound engine was only built in 1907, and this is one of just seven made. Steam exhausted from the 10.25-inch (25.625-cm) high-pressure cylinder to be utilized again in the 15-inch (37.50-cm) low-pressure cylinder. The stroke was 12 inches (30 cm). Owner: Norman Pross.*

16

Case
J. I. Case Threshing Machine Company
of Racine, Wisconsin

Jerome Increase Case's company built many of the most significant farm engines of the steam era. Case began experimenting with steam in the early 1860s after its Sweepstakes threshing machine was introduced. The Sweepstakes utilized horse-powers driven by as many as eighteen horses. About the same time, Case began using steam factory power.

The first Case-produced steam engine, called "Old No. 1," made its debut in 1869. It was not self-propelled, but pulled to the job by a team of horses. Once belted up, it produced about 8 hp.

Between 1869 and 1880, various inventions were devised for steering and propulsion of steamers. C. and G. Cooper of Mt. Vernon, Ohio, invented a bevel-gear set that could be added to most any portable engine for propulsion. Steering was still done by the team of horses, however.

Case added propulsion to its engines in 1878, but retained horse steering. Case's drive incorporated a ratchet-type differential. A 10-hp engine was added to the line that same year, with the same type of propulsion.

In 1880, Jessee Walrath was made manufacturing superintendent of Case. In those days in many factories, the person with that title had the responsibility for new designs and improvements. Walrath contributed mightily to the development of Case engines over the next sixteen years, his inventions including the straw-burner chute, the best steering mechanism in the industry, a full spur-gear differential, and a friction clutch. Models were offered over the years with side and center cranks, direct and reverse flues, chain and gear drives.

Case steamer and plow, 1900s
A plowing crew rests while breaking the prairie sod with their Case steamer.
(Glenbow Archives)

In 1887, Walrath devised a totally enclosed double cylinder featuring a rocker valve. This type of cylinder became known simply as the "Walrath." Use of the Walrath reduced the weight of a 12-hp engine by almost 3,000 pounds (1,350 kg).

George Morris became superintendent in 1897 when Walrath resigned. Morris also made continuous improvements in the engines over the years. He is most famous for putting springs between the boiler and wheels, allowing lighter engines, as the springs isolated the boiler from stresses and shocks when traveling on the roads. The unique and patented feature allowed the gears to stay in proper mesh while the drive axle moved up and down on the springs. By 1900, Case engines were outselling all competition.

As experience was gained and engine design matured, Case began experimenting with larger engines. In 1904, Case offered a 150-hp behemoth weighing 40,000 pounds (18,000 kg) that was obviously too big for field use. A few were built in the following years for road use before the design was abandoned.

Of greater importance was the famous Case 110, possibly the best and most popular steamer of the period. The Case 110 took more gold medals at the famed trials in Winnipeg, Manitoba, Canada, than any other engine.

In 1912, Case's steam engine production peaked at 2,250. After that, production diminished more rapidly than it had risen. By 1915, production dropped to 950 engines, and by 1920, only 346 were built. Production ceased in 1926 after fifty-seven years. Interestingly, the last engine built was a portable, like Case's Old No. 1.

1890s Case advertisement
"There are no others!" shouted this advertisement for Case's new spring-mounted steam engine.

1890s Case steamer advertisement

Right: *A colorful advertisement for Case's steam engines "for farmers, contractors and municipalities."*

1913 Case 110

Below: *A 110-hp Case steamer blows out a plume of smoke as it pulls a twelve-bottom gang plow at a modern-day tractor show. The 110-hp boasted a 12x12-inch (300x300-mm), "simple-cylinder" engine. It weighed an amazing 18 tons (16,200 kg), complete with the fancy locomotive-style cab. Owners: Jim Briden and Norman Pross.*

Case steamer, 1941

Above, top: *Many Case steamers were still going strong decades after the company halted production. This steam engine was still at work in Montgomery, Minnesota, in 1941.*

1913 Case 80

Above, bottom: *This 80-hp Case utilized an 11x11-inch (275x275-mm), "simple-cylinder" engine and up to 150 psi of steam pressure.*

1917 Case 80

Above: *The Vouk family of St. Stephen, Minnesota, has owned this 1917 Case steamer since new. It was bought new by grandfather Frank Vouk when he was nineteen years old. He was a horse trader, sawmill operator, and custom thresherman, and put the Case to good use over the decades.*

1913 Case 110 logo

Right: *Case used this trademark transfer on its steam engines in 1913. It showed the Case factory on the Racine River in Racine, Wisconsin. At each end of the transfer are "Old Abe" eagles perched on globes, signifying the worldwide scope of Case by that time.*

PLOWING AND HARVESTING BY STEAM
A SUCCESS.

Daniel Best Agricultural Works,
SAN LEANDRO, CAL.

1890s Daniel Best steamer advertisement

"A Revolution in Plowing," promised this ad. Labeling its machines "The Monarch of the Field," Daniel Best stated that his steamers "will do the work of 100 horses."

Holt steamer, 1900s

A Holt steamer hauls a train of three wagons laden with massive loads of cut boards from a sawmill in the Pacific Northwest. Ben Holt and his Holt Manufacturing Company of Stockton, California, followed the lead of arch-rival Daniel Best in building a steam traction engine. Both firms initially built their steamers to power their own separate advanced combined harvesters. (Eastman Collection, University of California–Davis)

Best
Daniel Best Agricultural Works of San Leandro, California

Daniel Best was born in Ohio in 1838. His family moved to Keokuk, Iowa, from where Daniel, then twenty-one, left for Oregon. After several years in the sawmill business in Oregon and Washington, he moved to California where he had three brothers farming large wheat ranches. While assisting his brothers harvest wheat, Daniel came up with the idea of a portable grain cleaner. Previously, the grain was hauled to a cleaning establishment, which was not only time consuming but also expensive. The following winter, he made three of his cleaning machines, which could be moved from farm to farm. The next fall, he and his brothers ran these machines for other farmers.

This was the start of a firm called Best Manufacturing Company. Cleaners were manufactured at first, but Daniel Best soon had developed a header-thresher-cleaner machine called a combined harvester. In fall 1886, he sold six of these to neighboring farmers. To power the combined harvester, or "combine" as they came to be called, a large team of draft animals was required.

An acquaintance of Best's from his Oregon days named Marquis DeLafayette Remington had patented a steam traction engine in 1888. The engine was unique in that it used a vertical boiler set far to the rear between the large drive wheels. A single front wheel was steered by steam power steering. The boiler arrangement reduced stresses on the pressurized components when traversing rough ground and made the machine lighter than others of its time. Remington's engine was designed primarily for traction work, with belt work a secondary consideration. Several of his engines were employed in the big western logging operations, where the Remington steamer was probably the first traction engine to be used to skid the giant logs.

Unfortunately, Remington's factory was nearly destroyed by a disastrous fire. To get cash to rebuild, he drove his remaining engine to Best's operation. After a brief demonstration, Best bought the patent rights to the engine for all but Oregon.

Best then set to work improving and enlarging the engine and integrating it with his combine. A steam hose from the engine provided power to operate the cutter, thresher, and cleaning mechanisms. It also powered a conveyor belt that brought straw forward to be used for fuel. Thus, the rig provided its own fuel as it went along.

The Best steamer was a great success with the large-acreage farmers of California, but the Best steamer still found most of its work in logging. By 1900, Best was turning out about twenty engines per year, some of which were being shipped to the far reaches of the globe.

Daniel Best steamer, 1894

Lumberjacks pause while hauling a gigantic load of monstrous logs behind their Daniel Best steamer. Best made fine use of his own name in advertising his machines as "The Best." Best's steamers burst onto the logging scene in the Pacific Northwest in the 1890s, revolutionizing the industry. In creating his steamer, Best bought the rights to the steam engine of DeLafayette Remington of Woodburn, Oregon, improved on the design, and went into production in 1889. The Remington was designed for use in the woods; the Best engines were suitable for logging as well as for farm use. (Eastman Collection, University of California–Davis)

The Romance of Steam

"A good steam engineer should be sober, industrious, careful, and faithful to his charge."
—Case's *Young Engineer's Guide* steam-engine instruction book, 1900s

1900s Lion steamer
Above: *Threshing machines and steam engines of the Canadian Waterloo Manufacturing Company were sold as the Lion brand from 1850 to 1925. This trademark transfer graced a 16-hp engine. Owner: Ontario Agricultural Museum.*

To many a young farm boy or girl, the traveling steam engineer was the icon of achievement. The grease-covered, tobacco-chewing, well-traveled boss of the crew held the highest fascination for the rural lad or lass, who had probably not been more than twenty miles from his or her birthplace, nor handled more power than a two-horse team. To be asked by the engineer to fetch something could make a day.

The steam engineer held the place the test pilot or the astronaut does today, but was much more accessible. Auto magnate Henry Ford stated in his 1922 autobiography, "The greatest experience of my young life was encountering a steam engine on the road to Detroit. I was off the wagon and talking to the engineer before my father knew what I was up to. It was that engine that took me into automotive transportation." Ford later became a steam-engine expert, having the job of field service man for G. Westinghouse & Company of Schenectady, New York, and later being the chief engineer for the Edison Illuminating Company in Detroit, Michigan.

Being a steam engineer was a tough, dangerous job. Early engines were made from uncertain metal—metal that could have dangerous weak spots. Construction methods in the early days were also lacking. Rivets could pop, castings could be porous, and the steam vessel might rupture. The engineer was also blamed for horse runaways, bridge collapses, and fires. Mechanical breakdowns required the utmost in ingenuity as parts had to be hand forged in many instances. Dirty water caused problems of foaming, which tended to

1913 Case 110
Below: *"Let 'er smoke!" A 110-hp Case steam engine leans into the traces pulling a twelve-bottom gang plow at the annual Rollag, Minnesota, show.*

carry water into the cylinder. Too much water in the cylinder could result in cylinder breakage. Other impurities in the water coated the heat-transfer surfaces. Suitable fuel was also a continuous problem. Coal was the best, but seldom available. Various kinds of wood did well, but a source close to the job was necessary. Eventually, on the Great Plains, straw was the fuel of choice, but it worked best in engines designed for that fuel.

During their heyday, there were as many as 75,000 custom-thresher engineers. They followed the harvest from south to north. Sacrificing a normal home life, they mostly slept outside under the machines. They returned year after year, lured not by financial reward, but by their love of machinery, the satisfaction of a job well done, the excellent food served by the farm women, and by the high esteem of the farm lads.

Steam power also seemed to have an almost mystical charm for those associated with it—and still does today. When thus infected, a train whistling for a distant grade crossing could not be ignored, nor could the chuckling sound of a steam engine operating a thresher or a sawmill. Old-timers would try to explain their fascination to the younger generation, but explanation was either unnecessary or ineffective: You either had the steam bug, or you were immune.

1918 Sawyer-Massey 76

The Sawyer-Massey Company of Hamilton, Ontario, was one of Canada's leading builders of threshers and steam engines. It all began from a humble blacksmith shop started by John Fisher in 1835. In 1840, a relative, L. D. Sawyer, bought into the fledgling firm, and they began building threshing machines. When Fisher died, the name of the firm was changed to the L. D. Sawyer Company. In 1892, Hart Massey, of Massey-Harris fame, bought a 40 percent interest, and the name was changed to Sawyer-Massey. The Massey family withdrew in 1910, however, but the name continued. Owner: Ontario Ministry of Agriculture and Food.

Wood Brothers
Wood Brothers Inc. of Des Moines, Iowa

1914 Wood Brothers 30
Wood Brothers's 30-hp "double-geared" steamer of 1914 was novel in providing geared engine power to each rear wheel, resulting in steady, balanced pull. Most steam engines of the day were single geared.

F. J. Wood and his brother, R. L., founded the Wood Brothers Thresher Company in Rushford, Minnesota, in 1893. In 1899, they moved their operations to Des Moines, Iowa, where the firm was renamed Wood Brothers Inc. F. J. Wood remained head of the company until he retired in 1945. Shortly thereafter, Henry Ford bought the company.

An inveterate inventor, F. J. Wood conceived of a double-geared, 30-hp traction engine with a center crank, which debuted in 1915. The dual power paths to the drive wheels lessened the strain on each gear. Highly stressed gears were submerged in oil, and other components were designed for durability when plowing.

This 30-hp engine was the largest made by the Wood Brothers. Others followed in the 20- to 25-hp range.

Avery
Avery Company of Peoria, Illinois

Brothers Robert and Cyrus Avery founded the Avery Company in 1874 in Galesburg, Illinois. After ten years in the corn-planter business, they moved their operation to Peoria, Illinois. They built their first steam traction engine in 1891. It was a single-cylinder, straight-flue machine with a robust boiler, allowing higher pressures than the competition. Avery also branched out into the thresher-manufacturing business at that time.

John Bartholomew, a relative of the brothers, became company vice-president in 1893. After the Avery brothers died, Bartholomew, who had been with the company since he was fifteen, became president. He was an energetic man with talents both in mechanical things and in finances. Bartholomew moved Avery into building gasoline tractors, including an unsuccessful attempt at a combination tractor-truck in 1909.

1912 Avery Undermounted 18
Avery's Undermounted was a two-cylinder, locomotive-type engine noted for smoothness and quietness. The firm built engines of this style with up to 50 hp; this engine was rated at 18 hp.

The crowning achievement of Bartholomew's presidency was the Avery Undermounted, which came out in 1903. The Undermounted was a locomotive-style steam traction engine with two cylinders mounted beneath the boiler. Tractors of 16, 18, 20, 30, 40, and 50 hp were built in this arrangement and were noted for their smoothness and quietness. Avery continued building the conventional single-cylinder type as well with power ranging from 12 to 50 hp.

In the early 1920s, Avery fell on hard times, becoming over-extended both in customer credit as well as in its attempts to compete in the gasoline tractor market. It was re-organized as the Avery Power Equipment Company in 1924. Bartholomew died in 1925, but the company did well until 1931 and the depths of the Great Depression. It was again revived and survived until 1941, building the famous Avery Ro-Trak gasoline tractor.

Advance-Rumely

Advance-Rumely Thresher Company of La Porte, Indiana

With the exception of Case, Advance-Rumely built more steam engines than any other firm.

The roots of the Advance-Rumely Thresher Company stretch back to German immigrant Meinrad Rumely's blacksmith shop, founded in La Porte, Indiana, in 1852. Rumely and his brother John began making threshers around 1854. By 1910, the Rumely Company, now in the hands of Dr. Edward Rumely, the grandson of one of its founders, began building the highly successful line of Rumely OilPull kerosene tractors.

Rumely went on to buy out numerous other firms over the years. It acquired the Advance Thresher Company of Battle Creek, Michigan, followed by Gaar, Scott & Co., and the Canadian firm of American-Abell Engine & Thresher Company of Toronto, Ontario. Soon after, the venerable Northwest Thresher Company of Stillwater, Minnesota, was also added. The company had grown too fast, however, and financial difficulties were insurmountable by 1915, when the whole was re-organized as the Advance-Rumely Thresher Company. In 1923, another great name came under the Advance-Rumely banner: the Aultman & Taylor Machinery Company of Mansfield, Ohio. The Advance-Rumely firm was taken over by the Allis-Chalmers Company of Milwaukee, Wisconsin, in 1931.

Rumely built a variety of steam engines over the years, including single- and cross-compound types. Power ranged from 12 to 35 hp under the old rating system, and up to 140 hp in the new system.

Gaar-Scott steamer, 1900s

"Built for the Pioneer Ranch, Macleod, Alberta," read the writing on the water tank of this Gaar-Scott steamer pulling gang plows to break the Canadian prairie. Gaar, Scott & Company of Richmond, Indiana, was founded in 1870 and acquired by Advance-Rumely in 1911. (Glenbow Archives)

1919 Advance-Rumely 22/65

Advance-Rumely built more than 12,000 steam engines. Originally founded in Canada, Advance was taken over by Rumely in 1911. This engine was built at Rumely's works in La Porte, Indiana. Owner: Kurt Umnus.

CHAPTER 2

The Genesis
of the
Gasoline Tractor, 1889–1920

"The infant gas tractor can stand the emergency endurance test where the horse and the mule fall down. He will pull all your tillage apparatus by moonlight as well as by daylight. If there is no moon all you have to do is to attach a searchlight."
—Barton W. Currie, *The Tractor*, 1916

1916 Avery 12/25
Main photo: *Built by the Avery Company of Peoria, Illinois, from 1912 to 1919, the 12/25 had a transverse two-cylinder, horizontally opposed engine with exhaust draft cooling.*

1919 Avery brochure
Above: *Avery promoted "Motor-Farming" as the way of the future.*

The Age of Invention

1889 Charter

Both photos: *John Charter's Charter Gas Engine Company of Sterling, Illinois, built what is considered the first internal-combustion-engine farm tractor in North America. The 10/20-hp Charter single-cylinder engine used liquid fuel rather than natural gas, as was typical of some earlier "gas" engines. Charter mounted his engine atop a typical Rumely steam-engine chassis. He built six machines in 1889 and shipped them to northwestern United States farmers.*

Timeline

1901: Radio signals span the
    Atlantic

1906: San Francisco earthquake
    and fire

1906: Alzheimer's disease
    identified

1907: Leo Baekeland patents
    the first plastic,
    known as Bakelite

1908: William Hoover invents
    the vacuum cleaner

1909: Radio broadcasts begin

1914: Panama Canal opens

1925: Scotch tape invented

At the dawn of the twentieth century, civilization was enjoying an explosion of technological advances akin to those at the turn of the twenty-first century. In the 1890s, many Americans had fought in the Civil War. They had then seen frontier log cabins and stumpy fields replaced by prosperous farms with frame houses and huge barns. Barely discernible wagon ruts across the prairies were replaced by railroads. In their lifetimes, the telephone, electric light, phonograph, and safety bicycle had been invented. But that was just the beginning. As the internal-combustion engine was developed, the automobile, tractor, and airplane followed.

The horseless carriage, as the automobile was first called in America, got off to a slow start. Automotive terms suggest French primacy—chauffeur, garage, chassis, sedan, and even Detroit, were French terms—and the automobile (another French word) really got going first in France. At the time of the Paris Exposition of 1900, cars were beginning to outnumber horses on Paris's Champs-Elysées. When Henry Ford founded his Ford Motor Company in 1903, the automobile was still considered a plaything for the rich. A good number of common people resented the rich in their noisy, smelly, horse-frightening automobiles. As Woodrow Wilson commented in 1907, "Nothing has spread socialistic feelings in this country more than the automobile, with its picture of arrogance and wealth."

There were two main obstacles to the acceptance of the automobile in the United States. One was price; the other was the lack of decent roads. Ford solved the first problem with his mass-produced Model T. The Good Roads Movement, founded in 1902 by the American Road Builders Association and the American Automobile Association, began to solve the other. What the Good Roads Movement needed was the tractor to power the implements of road building.

The early development of the gasoline tractor followed that of the steam engine. First, stationary engines were mounted to skids to make them portable. Then wheels were added, then a drive mechanism, and then a means of steering. Finally, a drawbar was forged, and the concept was complete.

The first such tractor was built by the Charter Gas Engine Company of Sterling, Illinois. Issued in 1889, John Charter's patent covered the use of liquid fuel, or gasoline. Prior to that, engines used everything from natural gas to coal dust for fuel. The need for lubricants in the machine age had brought forward the petroleum industry. When refining petroleum to make oil and grease, gasoline was a highly volatile byproduct that was distilled off. With the acceptance of gasoline as an engine fuel, both petroleum and engine companies flourished. Charter mounted his gasoline engine on Rumely steam-engine running gear and eventually sold six of these machines.

The first tractor able to propel itself both backwards and forwards was the 1892 Froelich. John Froelich of Froelich, Iowa, mounted a Van Duzen gasoline engine on a Robinson steam-engine frame and devised his own drive and steering systems. Froelich took his machine and his 40-inch (100-cm) Case thresher on a fifty-day threshing run. As he traveled from place to place, he pulled the thresher with the tractor. Once set up, he then powered the thresher by means of a flat belt from the engine's flywheel. In the fifty-day run, Froelich threshed some 72,000 bushels of small grain. Later, Froelich joined with venture capitalists to form the Waterloo Gasoline Traction Engine Company of Waterloo, Iowa. This company later built the famous Waterloo Boy tractor.

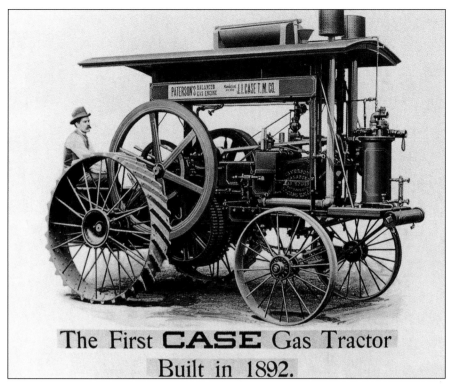

1892 Paterson-Case

Left: *Engineer William Paterson of Stockton, California, came to Case to build an experimental gas engine in the early 1890s. The "balanced" engine was a horizontal two-cylinder inline with water-jacketed combustion chambers. The Paterson was one of the first practical gasoline tractors, and it worked—but not well enough for it to enter production. The Paterson suffered from ignition and carburetion problems, the bane of all early gasoline engines. Undeterred, Paterson patented his engine design on October 30, 1894.*

1914 Townsend Model 30/60

The peculiar Townsend oil tractor was built on what was called a "boiler frame." Five different sizes of these steam engine–lookalikes were offered by Roy C. Townsend's Townsend Manufacturing Company of Janesville, Wisconsin. The Model 30/60 featured a two-cylinder, horizontal side-by-side engine that used oil for cooling. The "boiler" contained tubes around which air was circulated to cool the oil. Airflow was induced by the exhaust in the stack.

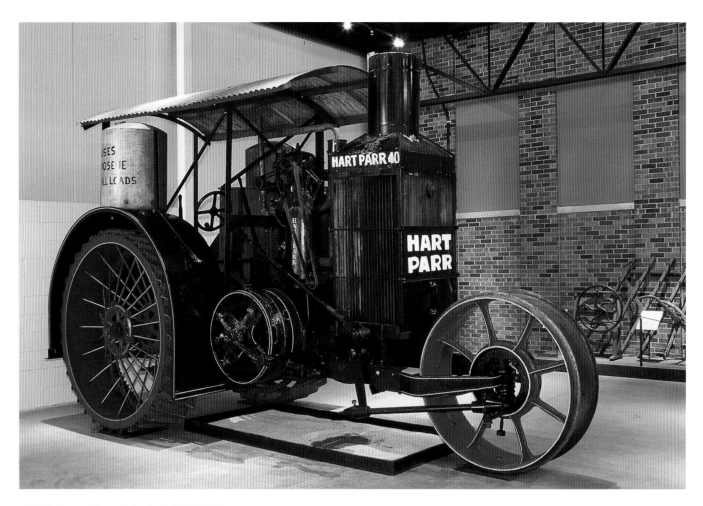

1914 Hart-Parr Model 40 20/40

This Hart-Parr 40 was on display at the Floyd County Historical Society's museum in Charles City, Iowa. This tractor was built in 1914, but others of the type were built from 1912 to 1914. The Model 40 was powered by a vertical, two-cylinder, oil-cooled engine rated at 400 rpm.

1910s Pioneer 30 advertisement

The Pioneer Tractor Manufacturing Company of Winona, Minnesota, began making tractors in 1910 with its Pioneer 30. "First in Gas Traction," promised this ad for the Pioneer's 7x8-inch (175x200-mm) four-cylinder, horizontally opposed engine. The drive wheels on the massive Pioneer 30 were 8 feet (240 cm) in diameter.

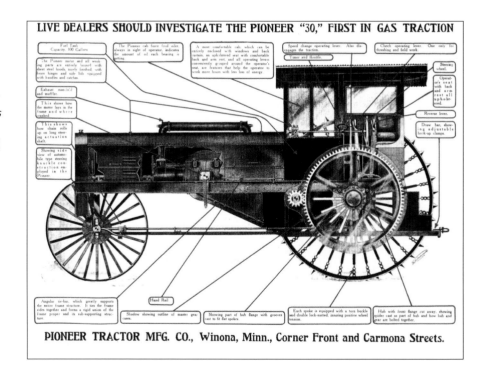

1910s Twin City Model 40

Minneapolis Steel & Machinery Company of Minneapolis was founded in 1902 to make steam engines and other agricultural equipment. MSM entered the gas-tractor business in 1911, naming its machines the Twin City line. Owner: the Vouk family.

Deere & Company of Moline, Illinois, purchased the firm in 1918, thereby jump-starting Deere into the tractor business.

In 1892, Case, well known for steam engines, also made an experimental gas-fueled tractor. This machine was based on an engine design proposed to Case by inventor William Paterson. Paterson had come to Case with a threshing-machine invention. In the course of trying to interest Case in that, he mentioned his idea for a two-cylinder "balanced" engine. Case President Stephen Bull said the firm had no interest in Paterson's threshing ideas, but was interested in the engine.

Case created a chassis design along the lines of its steamers and helped Paterson put his engine together. The Paterson engine had opposed pistons with a crankshaft on one side and linkage from the other side. Despite its complexity, the engine ran smoothly, but ignition and carburetor problems eventually spelled its demise. Case then wisely waited until 1912 to re-enter the gas-tractor business.

In 1897, Charles Hart and Charles Parr founded the Hart-Parr Gasoline Engine Company while they were both engineering students at the University of Wisconsin in Madison. When they had trouble raising capital for expansion, they moved their operations in 1900 to Charles City, Iowa, Hart's home-

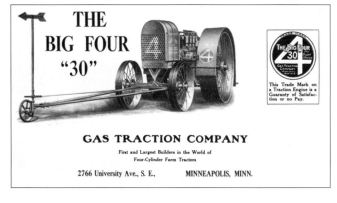

1910s Big Four 30 advertisement

The Big Four 30 from the Gas Traction Company of Minneapolis, was one of the most influential of the early gasoline tractors. The gigantic engine featured four cylinders with 4x5-inch (100x125-mm) bore and stroke. Big Four 30 machines were widely sold—especially by Deere & Company branch houses—and even more widely copied by other makers.

town. Since he and his family were well known there, local banks provided the cash necessary for the pair of youngsters to venture into the tractor business.

The duo built their first tractor, Hart-Parr No. 1, in 1901 and sold it in 1902. An improved version, Hart-Parr No. 2, was completed in 1903. Fifteen of the No. 2 were delivered that same year. By 1905, Hart and Parr had established the only business in America devoted exclusively to tractor manufacturing. Hart-Parr Sales Manager W. H. Williams was even credited with coining the word "tractor" in sales brochures in 1906; previously, these devices were called "traction engines." By 1907, one-third of the 600 tractors at work in the United States were Hart-Parrs.

In the first decade of the twentieth century, many of the firms that would have a significant influence on the future of power farming first appeared—including the Wallis Tractor Company of Racine, Wisconsin; Henry Ford & Son of Dearborn, Michigan; McCormick Harvesting Company of Chicago; Wm. Deering & Company of Chicago; Gas Traction Company of Minneapolis, maker of the Big Four tractor; and Minneapolis Steel & Machinery Company of Minneapolis, builder of the Twin City line. Tractors did not have a conventional configuration at this time, so many unusual arrangements of engines and drive systems were on the market. Some of the companies were solidly in the implement business, while others were following a single patent or idea. Ignition systems and carburetion were the big problems; external drive gearing also caused problems. The friction clutch, so common today, defied the ingenuity of designers of the day.

1917 Twin City advertisement
Left, top: *Minneapolis Steel & Machinery offered four sizes in its Twin City line, ranging from 15 to 60 hp.*

1910s Twin City Model 40
Left, both photos: *The Twin City Model 40 was powered by the company's own OHV four-cylinder motor of 1,590 ci (26,044 cc) rated in Nebraska tests at 40 drawbar and 65 belt hp. The tractor weighed more than 25,000 pounds (11,250 kg). The TC-40 was popular with custom thresherman and was built in Minneapolis from 1911 to 1924. The huge radiator on the nose held some 100 gallons (330 liters) of cooling water.*

1916 Russell Giant 30/60

Above: *A Russell Giant pulls a John Deere nine-bottom plow in a plowing contest. The Giant had a vertical four-cylinder engine and two-speed transmission. Russell had been a big player in the steam-engine business before it began making kerosene-burning tractors in 1911 in Massillon, Ohio. The company was founded in 1842 and survived until 1942.*

1913 Avery 40/65

Left: *Built by the Avery Company of Peoria, Illinois, the 40/80 four-cylinder model was a 22,000-pound (9,900-kg) behemoth. The 1,509-ci (24,717-cc) engine proved to be a little short of power on the belt, so the tractor was later rated as a 40/65. It had a production life from 1913 to 1920.*

Besides the technical problems, the automobile and gasoline tractor were causing social upheaval in both cities and rural areas. These were also times of social and political unrest. The Progressive Revolt began in 1896, with both agrarian and urban people fighting against the perceived takeover of the federal government by big business and railroads. The socialists were also gaining political influence among factory workers as Eugene Debs organized his Social Democratic Party in 1896. Most of the problems stemmed from the cities, where slums, crime, and poverty were rapidly spreading and where the exploitation of laborers, especially women and children, was rampant. Immigrants were at the mercy of big business and were also resented by the previous wave of immigrants. Banking empires, mostly unregulated, caused financial fluctuations with little regard for the human suffering they inflicted.

1918 Gray advertisement

1917 Gray 18/36

Above, both photos: *Gray tractors, built by the Gray Tractor Company of Minneapolis, featured a bizarre "wide drive drum" at the rear and a strange sheet metal cover. The drum was 70 inches (175 cm) wide and was designed to distribute the tractor's weight over a broad "footprint" in soft soil, a problem solved by other makers with crawler tracks. The Gray's power came from a 478-ci (7,830-cc) Waukesha four-cylinder motor. The Gray was built between 1914 and 1925. It was an outgrowth of the Knapp Farm Locomotive, which was first built in 1908 in Rochester, New York.*

1920 Hart-Parr 30A 15/30

Hart-Parr built its Type A from 1918 to 1924. It had a two-cylinder, side-by-side horizontal engine and two-speed transmission. The writing on the front of the tractor read "Hart-Parr Co., Founders of the Tractor Industry, Charles City, Iowa U.S.A." Owner: David Preuhs.

1910s Short Turn tractor

Tractors came in all shapes and sizes in the pioneering years of the 1910s and 1920s. The Short Turn 20/30 could turn around in an area its own length at the end of rows. It was the brainchild of inventor John Dahl and was built by the Short Turn Tractor Company in both Bemidji and Minneapolis, in 1916–1918.

1917 Kardell Four-In-One advertisement

The Kardell Tractor & Truck Company of St. Louis, Missouri, offered its innovative Four-In-One machine to serve the lucky owner as a motor plow, truck, tractor, and all-round farm power to operate threshers and other farm machinery. Rated as a 20/32-hp machine, the Four-In-One featured a radical clutch release that operated automatically if the plow hit something solid.

1925 Minneapolis 17/30 Type A

Right: *With its transverse four-cylinder engine, the 17/30 looked much the same as the 27/44, but was some 10 inches (25 cm) shorter and a ton (900 kg) lighter. It was built from 1920 to 1929. Owner: the Timm family.*

1929 Minneapolis 27/44

Below: *The 27/44 boasted two speeds forward, a transverse four-cylinder engine, and a weight of some 4 tons (3,600 kg). Owner: the Timm family.*

Froelich
Waterloo Gasoline Traction Engine Company of Waterloo, Iowa

John Froelich's tractor of 1892 was the first to propel itself both forwards and backwards. Since steam engines were reversible and able to run backwards, a reverse gear and clutch were not required. Simply installing and connecting a gasoline engine on a steamer chassis did not allow for backing up. With something the size and weight of the converted steamers, it is no wonder their market was limited and that the Froelich machine attracted attention.

Froelich used a monster of an engine manufactured by the Van Duzen Gasoline Engine Company of Cincinnati, Ohio, displacing 2,155 ci (35,299 cc) in its single cylinder. The engine was a "square" design with a 14.00x14.00-inch (350x350-mm) bore and stroke. It was mounted vertically to avoid lurching motion when in transit. Ignition came from a contact point and battery system, and it was equipped with a flyball governor that held open the exhaust valve when it ran over the desired speed.

The chassis was built mainly of wood with wheels and gearing from a Robinson steam engine. Froelich designed and built his own clutch and reverse-gear arrangement and steering system. Steering came from the machine's front platform by means of a linkbelt chain used to pivot the front axle. The chain was controlled from a steering wheel through a worm-and-sector gear. Levers were provided at the operator's station to control direction of travel, clutch, and throttle.

The tractor was successful in the hands of Froelich, but after he joined with financial backers to form the Waterloo Gasoline Traction Engine Company and tractors were delivered, many customers were so unhappy they returned the machines for a refund. To generate cash flow, the firm turned to making stationary engines, a venture in which they had a modicum of success. Froelich left the company, however, when the word "Traction" was dropped from the firm's title.

The Waterloo Gasoline Engine Company completed two other tractor designs in 1896 and 1897, but only one of each was built. The firm continued in the engine business until 1912. In 1906, the trademark "Waterloo Boy" was adopted for its engines, and the tractors that emerged from the factory after 1912 were also called Waterloo Boys. It was this company and the Waterloo Boy tractor that was acquired by Deere in 1918.

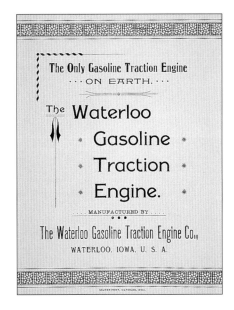

1890s Froelich brochure
The cover of the original Froelich brochure. Advertisements of the day touted the operator's visibility, since the platform was in front.

1892 Froelich replica
The first practical gas-engined tractor was built in 1892 by John Froelich. Twenty-six years later, it would evolve into the successful Deere tractor line. This replica was constructed by workers at Deere's Waterloo, Iowa, tractor works in 1937 to use in a documentary film. The Froelich replica was on display at Deere's Moline, Illinois, administration center.

1911 Hart-Parr 30/60 "Old Reliable"

Both photos: *The 30/60 was powered by a two-cylinder, horizontal side-by-side engine running at a constant 300 rpm. The "Old Reliable" used a dual jump-spark ignition from a low-tension magneto and a hit-and-miss governor, although the engine was started with dry-cell batteries. There were three tanks built into the 30/60: one for gasoline for starting, one for kerosene (the main fuel), and one for water for water injection. Engine exhaust was discharged into the cooling tower on the front to induce airflow through the radiators and out the chimney on top. This 30/60 is in original, unrestored condition. Owner: Ken Kass.*

Hart-Parr 30/60 "Old Reliable"
Hart-Parr Gasoline Engine Company of Charles City, Iowa

Although Hart-Parr built a full line of oil-cooled tractors between 1901 and 1918, it was the 30/60 "Old Reliable" that truly won the company renown. The 30/60 was introduced in 1907 and was the sixth design to be produced by the young firm.

The engine of the "Old Reliable" was a two-cylinder, horizontal side-by-side, kerosene-burner displacing 2,356 ci (38,591 cc) with a bore and stroke of 10.00x15.00 inches (250x375 mm) and rated at 300 rpm. A 1,000-pound (450-kg) flywheel helped smooth out the uneven firing caused by the pistons going in opposite directions and by the hit-and-miss governor.

Oil was used for cooling as it had a higher boiling temperature than water. Higher temperatures were required for successfully burning kerosene fuels, especially with the jump-spark ignition and low-tension magneto. The cooling-tower radiator was a hallmark of the Hart-Parr oil-cooled tractors for more than fifteen years. Hot oil from the engine was circulated through vertical tubes. Airflow was induced through the tubes and out the top of the tower by the jet-pump effect of the engine exhaust gases being injected in the tower chimney. This method had its roots in steam engines where exhausted steam was released in the smokestack to induce draft in the firebox.

The 30/60 weighed some 20,000 pounds (9,000 kg) and had one forward and one reverse gear. It was a four-wheel machine with swing-axle steering. The differential was in the left final drive.

Hundreds of these tractors were sold, as they were popular on the Great Plains where they were used for pulling the heavy sod-breaker plows. Many also found use in road construction. It was one of the first tractors that could be counted on by engineers with limited knowledge of internal-combustion engines to run day in and day out—hence the moniker "Old Reliable."

1911 Hart-Parr advertisement
Above: *"The Great General Purpose Engine," noted this Hart-Parr advertisement.*

1913 Hart-Parr 30/60 "Old Reliable"
Above, both photos: *The Hart-Parr 30/60 was manufactured in Charles City, Iowa, from 1907 through 1918. Hart-Parr sales manager W. H. Williams coined the term "tractor" while working on an advertisement for the machine. The 30/60 weighed in at 20,500 pounds (9,225 kg). It had a two-cylinder engine with a bore and stroke of 10x15 inches (250x375 mm) and was cooled by 80 gallons (264 liters) of oil. It gained an enviable reputation for dependability and earned the nickname "Old Reliable." Owner: Gary Spitznogle.*

The Age of Consolidation

The volatility of a pioneering industry such as the fledgling tractor business soon brought on an Age of Consolidation among tractor and farm-equipment makers. An economic recession in the early 1890s prompted whole industries to form trusts among themselves to eliminate competition and mulct the public. The big players in the farm-implement business were squeezed into following suit. In 1891, the Massey Manufacturing Company of Toronto, Ontario, and A. Harris, Son & Company of Brantford, Ontario, were forced to join together as the Massey-Harris Company in Toronto. McCormick, Deering, and five smaller outfits merged in 1902 to form International Harvester Company of Chicago. Case and Deere reorganized, and each acquired smaller companies to keep competitive and avoid being taken over.

Theodore Roosevelt became president of the United States in 1901 after William McKinley was assassinated. He was but forty-three years old at the time, the youngest president up to that point. The first object of Roosevelt's righteous zeal was the "Trust Problem," as it came to be called. Roosevelt invoked the Sherman Anti-Trust Law, which had been on the books since 1890.

International Harvester soon became a target, since five companies from which it was formed had made binders, mowers, and rakes. This, the government maintained, was restraint of trade, and IHC was ordered to dissolve. The company appealed to the U.S. Supreme Court, and legal wrangling dragged on until World War I erupted. The government realized that if it won the case against IHC, the seven other cases pending would automatically follow suit: The result could be the total disruption of war production. Government lawyers were granted an indefinite postponement, but IHC, not wanting this threat hanging over it, sought a settlement. In 1918, IHC agreed to divest itself of the Osborn, Champion, and Milwaukee lines of harvesting machines, and dual McCormick and Deering dealerships were to be eliminated.

1929 Twin City 21/32 brochure

The venerable Twin City line continued even after the Minneapolis Steel & Machinery Company merged in 1929 with Moline Implement Company of Moline, Illinois, and the Minneapolis Threshing Machine Company of Hopkins, Minnesota, to form the Minneapolis-Moline Power Implement Company.

1918 Twin City 16/30

Left and below: *The TC 16/30 rode on a totally enclosed chassis and a two-speed gearbox. Its L-head engine displaced 589 ci (9,648 cc). A starter and lights were optional. It weighed about 7,800 pounds (3,510 kg). Only 702 16/30s were made between 1918 and 1920. The example shown was built in 1918. Owner: Charles Doty.*

1926 Allis-Chalmers Model E
Allis-Chalmers Company of Milwaukee, Wisconsin, suffered through the post–World War I years and even acquired several other ailing firms. Its Model E tractor featured a four-cylinder, 461-ci (7,551-cc) engine with a 20/35 rating. Owner: Arland Lepper.

1920s Minneapolis 22/44
Above and left: *The Minneapolis 22/44 was introduced in 1921 by the Minneapolis Threshing Machine Company. It had a four-cylinder, 6x7-inch (150x175-mm), OHV engine. It featured an expanding clutch in the belt pulley and a contracting clutch in the flywheel for drawbar work. The 22/44 weighed 12,000 pounds (5,400 kg). Owner: Larry Maasdam.*

1910s Aultman-Taylor brochure
The famed Aultman & Taylor Machinery Company of Mansfield, Ohio, was plagued by financial woes following World War I and was eventually bought out by Advance-Rumely in 1924.

Mogul and Titan
International Harvester Company of Chicago

In 1914, International Harvester brought out its first "lightweight" tractor, the Mogul 8/16, followed in 1915 by the Titan 10/20. At that time, McCormick dealers sold Moguls, while Deering dealers sold Titans. The fact that the 8/16 Mogul was rated for two plows while the 10/20 Titan could handle three led to dealer friction. Therefore, the 1916 Mogul was upgraded to 10/20 hp and a three-plow rating.

The Mogul was a rugged one-cylinder, hopper-cooled workhorse. It featured a channel-iron frame with a kick-up, or arch, in the front. Close-set front wheels were placed under this arch, allowing tight turns. The final drive used a single roller chain with the differential in the left hub. The earlier 8/16 version had only a single-speed transmission with a planetary reverse, but the later 10/20 had two speeds forward with a single reverse.

The Titan used a two-cylinder engine. It had a frame and front wheel arrangement similar to that of the Mogul. Cooling was by the thermosyphon principle, with a large reservoir mounted above the front wheels. A two-speed transmission was used. A double-chain drive ran to the rear wheels.

These so-called lightweight tractors weighed in at around 6,000 pounds (2,700 kg). Nevertheless, they were a lot lighter, cheaper, and more maneuverable than their predecessors. They were also more powerful, affordable, and reliable than most offerings of the time and were an instant hit with the mid-sized farm owner.

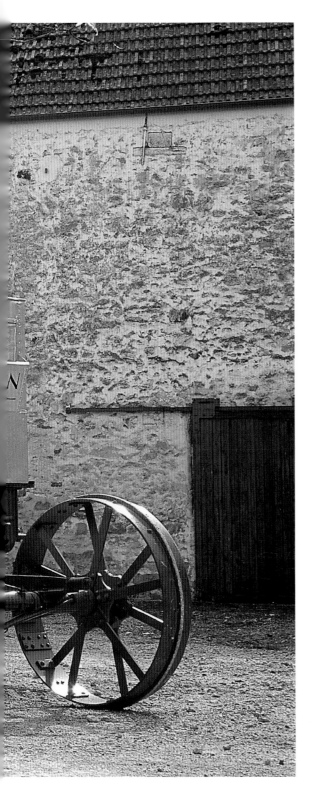

1910s International Harvester Titan Model D
Both photos: *The 20-hp Titan D was introduced in 1910 as a single-cylinder machine with a piston displacement of 902 ci (14,775 cc). Weight was 10,000 pounds (4,500 kg). Production ran to 1915, but only 259 were built.*

1908 International Harvester Mogul Type A
All photos: *Built from 1907 to 1911, International Harvester's first gear-drive (as opposed to friction-plate-drive) tractor was known as the Type A. It was built in three sizes: 12-, 15-, and 20-hp.*

1910s International Harvester Mogul 8/16

Sold by McCormick dealers starting in 1914, the Mogul 8/16 used a one-cylinder engine. It featured a chain final drive and single-speed transmission. Later versions were rated at 10/20 hp and had a two-speed transmission.

1919 International Harvester Titan 10/20

The Titan 10/20 was sold by Deering dealers and was a two-cylinder tractor with a two-speed transmission. Like its Mogul sibling, the Titan weighed about 6,000 pounds (2,700 kg).

1920s Mogul and Titan advertisement

International Harvester's English distributor sold both the 20-hp Mogul and Titan whereas in North America, McCormick dealers offered Moguls while Deering dealers had Titans.

49

1917 Dain–John Deere
All-Wheel-Drive brochure

1916 Dain–John Deere
All-Wheel-Drive prototype
By 1916, the Dain–John Deere was in its third prototype configuration. This one had the new McVicker-designed engine. The tractor performed well enough that production was ordered. The availability of the Waterloo Boy outfit, the high cost of the Dain–John Deere, and the death of Joseph Dain were all factors in the demise of the tractor.

Dain All-Wheel-Drive
Deere & Company of Moline, Illinois

Deere's Dain All-Wheel-Drive four-cylinder tractor was conceived in utmost secrecy. The reason for this concealment was the precarious nature of the tractor business in the 1910s as financial backers and bankers considered the business to be high risk.

Further, William Butterworth, Charles Deere's son-in-law who took over the company after the death of Charles, considered himself responsible for the family fortune and was not given to undertaking irresponsible development flyers. But there were powerful voices on the Deere board calling for tractor development. There also had been a successful, if unofficial, relationship between Deere branch houses and the Gas Traction Company in selling its Big 4 tractor as a quasi-Deere product. The result was authorization by Butterworth for low-key tractor experiments.

After an abortive attempt at building a tractor in 1912 designed by board member C. H. Melvin, another board member, Joseph Dain Sr., was asked to create a design in 1915. Dain had previously run his own company selling haying equipment to Deere. The competitive forces brought on by International Harvester prompted Deere to absorb such companies, putting their former owners on Deere's board.

The tractor Dain designed had specific limits put on it by the board. It had to be light, following the lead of the Bull Tractor Company of Minneapolis, whose Little Bull tractor had become the national sales leader. And it was to have a selling price of no more than $700, as the Little Bull sold for $400.

By February 1915, the first prototype was ready for testing. It was an interesting three-wheel design with drive to all three wheels. It weighed a little less than 4,000 pounds (1,800 kg). Originally, a Waukesha motor was employed, along with friction drive. Testing indicated the motor was short of power, and the friction drive would not work.

Second and third variations were built and tested. The friction drive was replaced by an all-gear power-shift transmission, after the fashion of the Model T, except it had two speeds in both forward and reverse. Engineer Walter McVicker was hired to design a new engine, and when this was ready in fall 1916, the tractor had ample power. The new engine had four cylinders with a bore and stroke of 4.50x6.00 inches (112.50x150 mm) and produced 24 belt hp.

Deere's board authorized construction of 100 of the final version of the Dain design, which were built and sold. The future looked bright for the Dain machine, but events quickly conspired against it. Dain died of pneumonia before the 100 tractors were finished, and with him died much of the push for his tractor. The board also became aware of Henry Ford's new low-cost, lightweight Fordson, whereas Deere's Dain would require a $1,600 price tag, far above the $700 goal the board set.

1917 Dain–John Deere All-Wheel-Drive

Besides being an all-wheel drive, the Dain–John Deere featured a two-speed (forward and reverse) power shift. The Dain–John Deere had a lever on the left that was connected to the drawbar. The lever on the right was the gear shift. The first prototypes of the Dain used a Waukesha engine that did not develop enough horsepower. Engine designer Walter McVicker was retained to create the engine eventually used. This is one of only two remaining Dain–John Deere tractors. Approximately 100 of these were built in 1917 and sold in the Huron, South Dakota, area. No record remains as to the disposition of the other 98. This one was donated to the Northern Illinois Steam Power Club of Sycamore, Illinois, by F. L. Williams, now of Sebastopol, California. Club member Bill Karl of Maple Park, Illinois, is the monitor and operator of the machine.

Finally, Deere heard that the Waterloo Gasoline Engine Company, maker of the Waterloo Boy tractor could be bought for $2.3 million. At the time, both the Waterloo Boy Model R and Model N were in production. They had an excellent reputation coupled with a selling price of $985 for the R and $1,150 for the N. On March 14, 1918, Deere bought the Waterloo outfit, rights to the famous Waterloo Boy, and the Waterloo Foundry, a separate but related company.

Waterloo Boy

Waterloo Gasoline Engine Company of Waterloo, Iowa

The well-known Waterloo Boy was a direct descendant of the original Froelich tractor of 1892. The Waterloo Gasoline Traction Engine Company, formed by Froelich and others, did not set the tractor world afire. When the other investors insisted on building engines only, Froelich left the company. Two more abortive attempts at tractors were made, but it was not until 1911 that things began to improve for the new Waterloo Gasoline Engine Company.

In 1911, A. B. Parkhurst of Moline, Illinois, joined the firm, bringing with him some of his own tractor designs. A feature of his creations was a two-cylinder, horizontally opposed, two-cycle engine. Two tractor models were built using this engine, the Models L and LA. The L had three wheels with one-wheel drive; the LA was the same tractor, but converted to four wheels with two-wheel drive.

The two-cycle engine did not prove satisfactory, however, and since the company was familiar with four-cycle engines, it decided to convert the Model LA to a new four-cycle, two-cylinder engine. A horizontally opposed type became much too wide for the chassis, so it was changed to be a side-by-side type. While the former type is naturally balanced and has even firing, the side-by-side type requires compromises. If the two cylinders moved in unison, even firing resulted, but tremendous counterbalances were required. If the cylinders moved in opposition to each other, the counterbalance problem was minimized, but uneven firing resulted. While the competitive International Harvester Titan opted for the cylinders moving in unison, Waterloo chose the other option, casting in iron the characteristic Poppin' Johnny sound of subsequent Waterloo Boy and John Deere two-cylinder tractors. Some believe that this distinctive sound, as much as anything, accounted for their success.

With the new engine, the Model LA became the Model R, built from 1915 to 1919. The engine originally had a bore and stroke of 5.50x7.00 inches (137.50x175 mm), which was changed in 1915 to 6.00x7.00 inches (150x175 mm). In 1917, when the Model N was introduced, the R was switched to the N's larger, 6.50x7.00-inch (162.50x175-mm) engine. The R featured one forward and one reverse speed as well as chain-driven, swing-axle steering.

The Model N was the final version of the "Boy." It could be distinguished from the R by the size of the final drive gear inside of each rear wheel. On the N, which had a two-speed transmission, this gear was as large as possible to maximize torque. On the single-speed R, this gear was much smaller. After 1921, the steering was changed to automobile-type steering. Production continued into 1924.

The name "Waterloo Boy" was believed to have been a play on the then-widely used term "water boy" and the fact that these farm engines were often used to pump water. A lad was employed to run from the pump to the locations where the various men were working, carrying a wooden pail of cold water and a dipper. Needless to say, on a hot, dry harvest day on the Great Plains, the water boy was a welcome sight!

1917 Waterloo Boy advertisement

Above: *"Farmers are clamoring for the Waterloo Boy,"* promised this advertisement to potential dealers.

1910s Waterloo Boy Model R

Facing page: *The Waterloo Boy was a direct descendant of the Froelich tractor of 1892 and was the forefather of the John Deere tractor. It was the first to use the two-cylinder side-by-side engine that would characterize Deere tractors for more than forty years. The Model R Waterloo Boy was built between 1915 and 1919. The Model N was introduced in 1917 with a two-speed transmission and other improvements. Deere & Company bought the Waterloo Boy outfit in 1918. The Waterloo Boy N was continued into 1924, overlapping in production both the Model R and the first two-cylinder Deere, the Model D.*

1910s Waterloo Boy Model R

Right: *Kenneth Kass of Dunkerton, Iowa, drives his Waterloo Boy Model R. Ken and his father, Art Kass, farm in east-central Iowa. Art Kass remembers farming with a Waterloo Boy when he was a boy. He noted that the front axle was held on by a pin that allowed for swing-axle steering. Sometimes, the cotter pin on the end of it would wear out—which happened to him on the far end of the farm. Due to a jerky clutch, the front end lurched up and the steering pin fell out, dropping the nose of the tractor on the ground. It was a long walk home to get the team, wagon, and jacks to get it up again. Once he got the tractor back together, he first had to take the team and wagon home, then walk back to the tractor, and resume plowing where he left off.*

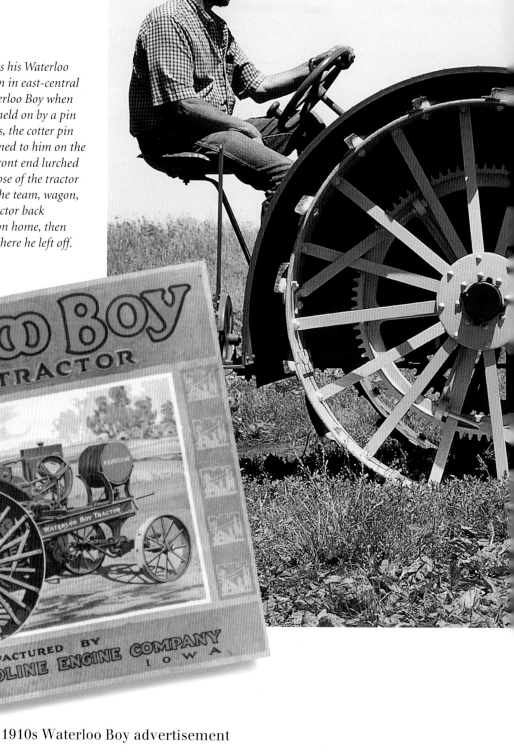

1910s Waterloo Boy advertisement

Rumely OilPull

Advance-Rumely Thresher Company of La Porte, Indiana

The OilPull line of tractors began in 1909 when Dr. Edward Rumely, grandson of the company founder, collaborated with John Secor, who had been doing engine experiments for more than twenty years. They developed a line of one- and two-cylinder tractors that used oil, rather than water, as an engine coolant. The oil, with its much higher boiling point, allowed higher engine temperatures for more efficient use of the low-volatility kerosene fuel.

Engine cylinders were offset from the crankshaft centerline to reduce piston side loads. The engines used water injection, sometimes consuming as much water as fuel. Cooling oil was circulated by a centrifugal pump. Engine exhaust was used to induce airflow through the chimney-type radiator. High-tension magneto ignitions were used, except on the early versions. The tractors were driven through an expanding shoe clutch

1928 Rumely OilPull advertisement

The OilPull was "the Symbol of Power and Dependability," according to this Rumely ad.

and a spur-gear final drive. One-, two-, and three-speed transmissions were used.

The OilPull line was noted for its large-displacement, slow-turning engines. OilPull tractors could generally best their official power and pull ratings, a fact that endeared them to their owners.

Over the years, Rumely built a long line of OilPull models and variations, including the 25/45 Type B of 1910–1914; one-cylinder 15/30 Type C of 1911–1917; one-cylinder 18/35 Type D built only in 1918; 30/60 Type E of 1911–1923; 14/28 Type F of 1918–1919; 16/30 Type F of 1919–1924; 12/20 Type K of 1919–1924; 20/40 Type G of 1920–1924; 25/45 Type R of 1924–1927; 20/35 Type M of 1924–1927; 15/25 Type L of 1924–1927; 30/60 Type S of 1924–1928; 20/30 Type W of 1928–1930; 25/40 Type X of 1928–1930; 30/50 Type Y of 1928–1930; and 40/60 Type Z of 1929–1930.

1929 Advance-Rumely Type Z
Rated at 40 drawbar and 60 belt hp, the OilPull Type Z used oil for cooling because of its higher boiling temperature. The higher temperatures allowed for better burning of kerosene fuel. Owner: Don Wolf.

1928 *OilPull Magazine*
Left: *Advance-Rumely published an OilPull owner's magazine throughout the 1920s that featured everything from agricultural tips to farming poetry.*

1923 Advance-Rumely OilPull Type G

Above and right: *The 20/40 Type G was introduced in 1920, and production continued through 1924. Like other Rumelys, it used oil as a cooling medium. Engine exhaust induced airflow through the chimney-type radiator. Owner: Glen Braun.*

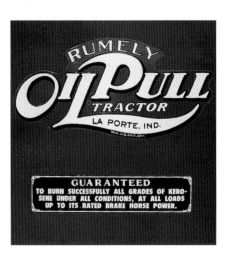

CHAPTER 3

The Debut *of the* Lightweight Tractor, 1913–1935

"I think it safe to eliminate the horse, the mule, the bull team, and the woman, so far as generally furnishing motive power is concerned."
—W. L. Velie, Director of Deere & Company, 1918

1920 Hart-Parr 30A
Main photo: *The 30A of 1920 was a departure from the previous large, oil-cooled tractors from Hart-Parr. It was the first of a line of comparatively lightweight water-cooled machines from the Charles City, Iowa, works.*

1920s Fordson advertisement
Above: *Henry Ford termed his creation the "modern tractor." For its day, the Fordson was indeed revolutionary.*

The Age of the Lightweights

Timeline

1912: Steamship *Titanic* sinks in the Atlantic

1913: Federal income tax adopted as the Sixteenth Amendment

1915: Alfred Einstein publishes his theory of relativity

1915: British passenger ship *Lusitania* sunk by a German U-boat

1916: Mexican revolutionary Pancho Villa attacks Columbus, New Mexico

1919: Treaty of Versailles signed ending World War I

1923: Colonel Schick patents the first electric shaver

1929: Stock market crashes

1931: Empire State Building opens in New York

1932: Franklin Delano Roosevelt becomes U.S. President

1934: Adolf Hitler takes power in Germany

1935: Social Security Act passed

The decade leading up to World War I was one of tentative steps as technology found its footing. Roads, motor cars, tractors, and fuels all were developed together, finally achieving practical efficiency levels. Although pioneered in the United States, the aviation industry flourished mainly in Europe. Electrification came to the city, giving urban people a taste for modern conveniences—and driving a cultural wedge between them and their country cousins.

With the advent of the automobile, country folk were much less isolated, however. The Great War, as it came to be called, had a profound coalescing effect as city and country people came to appreciate their reliance upon one another. After the United States was drawn into the conflagration, the American people realized that they were not as isolated from the rest of the world as had been thought.

In the fifteen years that gas tractors had been available to farmers, two characteristics emerged: First, gas tractors took on the general appearance of steam tractors; and second, like steamers, they got larger and larger. While the Froelich tractor was relatively small—it boasted 20 hp and weighed some 2 tons (1,800 kg)—the average size was soon represented by the monstrous 1913 Avery 40/80, which weighed more than 11 tons (9,900 kg).

The famous Tractor Trials in Winnipeg, Manitoba, focused attention on the big tractors' plowing acreage-per-hour rate. The 21,000-pound (9,450-kg) International Harvester Titan demonstrated a plowing rate of 2.54 acres (1 hectare) per hour in 1913. This, of course, was impressive—especially if you farmed in the Great Plains, or had one of the huge California spreads. But by 1900, fully two-thirds of American farmers had less than 40 acres (16 hectares) of land. By the time the typical farmer pastured and hayed enough land to feed a team of horses or mules and several cows, there was not much land left for cultivation. There was no way most farmers could even consider power farming.

By 1913, several factors combined to change the plight of the small-acreage farmer. The first was the drive to consolidate small farms into larger holdings. The second was the opening of the vast areas of the Great Plains to homesteaders, with 160 acres (64 hectares) of land allotted to each. And finally, in September 1913 a tractor sensation, the Little Bull, was offered for sale at the affordable price of $335. This price was about the same as for a good horse team.

The Bull Tractor Company introduced its lightweight Little Bull at the 1913 Minnesota State Fair. The Little Bull employed a single driving wheel on the right side, an unpowered balancing wheel on the left, and a single front wheel for steering, which was also on the right. The front wheel and drive wheel ran in the previously plowed furrow. A leveling arrangement was included with the balance, or idler wheel, so that the tractor would run level whether or not its two right wheels were in a furrow. A two-cylinder, horizontally opposed engine provided 12 hp. This trim little 3,000-pound (1,350-kg) machine rattled the industry and, by the end of 1914, more than 4,000 had been sold. The Bull Tractor Company was first in sales, displacing the mighty International Harvester.

Prosperity was fleeting for the fledgling Bull firm, however. Most purchasers were howling that they had been stung before the year was out. The

1913 Bull

The Bull Tractor Company of Minneapolis introduced its Bull tractor in 1913, and the lightweight design became influential in the tractor industry for a number of years. The Bull used a large drive "bull" wheel on the right side and an idler wheel on the left, circumventing the need for a differential. The three-wheel design aligned the single front wheel with the right driving wheel. The Bull had a two-cylinder horizontally opposed engine producing 5 drawbar and 12 belt hp.

1913 Bull

Above, both photos: *The Bull, or "Little Bull" as it was later known, made waves in the tractor industry because it was light at 3,000 pounds (1,350 kg) and inexpensive at a mere $335. The 5/12-hp tractor had a two-cylinder engine and was of the three-wheel design with single-wheel drive and an idler, or balance, wheel at the rear. The design was updated in 1915 to two-wheel drive with more power and called the Big Bull. Despite the influential design of the Bull, the company did not survive past 1917. This Little Bull is displayed at the Heritage Hall Museum in Owatonna, Minnesota. Owner: Bill Thelemann.*

Little Bull had not been sufficiently tested over a long period: While it performed well enough at the start, failures occurred with time and heavy use. For 1915, the Big Bull was introduced. It had the same configuration, but included a larger, 20-hp engine and beefier components. By 1917, engine power was again increased to 24 hp and the balance wheel was powered. At this point, Massey-Harris became interested in acquiring rights to the Big Bull, but manufacturing difficulties drove the Bull Tractor Company into bankruptcy.

Nevertheless, the Bull's impact on the tractor industry was permanent. A plethora of lightweight machines flooded the market. Numerous machines were unabashed copies of the Little Bull, such as the Model 10/20 from Case; the Little Devil from Hart-Parr; the Model 10/18 from Allis-Chalmers; the Happy Farmer from La Crosse Tractor Company of La Crosse, Wisconsin; the Model L 12/20 from Emerson-Brantingham Implement Company of Rockford, Illinois; and the Light Four from Huber Manufacturing Company of Marion, Ohio. Some were good, some were not. Some were not truly lightweights, such as the 4,000-pound (1,800-kg) Wallis Cub, 5,700-pound (2,565-kg) International Harvester Titan 10/20, and 6,000-pound (2,700-kg) Waterloo Boy. Tractors in this class, although expensive, were more likely to satisfy their owners.

1918 International 8/16

International's lightweight 8/16 looked more like an automobile than a tractor.

One interesting lightweight did enter the field during this period—the Universal tractor. The Universal was introduced in 1913 by the Universal Tractor Company of Columbus, Ohio. Rights to the Universal were quickly bought out in 1915 by the Moline Plow Company of Moline, Illinois, which popularized the machine. Copies of the Universal were also built by Allis-Chalmers as its Model 6/12 and as the Indiana from the Indiana Silo & Tractor Company of Anderson, Indiana.

1919 International 8/16

Built from 1917 through 1922, this tractor featured an inline four-cylinder, 4x5-inch (100x125-mm), OHV engine that was taken from the International Model G truck. In fact the entire configuration was similar to that of the truck with the radiator behind the engine.

1910s Happy Farmer

Above and below left: *The Happy Farmer Tractor Company was incorporated in 1915, with its headquarters in Minneapolis. However, most of the Happy Farmer tractors were made in La Crosse, Wisconsin. It was one of the first of the truly lightweight tractors. Power was provided by a two-cylinder engine of 255 ci (4,177 cc). Owners: Wendell and Charlene Shellabarger.*

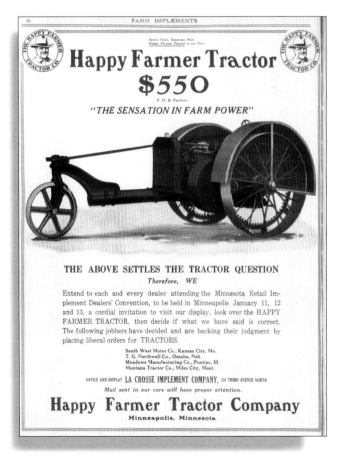

1917 Happy Farmer advertisement

1910s Moline Universal Model C

The Moline Plow Company got into the tractor business in 1915 when it bought out the Universal Tractor Company of Columbus, Ohio. Capitalizing on the firm's experiments, Moline brought out a truly unique machine, the Moline Universal. Owner: Walter Keller.

1919 Allis-Chalmers 6/12

Built in 1919, the 6/12 was an unlicensed copy of the Moline Universal—and Moline demanded royalties from Allis-Chalmers. The 6/12 required an implement sulky to hold up the back end. Steering was by an articulation in the middle. Owner: Norm Meinert.

1918 Case 10/20

Like the Bull, Case's tractor had one powered wheel, a front guide wheel on the right, and a "land," or "balance," wheel on the left that could be clutched in for more pull. Case's first four-cylinder, the 10/20 was offered from 1915 to 1922.

1919 Wallis Model K

The Wallis Tractor Company of Racine, Wisconsin, built the Model K, which was sold by the neighboring J. I. Case Plow Works. This Model K was photographed at the Colfax School, part of the Old Midwest Threshers Museum of Mount Pleasant, Iowa. Owner: Alan Buckert.

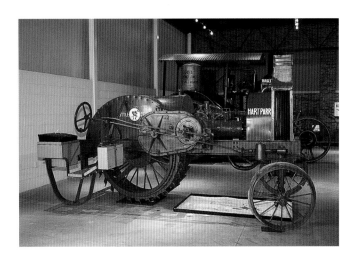

1910s Hart-Parr Little Devil

The Hart-Parr Little Devil was built between 1914 and 1916, and was powered by a 22-hp, two-cylinder, two-cycle engine and one-wheel drive. It was one of the less successful Hart-Parrs.

1920 Massey-Harris Parrett No. 2

Massey-Harris marketed three versions of the famous Parrett tractor between 1918 and 1923. The Parrett Tractor Company was in Chicago, but castings are stamped "MH," indicating some re-engineering and Canadian manufacture. The tractor had a four-cylinder Buda engine giving it a 12/22 rating. Owners: Rich and Joyce Holicky. Rich bought the tractor in Canada; the former owner had purchased a tract of land and found the Massey No. 2 in the woods.

Universal

Universal Tractor Company of Columbus, Ohio;
Moline Plow Company of Moline, Illinois

1917 Moline Universal advertisement
Moline attempted to sell its Universal by comparing it to farming with a horse team and horsedrawn implements.

Not many Moline Universal tractors ever made their way into the hands of farmers, but the machine nevertheless had a great impact on future tractors. It originated both the all-purpose idea and the concept of integrating the tractor and implement, which is what eventually became the concept behind the ubiquitous three-point hitch.

The nominal Universal Tractor Company developed in 1913 the world's first all-purpose tractor—a tractor that could be employed to do all tasks that could be done by horses on the farm. At the time, other tractors could only pull tillage implements and power other machines via the flat belt and pulley. The Universal could plow, harrow, plant, cultivate, mow, rake, harvest, pull a spreader, and do belt work.

The Universal was a light tractor, weighing less than 3,500 pounds (1,575 kg), and had a unique two-wheel configuration with the engine between the wheels. The driver and implement came behind, the wheels of the implement holding up the back end and providing a place for the driver to ride. Steering was by means of a hinge, or articulation, in the middle and a sector gear driven by the steering wheel.

In 1915, the Moline Plow Company bought the rights to the Universal. As acquired, the tractor needed work. Its two-cylinder, horizontally opposed engine was weak and unreliable. The tractor itself was top heavy and somewhat unstable. Most of all, it was expensive. The Moline firm set about correcting its flaws.

In 1918, Moline launched the Universal Model D with a more-powerful four-cylinder, overhead-valve engine capable of 27 hp—although the tractor was rated at just

1918 Moline Universal Model C
Above and right: *The C version of Moline's Universal was an upgrade from the earlier model. This one had a four-cylinder engine, cement wheel weights, a starter, and lights with an electric governor. It was built from 1918 to 1923. The four-cylinder engine produced over 27 hp at 1,800 rpm. Weight, with the cement, was 3,400 pounds (1,530 kg). Owner: Sue Dougan.*

70

9 drawbar and 18 belt hp. Top-heaviness was corrected by factory-installed cast-concrete wheel weights, and traction was improved through the use of one of the first differential locks. A starter and lights were standard equipment, as was an electric engine governor. Axle clearance for cultivating crops such as corn and cotton was just under 30 inches (75 cm). This high clearance set the Universal apart from other tractors and allowed it to do row-crop work that others could not.

Besides having only a single-speed transmission, the Universal's major shortcoming was its price. The 1920 price tag of $1,325 was three times that of the Fordson. Indeed, it cost more money than the offerings from either Deere or International Harvester, and special implements had to be acquired or made. The Universal's price ultimately caused its demise as it did not survive the great Tractor Price War of the 1920s. The innovative Universal was history by 1923.

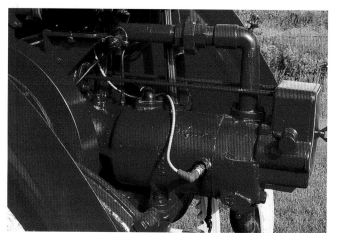

1910s Moline Universal Model C

The Moline Universal Model C was powered by a two-cylinder Reliable engine, but it proved somewhat weak, so the subsequent Model D was offered with a four-cylinder motor. Steering was accomplished by means of a center pivot and a sector gear, which caused the tractor-sulky plow combination to bend in the middle.

Doodlebugs, Jitterbugs, and Puddle Jumpers: Home-Brewed Iron Horses

By 1915, a farm tractor cost anywhere from $400 to more than $4,000. Naturally, quality and reliability went hand in hand with a high price tag. International Harvester's Titan 10/20 cost $900 in 1914; the 12/25 Waterloo Boy Model N cost just under $1,000 in 1916. Both were creditable tractors, but that was a lot of cash for the small farmer.

By 1915, the price of Henry Ford's Model T automobile was down to an amazing $450. It was the most popular car among rural people and had a great emancipating effect on their lifestyle. The Model T was their car of choice partly because of the price, partly because it was rugged and durable and could negotiate the mud and ruts of country roads that left high-priced autos stranded—and partly because Henry Ford was a hero to the common man. Ford knew he was held in high regard by farm folk and used every ploy to further the notion that the Model T was built just for them. One much-publicized photo showed Ford himself buzzing up cordwood using the jacked-up rear wheel of a Model T and a belt to drive a circular saw. This method of powering tools such as choppers and feed grinders was widely touted.

With all this emphasis on the usefulness of the Ford on the farm, it was only natural that wily inventors would take the next step and create adaptations to make the trusty Tin Lizzie do tractor duty. The idea was to provide kits that could quickly convert the family car for pulling implements; then on Saturday afternoon, it could be converted back into a passenger car ready to take the family to Sunday morning church. Such conversions, either factory kits or homemade jobs, came to be known affectionately as "doodlebugs," "jitterbugs," or "puddle jumpers."

Forty-five factory conversion kits were listed in the January 1919 issue of *Chilton's Tractor Index* alone and more were available elsewhere. Of these, none were truly as "convertible" as was hoped. Only a few performed well enough to be considered successful tractors. All suffered from shortcomings inherent in the basic Model T. Simply put, the T was not designed for steady heavy pulling, as was required in plowing. On lighter jobs, such as dragging or raking, it did well. While most of the conversions provided reduction

"Don't let your old Ford or Chevrolet go to waste. Use it to make a practical general-purpose tractor that has the pulling power of from two to four horses, yet costs less than the price of one horse."
—Sears, Roebuck catalog, 1939

1918 Staude Mak-A-Tractor brochure
The E. G. Staude Manufacturing Company of St. Paul, Minnesota, promised that it had signed and notarized affidavits from 363 farmers throughout North America lauding the firm's conversion kit that turned your everyday automobile into an iron-willed farm tractor. Such conversion kits were common in the 1910s and 1920s.

1917 Smith Form-A-Tractor advertisement

All you needed to build your own tractor was the $255 Smith Form-A-Tractor kit—"and a Ford" automobile or truck, as this ad noted in smaller type. The Smith Form-A-Tractor Company was based in Chicago.

gearing to the larger rear wheels, the friction-band planetary transmission was a weak point. Nevertheless, it was the first tractor with power downshift, a forerunner to the Farmall Torque Amplifier of the late 1950s.

With credit often unavailable for the purchase of a real tractor, the farmer was forced into ingenious solutions to his power problems. Homemade doodle-bugs were crafted from whatever was available. The vehicle frame was often shortened and a truck rear axle added. The Ford Model A automobile was a popular base, but other brands—and combinations of brands—were used as well. A foreshortened Model A truck could be assembled for as little as $25. Traction would be a problem, but some farmers framed up a box on the back and filled it with cement. Only first gear was useful for work, and because of the brakes, only second was safe on the road. Maneuverability was problematical at best. Adding a second transmission behind the original gave a good range of ratios and provided enough torque to break something downstream, if care was not exercised.

Often, these homemade farm tractors served their ingenious makers for years, if not decades. Some homegrown tractors were mere stopgap vehicles used until the farmer could afford a real, factory-built tractor. Others were well-engineered machines that rose above the sum of their disparate parts to become legends in their farm communities, bestowing renown on the farmer who eschewed the factory-built variety of tractor. Either way, they provided a sign and inspiration to the tractor manufacturers that there was a market for lightweight machines.

Doodlebug

Built about 1936, the "Mogg Tractor" was more refined than the average doodlebug—it had headlights and a front bumper. It was the product of one Peter Mogg, a car dealer from Mt. Pleasant, Michigan. Mogg's son-in-law Harold Taylor is at the controls. (Donald A. Tietz collection)

74

1910s Doodlebug

This was the fate of most homemade tractors, may they rust in peace. Such doodlebugs were common on smaller farms from the early days of the Model T Ford through the 1950s. Most were made from cut-down trucks. Sometimes two transmissions were used in series to gain enough reduction. Generally, however, first gear was used for just about everything.

1910s New Deal

Above: *The New Deal was basically a factory-made doodlebug, incorporating Model T Ford components. Only about 100 were made by the New Deal Tractor Company of Wyoming, Minnesota, and about six are still in existence. Owner: Dean Zilm.*

1941 Sears, Roebuck Economy Tractor

Left: *As late as 1941, the famous Sears, Roebuck and Co. still offered two "doodlebug" tractor kits through its mail-order catalog. The Economy Tractor was essentially a converted Ford Model A automobile and was powered by the Ford's engine. Sears also offered a "thrifty" conversion kit to build your own farming machine.*

The Decade of the Fordson, 1918–1928

"The farmer must either take up power or go out of business."
—Henry Ford, *My Life and Work*, 1926

With the advent of World War I in 1914, the armed services acquired all the horses they could find for the war effort; this bolstered the demand for tractors as North American farmers were called upon to provide food for much of the world. Also, many young farm men were inducted into the services, so mechanical help was needed on the farm. Tractor companies flourished.

In 1917, when the United States officially entered the war, tractor production doubled. At the same time, some eighty-five new manufacturers entered the field bringing the total number of U.S. manufacturers to more than two hundred.

Among these myriad makers was one machine that stood out from all the rest—so much so, in fact, that it was perhaps the most significant development in the history of the tractor. It was called the Fordson.

Henry Ford founded his Ford Motor Company in 1903, and in 1908 introduced his revolutionary Model T automobile. Ford then turned his attentions to making tractors.

True to his philosophy that excess weight was the enemy of a motor vehicle, Ford's first tractor, made from car components, weighed less than 2,000 pounds (900 kg), about one-tenth of what others of the time weighed. This tractor, which Ford called the Automobile Plow, proved to be too light for traction and endurance, however. Nevertheless, over the next several years, variations of the Automobile Plow were tested, but no production versions resulted. Following this, several new tractors were tried, which were generally identified by the name of the chief engineer responsible for them, such as Joe Galamb's tractor of 1914 and Eugene Farkas's design of 1916.

The year 1914 was pivotal for the Ford Motor Company and, indeed, the world. Ford introduced assembly-line practices, and the Model T's price came down so it was affordable to the masses. And the year saw the start of World War I in Europe.

Fordson assembly line, 1920s
After production details were settled, the Fordson began rolling off Henry Ford's new assembly lines in numbers never even considered by other tractor makers.

In England, the war sparked an immediate need for farm tractors, and the British Ministry of Munitions (MOM) asked Ford and his tractor-building company, Henry Ford & Son, to send the first 6,000 of his Farkas-designed tractors to Britain. Ford swung into action. A series of pre-production prototypes were built and tested. When by September 1917, tests were still going on, the MOM dispatched Lord Northcliffe to encourage Ford to stop improving and start producing. He was successful, and the first production MOM tractor was delivered on October 8, 1917. By year's end, 254 had been completed. The London *Daily Mail* reported that Ford's tractors were good news for Britain, describing them as "wonderful instruments of war." Although off to a slow start, production of the remainder of the 6,000 MOM tractors (which were not yet identified as Fordsons) were completed in a mere sixty days.

Henry Ford & Son turned to domestic production. Now the name "Fordson" was cast into the radiator head tank. The name, a contraction of Henry Ford & Son for use in transatlantic cable shorthand, had caught the fancy of the senior Ford, and so it became one of the world's most famous trademarks. Another 34,000 Fordsons came off the assembly line in 1918.

1918 Samson Model M advertisement

Above: *The Fordson became the quintessential tractor of the 1910s and 1920s, and other makers rushed to copy its design. Wanting an entry into the tractor market, Ford arch-rival General Motors of Pontiac, Michigan, bought the Samson Tractor Company of Stockton, California, and moved its operations to Janesville, Wisconsin, where it introduced its Fordson lookalike, the Samson Model M, in 1918. Sadly, the Model M never matched the Fordson's sales record, and GM eventually made a quiet exit from the tractor market.*

1917 Fordson prototype

Above and right: *Henry Ford & Son of Dearborn, Michigan, built sixteen experimental tractors following Ford's acceptance of an order for 6,000 machines from the British Ministry of Munitions. These were built in pairs for testing in late 1917, each pair incorporating improvements found to be necessary in previous testing. These tractors were designed by Eugene Farkas and incorporated a "unit-frame" with the engine, transmission, and rear-end castings being bolted together to form the frame as well as a 251-ci (4,111-cc) Hercules engine and an undershot worm final drive. These machines were not yet Fordsons and had no name emblems applied. The name "Fordson" was applied after the order from the M.O.M. was completed. Owner: Duane Helman.*

Just as he had amazed the world with his revolutionary Model T car, Ford again stunned everyone with the introduction of his radical Fordson. It was conceived as a lightweight, inexpensive tractor to replace not the gigantic steam engines of the large farms but the mules, oxen, and horses of the more numerous small farms. The timing was right, the $785 price was right, and the Fordson became the Model T of farm tractors. By 1920, Ford had 70 percent of the world tractor market.

Fordson
Henry Ford & Son of Dearborn, Michigan

The Fordson was undoubtedly the most significant tractor of the era. With more than 750,000 built in the United States alone from 1917 through 1928, the Fordson was so popular that it virtually personified the normal configuration for tractors of the period. Previously, the configuration was generally that of the Waterloo Boy or IHC Titan.

The Fordson F was the first model built both in the United States and Ireland. It featured a unit frame where the engine, transmission, and axle castings were the frame. It's four-cylinder engine of 251 ci (4,111 cc) produced 10 drawbar and 20 belt hp. It had a three-speed transmission while many of its higher-cost competitors offered only two. It weighed a mere 2,700 pounds (1,215 kg). Over the years, its price would range from a low of $395 to a high of $785; the average price was closer to $500.

After Ford transferred all Fordson production to Cork, Ireland, in 1928, the original Fordson concept was produced in Ireland and England through 1946 with minor modifications as the Model N. The same engine was used in the post–World War II British E27N Fordson Major.

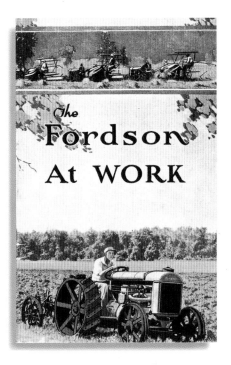

There is no question that the Fordson F had shortcomings. The flywheel magneto made them notoriously difficult to start. They had disgraceful traction and the embarrassing tendency to tip over backwards when pulling hard. The use of a worm drive in the rear end caused a howling sound that was recognizable for miles.

Nevertheless, the Fordson introduced most farmers in the United States, Canada, and England to power farming. The Fordson was well loved in Britain where it saved the people from food shortages in two world wars. It was not as appreciated in North America, where farmers readily junked their old Fordsons and switched over to the new row-crop machines of the 1930s.

1920s Fordson brochure

1918 Fordson Model F

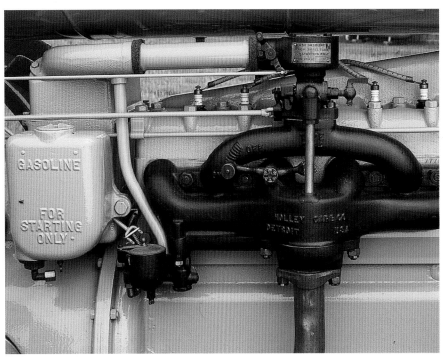

1918 Fordson Model F

Above and left: *The Model F was the first of the Fordsons and the first Ford-built tractor for North American use. To buy one during World War I, a farmer had to obtain a permit from his County War Board. The first of these went to Henry Ford's close friend, botanist Luther Burbank. The Fordson F was much the same as the tractor produced for the British food program, but the engine was soon changed from a Hercules unit to a Ford motor. The earliest Fordsons can be identified by the ladder-side radiator frame. Owner: Duane Helman.*

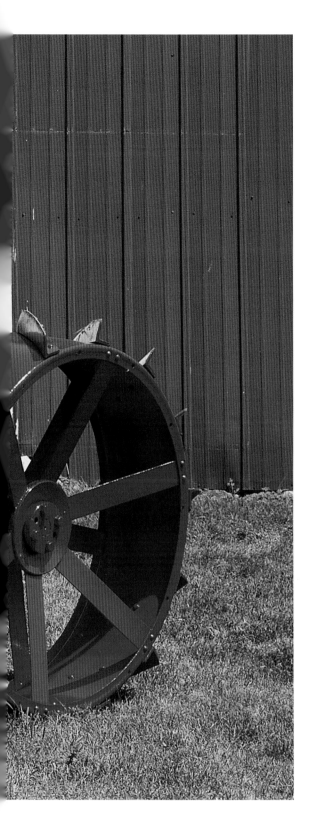

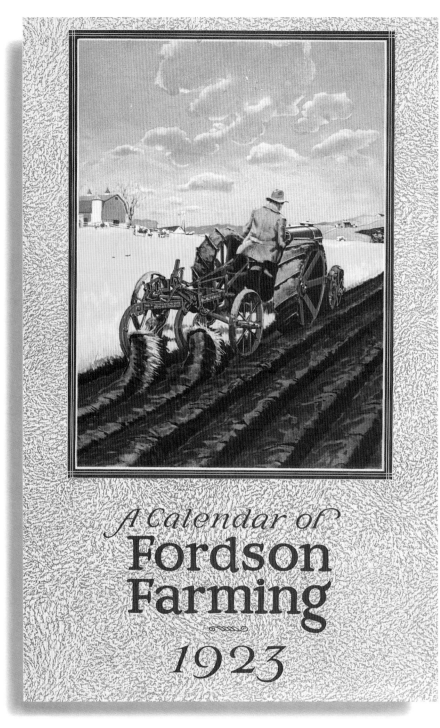

1923 Fordson calendar

THE HENRY FORD STORY: A MIDWESTERN FARM BOY MAKES GOOD

"By the dreams he had, pursued and achieved, the burdens of drudgery were taken from the shoulders of the humble and given to steel and wheel."
—Requiem for Henry Ford by Edgar A. Guest, 1947

If you were born before 1940, you are undoubtedly aware of the aura surrounding Henry Ford. He was reputed to be the richest man in the world. He owned the Ford Motor Company outright. He was famed for being a builder of cars, trucks, airplanes, and tractors. He was respected in political circles; even pressured to run for the U.S. presidency.

If you were born after 1940, you may not have much of an awareness of Ford, the man. You may not know that the Ford Motor Company, founded in 1903, was Henry's third attempt at the automobile business. The first two were failures. (However, his second attempt, the Henry Ford Company, was reorganized to become Cadillac.) You may not know that Henry Leland fired Ford from his second company. Leland later founded Lincoln, and when Lincoln foundered in the early 1920s, Ford bailed Leland out financially—and then promptly fired him.

Such facts and fables of Henry Ford have filled many volumes. But Ford was really two men: He was a cantankerous, self-appointed philosopher; and he was a hands-on, master maker of machines. Like so many other people that rise above their peers, Ford's real genius was his ability to surround himself with loyal followers who had the capability to execute Ford's dreams.

Henry Ford was born in 1863 to Irish immigrants on a prosperous Michigan farm, not far from Detroit. When he died in 1947, his funeral caused a massive traffic jam on the streets of Detroit. These were streets that saw their first car, a Ford, a mere fifty-one years previously. Such were the changes wrought over the eighty-three years of his life. *Time* magazine said, "More than any man in the Twentieth Century, Ford changed the way people lived. He did so by originating a means of getting a useful instrument in many people's hands at lower and lower cost, and in so doing had shown the way to distribute many other useful instruments to millions."

Although Henry Ford's father tried to get him interested in farming, Henry never quite took to it. Instead, he gravitated towards things mechanical, becoming an engineer for the Detroit Edison Illuminating Company. He and his wife, Clara, and their newborn son, Edsel, lived in rented quarters in Detroit. Henry tinkered in his spare time at work, in his shop, and in the kitchen at home. He made himself a two-cylinder engine out of pieces of pipe and other hardware that he found or crafted. With the engine clamped to the kitchen sink, and Clara dribbling gasoline into the intake, Henry spun the flywheel, and the first Ford engine roared into life just a few feet from the sleeping baby Edsel.

Ford soon had the engine mounted in an automobile, which he called a quadracycle since it looked like two bicycles with a box between. The door to the shop behind the house proved too narrow to get the vehicle out, so an ax and sledge were employed to enlarge the opening of the brick structure. It was near midnight in June 1896 when Henry, followed by a friend on a bicycle, took off on the first test run.

Ford made a variety of cars before hitting on the one that made him famous—the Model T, which made its debut in 1908. At first, the Model T was not all that successful or inexpensive. But in 1914, Ford began using the assembly-line technique, and prices dropped to where it was the most affordable car. He soon had 50 percent of the U.S. market, and over a nineteen-year period, Ford built 15 million Model Ts.

Ford never got along well with the investors in his companies. In 1917, he formed a separate, wholly owned company, Henry Ford & Son, to manufacture his Fordson tractor without stockholder interference. By early 1919, Ford was able to buy out all the non-family stockholders in the Ford Motor Company. He then folded the tractor entity into the car company.

Ford also resisted unionizing his factories. The streets around his Dearborn and River Rouge plants were the scenes of some bloody battles between Ford "guards" and union men. Abruptly, however, in 1941, with his factories ringed by pickets, Ford suddenly acceded to all of the union's demands. Clara, he said, would not let him fight it out. The strike was averted just in time to begin conversion to wartime production.

Ford was an ardent pacifist. Nevertheless, with the bombing of Pearl Harbor, Ford threw himself and his resources into the war effort. With characteristic energy, he turned Ford into an arsenal of democracy. By World War II's end in 1945, his plants and people had built 278,000 jeeps, 8,900 B-24 Liberator bombers, and 57,000 airplane engines.

Before the war ended, however, Ford's only son, Edsel, died suddenly at age fifty. Edsel's son, Henry II, was released from the Navy and called home to help with the business, which because of Henry's crotchetiness and fragility—he was by then over eighty—had always been worrisome to the War Department.

Henry Ford and Automobile Plow, 1907
Henry's 1907 version of the Automobile Plow had an automobile-type radiator, and used the four-cylinder engine and transmission from the luxurious Ford Model B car. The axles and differential came from a Ford Model K six-cylinder car as seen in the background.

After the war, Henry spent most of his time at Greenfield Village, the museum he erected in Dearborn. On April 7, 1947, there was a heavy rainstorm in the area. By evening the basement and power plant of his beloved Fair Lane estate were flooded, leaving the Fords with kerosene lamps and candles for light and fireplace fires for warmth. Ford went to bed early, saying he didn't feel well. He later worsened, called for Clara to bring him a drink of water, and then, just before midnight, he died. With candles for light and wood fires for heat, Henry Ford left the world as he entered it back in 1863, but he had forever changed it nonetheless.

Henry Ford and Fordson, 1910s
Henry Ford, center, was not afraid to get his hands dirty working on the development of his Fordson.

The Minneapolis Ford Tractor and the Nebraska Tractor Tests

1917 Ford advertisement
"At last!! The right tractor at the right price," shouted this ad for the Ford Tractor Company of Minneapolis. The Ford was not the right tractor for Nebraska farmer Wilmot Crozier, however. He was so incensed by the machine's shortcomings that he ran for state legislature and introduced the Nebraska Tractor Test Bill to weed out tractors like the Ford.

Henry Ford tinkered with tractors as soon as he got his Ford Motor Company on solid footing. He boasted to folk that he would make a tractor that would be to the farmer what the Model T was to the public at large. He mentioned such things as a $250 price tag. All of this whetted the appetite of farmers anxious to make the switch to power farming.

Taking advantage of these expectations, a group of investors lead by financier W. Baer Ewing organized the Ford Tractor Company of Minneapolis in 1914. In the organization there really was a man by the name of Ford—Paul B. Ford, to be exact—but he bore no relation to Henry. This Ford knew nothing of tractor design, but was merely recruited so that his name could be used. A few tractors were actually built and sold, but the real purpose of the firm was to force Henry Ford to pay them off so he could use his own name on his forthcoming tractor.

Henry Ford was not about to be trapped in such a scheme, however. Ford and his son, Edsel, launched their tractor enterprise, calling it simply Henry Ford & Son. The Minneapolis Ford outfit soon went into receivership, but not before leaving a legendary legacy in helping to create one of the greatest boons to farmers up until that time—the University of Nebraska Tractor Tests.

Nebraska farmer Wilmot Crozier ordered one of the Minneapolis Ford tractors in 1915. When the tractor was delivered, Crozier had trouble with it almost immediately. Not being one to put up with much, Crozier demanded the company replace it. They did, but the replacement was also unsatisfactory. He then bought a Big Bull tractor. This too was a total disappointment.

Farmer Crozier was beside himself. "I'll try one more before I give up," he said to a neighbor. In 1918, Crozier bought a Rumely "Three-Plow." This tractor was a pleasant surprise, being reliable and durable and regularly pulling five bottoms. The injustice of it all stuck in his craw. Unscrupulous companies were victimizing farmers—who were having enough trouble keeping up, anyway. Farmer Crozier decided to do something about it. He got himself elected to the Nebraska legislature.

During his first year in office, he teamed with Charles Warner to pass legislation requiring any tractor sold in Nebraska to be tested by the Agricultural Engineering Department of the University of Nebraska. The tests were to ascertain whether or not the machine lived up to advertised claims. If not, such claims could not be made, at least not in Nebraska.

Ag Engineering Department experts L. W. Chase and Claude Shedd devised the tests and test equipment. The first test was attempted in fall 1919, but snowfall prevented completion. The following spring, the Waterloo Boy Model N was the first to be certified. Since that time, the Nebraska Tractor Tests have become world renowned. To this day, tractors by all manufacturers are still submitted to the University of Nebraska for testing.

1910s Waterloo Boy Model R

Above: *Just as the Ford tractor holds an infamous place in tractor history for sparking the Nebraska Tractor Tests, the Waterloo Boy wears laurels as the first tractor to be tested. A Waterloo Boy Model N 12/25 was tested from March 31 to April 9, 1920, and passed with flying colors.*

Wilmot F. Crozier

Left: *Farmer-turned-legislator Crozier was a key figure in the history of truth in advertising for tractors.*

The Great 1920s Tractor Price War

"Henry Ford's presence in the implement province and the new type of competition he soon introduced returned the industry for a time to the atmosphere of battle."
—Cyrus McCormick III,
The Century of the Reaper, 1931

"What? What's that? How much? Two hundred and thirty dollars? Well, I'll be . . . What'll we do about it? Do? Why damn it all, meet him, of course! We're going to stay in the tractor business. Yes, cut $230. Both models. Yes, both. And, say, listen, make it good! We'll throw in a plow as well."

This quotation is from Cyrus McCormick III's great 1931 book, *The Century of the Reaper*, in which he recounts one half of a telephone conversation between International Harvester's Springfield, Ohio, office and the Chicago headquarters. The words are those of the company's hard-boiled general manager, Alexander Legge, who was visiting the Springfield works. This January 28, 1922, telephone conversation came on the eve of the 1922 National Tractor Show in Minneapolis where Henry Ford had just announced a price cut of $230, bringing the cost of a Fordson to the unheard of amount of $395. Most tractor companies spent more than that on their engines.

McCormick went on, "Harvester was waging the battle of the implement industry against mighty Henry Ford and the automobile. Ford was backed by the most popular commercial name of the time and the uncounted millions earned for him by his epoch-making car . . . ."

Harvester did fight back by cutting prices on its popular Titan and International 8/16 by $230 each. They still cost almost twice as much as the Fordson, but the inclusion of the P&O plow sweetened the deal. Harvester's sales people made every effort to turn Fordson demonstrations into field competitions. Harvester and other companies intent on survival, adopted Ford's manufacturing practices.

The real winner of the war was the farmer. The intense competition not only drove prices down, but led to great improvements in parts interchangeability, dealer responsiveness, and in tractor performance. Weaker companies were eliminated in this "survival-of-the-fittest" atmosphere. By 1929, only forty-seven of the original two hundred tractor builders were left.

The cause of the 1920s Tractor Price War was a post–World War I depression that started in 1921. The downturn cut tractor sales in half from their peak in 1920. At 6,000 tractors per month, Henry Ford & Son's shipping lots were jammed by the time the existence of the recession was realized. Ford had no alternative but to cut prices.

This was also a problem for the folks at Deere & Company, who had taken on the Waterloo Boy in 1918. Deere planned to sell forty tractors daily for the last half of 1921. In the end, however, it only sold seventy-nine tractors for the whole model year.

For Ford, the 1922 price cuts that signaled the start of the Tractor Price War were a success. At $395, the Fordson sold. In fact, more than 100,000 were sold in 1923 alone.

The great Tractor Price War was over by 1929. As the recession diminished, retail prices rose swiftly to profit-making levels. By 1929, annual domestic tractor sales were again around 200,000 units.

The Fordson, however, was not among them, as all production was transferred to Ford's new Cork, Ireland, plant in 1928. The Fordson, like the Model T car, had succumbed to determined competition. The new Ford Model A replaced the venerable Model T. The new "general-purpose" tractors—like International Harvester's Farmall—were what farmers wanted now.

1919 Case 10/18 Crossmotor
Case introduced its novel and innovative Crossmotor line in 1915 and soon reaped the rewards of the new machines. The 10/18 was a successor to Case's short-lived Model 9/18B and was built from 1917 to 1920. The two were much the same, except for engine improvements in the 10/18. Both used Case's rock-solid cast-iron frame and novel crossmotor engine installation.

1924 Fordson Model F
The Fordson tractor was essentially mature by 1924. Appearance was somewhat different from previous-year models in that a lighter shade of gray paint was used, and fenders became an option. Wheels were bright red, and the rears had seven spokes. A two-bung fuel tank was used beginning in 1924, with the small gasoline tank inside the main kerosene tank. A hard-rubber steering wheel rim replaced the wood. As before, the Fordson had a 251-ci (4,111-cc) four-cylinder, L-head engine; a three-speed transmission; and the infamous, noisy, and troublesome worm-gear final drive. The worm final drive was retained on the British Fordsons up to 1946. American production of the Fordson ran from 1918 to 1926. Owner: Palmer Fossum.

Orphan Tractors: The First Industry Debacle

1903 Flour City advertisement

Named for its home city of Minneapolis—the flour-milling capital of the world at the time—the Flour City tractor was built by the Kinnard-Haines Company of Minneapolis. The firm began building gas engines as early as 1896 but was forced from the field during the Great Depression.

In the 1910s, North America boasted of some two hundred tractor makers. By 1930, that number had been slashed to about forty-seven. Tough economic times in the years following World War I toppled many pioneer tractor manufacturers; the Great Depression of the 1930s wiped out numerous others who were still standing.

Throughout the ongoing history of the farm tractor, there has been a continuous trimming of the tractor's family tree. Many of those firms that fell out along the way built credible tractors; other machines, however, were bizarre Rube Goldberg creations, imperfect designs, or the brainchild of an engineer who marched to a different drummer. Many fledgling companies over-extended themselves financially as they sought to market their machines; others were simply victims of the numerous economic recessions. Despite financially strong parents, further tractor firms were victims of the intense competition in a marketplace where only the fittest survived.

These orphans—tractors not absorbed or acquired by surviving companies—are today some of the machines that collectors avidly seek out. Yet the orphan tractors are for the truly serious collector, as no help with parts or data can be expected. The reward in satisfaction and acclaim is proportionally great, however, as the restorer may own an incredibly rare or historically important machine.

1917 Interstate Plow Boy and Plow Man advertisement

Uncle Sam himself promised dealers that "America's Demand for Power Farming is Your Opportunity!" Many pioneering tractor makers in the 1910s heeded these words, but they were wiped out by the economic depression following World War I—including the Interstate Engine & Tractor Company of Waterloo, Iowa, that produced the Plow Boy 10/20 and Plow Man 13/30.

1919 Avery Model C

Above: *The Avery Company of Peoria, Illinois, had tunnel vision during the 1910s and 1920s: While other makers were experimenting with innovative lightweights, Avery stayed true to its outdated heavyweights. The firm finally introduced this six-cylinder cultivating tractor in 1919, but it was too late. Like many other smaller companies, Avery filed for bankruptcy shortly after World War I, re-organized in 1925, then closed its doors forever during the Great Depression of the 1930s.*

1919 Nilson 22/45

Left: *The unique Nilson 22/45 was made in Minneapolis. It featured a four-cylinder engine, two-speed gearbox, and three rear driving wheels. This Nilson was on display at the LeSueur, Minne-sota, Pioneer Power Show in 1999.*

1921 Huber Super Four

Facing page: *The Huber Manufacturing Company of Marion, Ohio, made a number of tractors of various configurations called the Super Four. This example was the first version. It used a transverse-mounted Midwest engine, which gave it a 15/30 rating. This configuration was produced through 1924, then engine improvements resulted in a rating of 18/36. In 1926, a Super Four 18/36 was introduced with the engine installed parallel to the tractor's centerline. During the Great Depression of the 1930s, however, Huber made its exit from the tractor field to concentrate on construction equipment. Owner: Cliff Peterson.*

1919 Wheat advertisement

Above: *Numerous firms rushed into the booming tractor market in the 1910s and 1920s, but the economic downturn following World War I weeded out the serious makers from the chaff. The Wheat tractor had a short production life in the early 1920s.*

1920s Little Giant

Left: *The Little Giant tractor from the Little Giant Company of Mankato, Minnesota, debuted in 1918 and won a strong following throughout the 1920s. Faced with the Tractor Price War of the 1920s and the roller-coaster ride that the economy took throughout the decade, the company ended production in 1927.*

McCormick-Deering 15/30

International Harvester Company of Chicago

1929 McCormick-Deering
15/30 advertisement

McCormick-Deering 15/30,
1920s

A McCormick-Deering 15/30 pulls a combined harvester-thresher through a wheatfield on the Great Plains.

The big 15/30 was introduced in 1921 to replace International Harvester's Mogul and Titan. It was designed to provide a modern alternative to the Fordson, which was ominously eroding Harvester's market share. While the 15/30 was expensive at about $900, it was everything the Fordson was not. On farms of more than 100 acres (40 hectares), the 15/30 could replace four teams of horses. In the early 1920s, a team cost about $200, so the price was really not insurmountable.

The 15/30 set the industry standard for reliability and durability. Its four-cylinder, overhead-valve, 284-ci (4,652-cc) engine ran on ball-bearing mains. Like the Fordson, it featured a unit frame, but its seat and steering wheel were offset to the right to enhance visibility when plowing.

The McCormick-Deering 15/30 weighed in at 6,000 pounds (2,700 kg), more than twice a Fordson. On the other hand, it was well balanced and boasted excellent traction, which the Fordson did not. It was equipped with a rear power takeoff (PTO) to power all kinds of trailing harvester implements.

Production continued through 1928 when an uprated version, the 22/36 was introduced with engine improvements. The 22/36 was built through 1934.

1920s McCormick-Deering 10/20

Right and below: *Built from 1923 to 1939, the 10/20 was McCormick-Deering's answer to the onslaught of the Fordson. It was a smaller version of the 15/30—14 inches (35 cm) shorter and a ton (900 kg) lighter. Its 284-ci (4,652-cc) engine was slightly larger than the Fordson's 251-ci (4,111-cc). Owner: Fred McBride.*

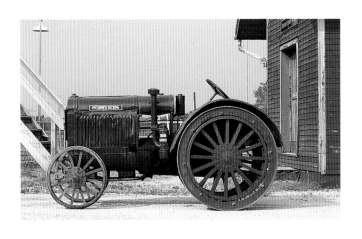

John Deere Model D

Deere & Company of Moline, Illinois

The John Deere Model D is famous for having the longest production run of any tractor. It was built from 1923 through 1953—thirty years. Certainly, the tractor was much improved over that time, but the original concept was still in evidence at the end of production.

Like many of the tractors of the era, the Model D was designed to overcome the Fordson's onslaught. The D featured a carlike hood and radiator, but under the skin, it was much like the Waterloo Boy it replaced. The Deere was unique among its competitors in that it was powered by a two-cylinder engine. The engine originally displaced 465 ci (7,617 cc); this was increased to 501 ci (8,206 cc) in 1927. It used the Waterloo Boy's two-speed transmission

up to 1935 when it was replaced by a three-speed unit. Following International Harvester's example, the steering wheel and seat were moved in 1931 from the left to the right to enhance plowing visibility. During its first two years of production, the exposed external flywheel had spokes; solid flywheels were used thereafter. In 1939, styled sheet metal was added.

The big, slow-turning engine in the Model D made a delightful sound when plowing. It ran at a mere 800 rpm; in 1932, engine speed was increased to 900 rpm. Besides the lower costs inherent to the two-cylinder engine, the exhaust note was a big factor in its popularity.

The D, like all of the Deere line, was exceptionally rugged. It was designed from the outset to pull three- or four-bottom plows. At the outset, the D weighed 4,000 pounds (1,800 kg)—a ton (900 kg) less than the McCormick-Deering 15/30 although they were in the same power class. As time went on, the weight grew to 5,300 pounds (2,385 kg) without ballast, still far less than the 15/30.

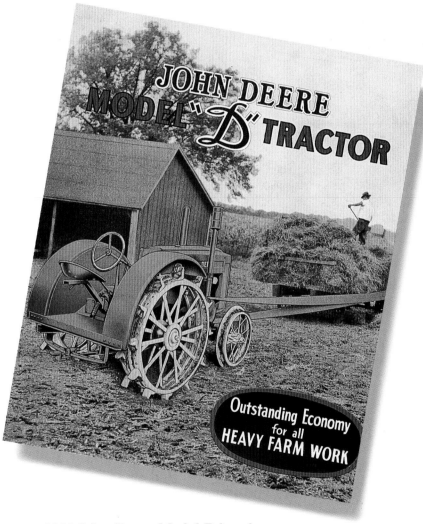

Above: 1939 John Deere Model D brochure

1924 John Deere Model D

Left: *After many false starts and Deere's successful Waterloo Boy acquisition, the Model D became the first truly successful Deere tractor. The Model D introduced in 1923 had a 26-inch (65-cm) spoked flywheel and ladder-side radiator; this successor had left-hand steering and a 24-inch (60-cm) spoked flywheel. The Model D was produced with several improvements for the next thirty years. Owner: Deere & Company.*

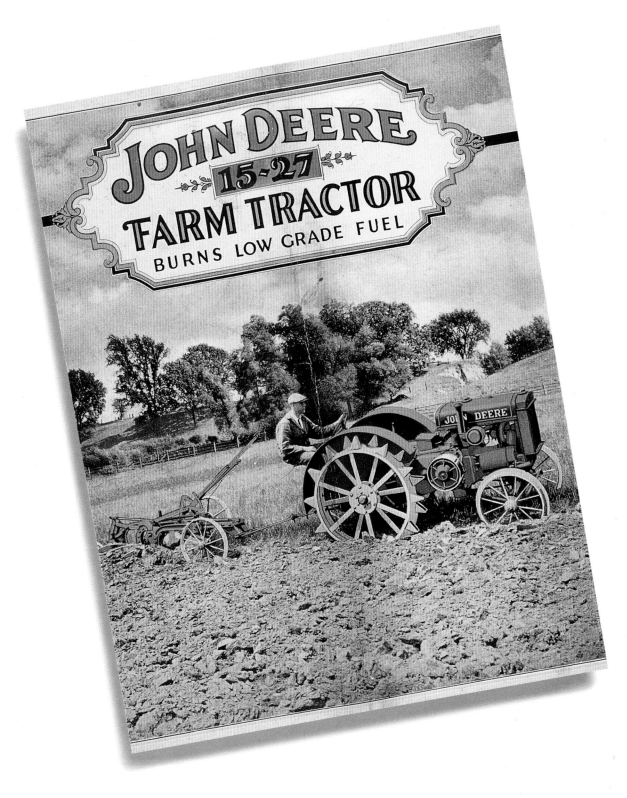

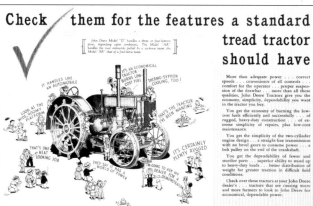

Above: 1927 John Deere Model D brochure

1920s John Deere Model D flyer
Left: *Miniature farmers swarm over a giant Model D in this advertisement reminiscent of* Gulliver's Travels.

1932 John Deere Model GP

Above: *The Model GP tractor was made between 1928 and 1935, and was Deere's first answer to the Farmall. This GP, serial number 228863, was one of only 385 Deere GP tractors made in 1932. It is carrying a GP301 check-row planter, made between 1928 and 1935. Owner: the Keller family.*

Right: 1930 John Deere Model GP brochure

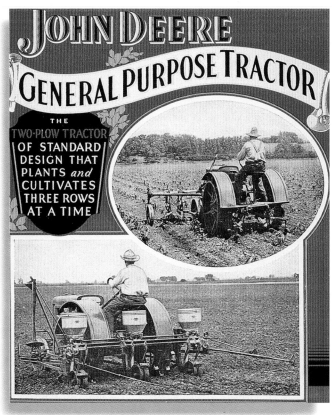

Farewell to the Horse, Hello to the Farmall

It was a sad time for "Old Dobbin": The general-purpose tractor was rapidly becoming the horse's replacement. Once farmers realized that horses were not needed on the farm, a great change took place. Acreage was added to the farm whenever possible, since more could be done with the same manpower. Farmers with extra tractor- and manpower did custom work. While farmers were, in some cases, reluctant to give up their horses, which had struggled along with them through good times and bad, the economics of it became too obvious to ignore.

This change was brought about in large part by the tractor makers. With the advent of the lightweight tractor, manufacturers recognized that their competition was not with the larger tractors, but with the horse. For every 15 acres (6 hectares) a farmer had under cultivation, one horse was needed. Hence, tractor power and indeed price was based on animal competition. The more horses a tractor could replace, the more dollars it could command. The advent of the Fordson and the Tractor Price War provided the impetus for International Harvester to come out with the first truly practical general-purpose tractor—the Farmall.

When the Fordson threatened the whole International Harvester empire in 1922, General Manager Alexander Legge called in Experimental Department Chief Engineer Edward A. Johnston. "What has happened," he asked, "to those versatile tractor concepts you have been working on for the last ten years?"

Johnston and his team had been experimenting with various designs of motor cultivators, some of which were quite innovative. He had, of course, kept Legge and other officials informed of his activities, but there was little corporate interest. In about 1920, the best features of these were combined into an all-purpose tractor, which the team called the Farmall. Several prototypes were constructed. When Johnston told this to Legge and assured him that the Farmall could best the Fordson in every way, Legge ordered twenty more examples built for testing, along with a full complement of implements. The engineers quickly worked on the design to improve performance as well as to make it compatible with new mass-production manufacturing techniques.

The Farmall, as it emerged from Johnston's shop, was built like a tall tricycle. It had large steel rear wheels. The rear axle did not run between the hubs like conventional tractors, but enclosed gear meshes at each end that drove the wheels. Thus, the rear axle could be up and out of the corn. The two front wheels were close together to run between two rows. The tricycle front wheels could rotate almost 90 degrees for steering, making the Farmall much more maneuverable than conventional tractors. In addition, turning the front wheels to their limits actuated cable-operated steering brakes.

Although the Farmall appeared spindly, it was heavier than it looked. It weighed 3,650 pounds (1,643 kg)—about 1,000 pounds (450 kg) more than a Fordson—but the weight was in the right place for traction and stability, two of the Fordson's most glaring shortcomings. Most importantly, the Farmall, as Cyrus McCormick III said in his book, *The Century of the Reaper*, "could handle all farm tasks except milking."

In 1923, more prototypes were ordered, and in 1924, a run of 200 pre-production models were built and sold to farmers. IHC representatives watched closely as the farmers put the Farmall to work, and changes were made as problems arose. The field representatives sent back estimates that the Farmall could reduce costs sixfold when compared to horse farming.

Farmall sales exceeded expectations in 1924, and by 1926, IHC's new Rock Island, Illinois, plant was on line, and Farmalls were rolling out the door. Sales averaged about 24,000 units per year, a far cry from the 100,000-plus Fordsons built annually during its heyday, but along with International Harvester's other tractors it was enough to put it ahead of its nearest competitor, John Deere, by a factor of three.

Junior and Farmall

After old Dobbin made way for the Farmall down on the farm, Junior had a new best friend. (Library of Congress)

Farmall

International Harvester Company of Chicago

1936 Farmall F-12
advertisement

1942 Farmall advertisement

The Farmall heralded the general-purpose tractor revolution when it was first introduced in 1924. It was well thought out and tested before large numbers got into farmers' hands. Thus, Farmalls were noted for living up to their owners' expectations, which more than anything gave farmers faith in power farming and spurred them to retire their horses.

Although not rated by the factory, except for its two 14-inch (35-cm) bottom plow capability, the original Farmall's four-cylinder, overhead-valve engine developed about 25 hp. It weighed a little less than 4,000 pounds (1,800 kg) and was a well-balanced machine. A four-speed transmission was offered. An engine-driven PTO was standard, as was a belt pulley.

Farmalls continued to set the pace for the industry as long as row-crop tractors were popular. Over the years, Farmalls were made in small, medium, and large sizes as well as high-crop versions with even more crop clearance. They became so popular that standard-tread versions of the three sizes were also made available, as were orchard and industrial versions.

Debuting in 1939, the Raymond Loewy–styled Farmalls were so strikingly beautiful they still look modern today.

1930 Farmall Regular

The Farmall was the brainchild of International Harvester's Experimental Department Chief Edward Johnston. It was developed to replace not just some horses on a farm, but all of the horses on the farm. It was introduced at a time when the inexpensive Fordson was glutting the market. Like many other tractor makers, International Harvester needed something dramatic for a counter punch. The Farmall was just that, changing the conventional configuration of the farm tractor from the standard tread to the tricycle row-crop. Owner: Larry Kinsey.

The first of the famous Farmall line was eventually called the "Regular" when subsequent versions were given identifiers. The Regular was built from 1924 to 1931, when it was replaced by the Farmall F-20. Although not rated by the manufacturer, the four-cylinder OHV engine gave the Regular about 20 hp on the belt. Owner: Larry Kinsey.

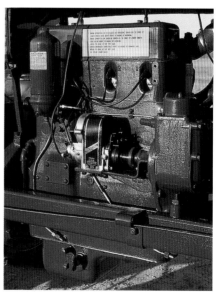

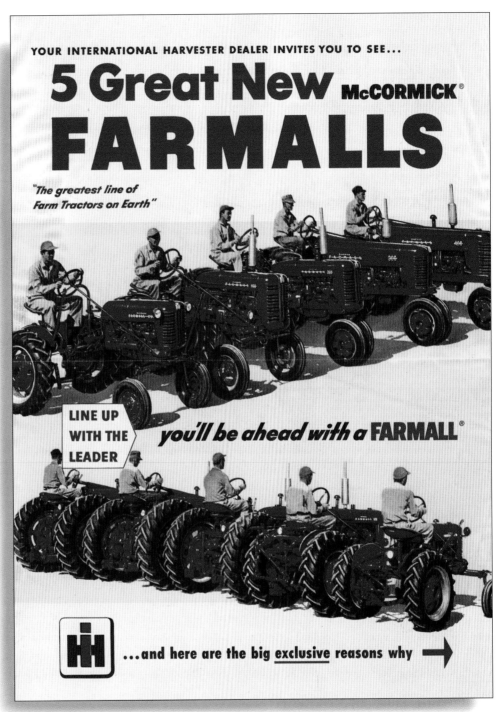

1950s Farmall brochure

"The greatest line of Farm Tractors on Earth," promised this International Harvester brochure. IHC was now offering five Farmall models: the Cub, 100, 200, 300, and 400.

Those New-Fangled Rubber Tires

1934 Allis-Chalmers Model U
Owner Jim Polacek pulls his 1948 Belle City Perfection No. 1 thresher to the next setup.

The "Farmer's Friend"—the Model T Ford automobile—rode on rubber tires, prompting the thought, why not use rubber tires on tractors? In the Model T's early days, rubber tires were not without their problems. People carried as many as four spare tires on trips of any distance, along with a complete tire-repair kit. Nevertheless, the idea persisted. Doodlebug tractors used rubber front wheels, and homemade doodlebugs sometimes used truck rear tires.

Non-pneumatic rubber tires (solid bands of rubber) were also used on some tractors. Early Fordsons and other standard tractors were often used as industrial "mules" on solid rubber tires. As early as 1871, a Thompson Steamer was entered in the California State Fair plowing contest using rubber blocks like cleats around both the front and rear wheels. Hard rubber did not provide the needed traction in soft earth, however.

The next avenue to be explored was prompted by orchard growers. Steel lugs were damaging tree roots during cultivation, so orchard tenders mounted discarded truck tire casings on their steel wheels so the natural strength of the rubber arch supported the weight of the tractor; several casings could be used side by side to get enough support. These proved so successful that in 1931 tire maker B. F. Goodrich brought out what was called a "zero-pressure tire."

As early as 1930, Allis-Chalmers began experimenting with real pneumatic tires. A-C engineers mounted a set of Firestone airplane tires on the rear of an Allis-Chalmers Model U. By working with tire manufacturer Firestone, these were developed into true low-pressure tractor tires. Allis-Chalmers then announced that for the 1931 model year, rubber tires would be standard equipment on the Model U.

Nevertheless, farmers were reluctant to make the change—some even offered dire predictions of polluted land unable to grow crops. Of course, some had made the same prediction about the tractor itself.

By 1934, all major manufacturers offered optional rubber tires. By 1936, 31 percent of all tractors were delivered on rubber, and by 1939 almost all were rubber equipped. During World War II, the rubber shortage forced many farmers to go back to steel, but as soon as possible, they returned to rubber.

1930s Model U tractor race
Allis-Chalmers organized tractor races at county and state fairs across North America to display the speeds possible with the new rubber-tired Model U. Here, famed race-car driver and Allis promoter Barney Oldfield leads two other Us around a horse-racing dirt-track. Oldfield always won his race—it was written into his contract.

1936 Allis-Chalmers Model U

The Model U was originally designed and built in 1929 by Allis-Chalmers for the United Tractor and Equipment Corporation of Chicago, but A-C took over the U completely when United folded. At the same time, Allis worked with Firestone in developing pneumatic tires, and the Model U became the first tractor to be equipped with the new-fangled rubber. Up to 1932, a flat-head Continental engine was used in the Model U. After that an OHV Allis-Chalmers engine was used. Production was continued through 1944. Owner: Alan Draper.

1938 Case CC-3

The CC was Case's first true general-purpose tractor. Owner: Jay Foxworthy.

1938 Minneapolis-Moline Twin City FT-A

Left: *"A tractor is like a horse—it pays to buy a good one," was the M-M advertising slogan in the 1930s. The FT-A was, indeed, a good one. It was introduced in 1929 by the Minneapolis Steel and Machinery Company, which called its line of tractors the Twin City. Originally known as the Twin City 21/32, the FT-A featured hardened steel gears in its three-speed transmission, dual air cleaners, and full-pressure lubrication. The designation was changed to FT-A in 1936 to be more in line with other M-M designations. Owner: the Timm family.*

1937 Fordson Model N

Above: *Henry Ford moved Fordson production to Cork, Ireland, in 1928 and, soon after, to Dagenham, England. Fordsons were then painted blue with orange trim. The Model N's four-cylinder flathead engine displaced 267 ci (4,373 cc). Owner: Eric Coates.*

1938 Fordson All-Around

Left: *Fordson offered its All-Around row-crop variation to satisfy demand in the North American market. Most All-Arounds were exported from England to the United States. Owner: Marlo Remme.*

Farm Crawlers, 1900–1960

"She crawls along like a caterpillar."
—Charles Clements, 1905

1937 Caterpillar Twenty-Two
Main photo: *Call it a tracklayer, crawler, or caterpillar, the steel-tracked tractor was created to spread the machine's weight over a larger surface, increase traction, and lessen soil compaction. Caterpillar's Twenty-Two had a 251-ci (4,111-cc), four-cylinder engine with overhead valves. It was virtually the same tractor as the R2, built in limited numbers for the U.S. government. Owner: Marvin Fery. Fery was one of the founders of the Antique Caterpillar Machinery Owners Club.*

1920s Bates Steel Mule 12/20 advertisement
Above: *Made by the Joliet Oil Tractor Company of Joliet, Illinois, the Steel Mule may have lived up to its namesake's proverbial stubbornness as it soon disappeared from the market.*

Caterpillars, Crawlers, and Tracklayers

Charles Clements, a photographer hired by Benjamin Holt to record scenes of his new crawler tractor for a brochure, coined the term "caterpillar" for the crawler tractor. Clements's view through his primitive camera was of an upside-down machine, the undulation of the topside of the track links reinforcing the "caterpillar" notion. Holt seized upon the descriptive term immediately and made it the now-famous trademark.

By 1905, when Holt made his first steam Caterpillar, crawlers were not a new idea. Attempts had begun in the 1850s to enlarge the footprints of the heavy steam traction engines, many of which tipped the scale at upwards of 50,000 pounds (22,500 kg). The first appears to have been the Minnis Steam traction engine of 1869, which was demonstrated in Ames, Iowa, but nothing more was heard of it.

There were other attempts after the Minnis, but the first to gain success was Alvin Oliver Lombard's Lombard Log Hauler of 1900 from the Waterville Iron Works of Penobscot County, Maine. It was a half-track steam engine with skis in front for steering. One of the reasons for its success was that the machine was only driven on snow and ice, therefore there was little grit to wear out the track pins and little resistance to sliding the tracks sideways for turning. It is interesting to note that the "pilot" sat in front where the cowcatcher would be on a railroad locomotive, controlling the skis with a steering wheel. The engineer rode in the cab, handling the throttle and reversing (brakes) control. About 200 Lombards were sold, and their patents were licensed to others who made similar machines.

Timeline

1903: Wright brothers fly their first airplane

1928: Walt Disney Productions introduces Mickey Mouse

1937: Amelia Earhart lost over the Pacific

1939: First flight by a jet plane, built by Germany's Heinkel Aircraft Company

1941: Aerosol spray can invented

1948: Transistor invented

1956: Interstate highway system approved

1957: Soviets launch first satellite

1960: First laser operated by U.S. physicist Theodore Maiman

1922 Fordson with Hadfield-Penfield crawler conversion
The lightweight Fordson was notorious for the lack of traction. The Hadfield-Penfield Steel Company of Bucyrus, Ohio, made half-track conversion kits for the Fordson in 1926. Besides increasing the ground-contact area, the tracks nearly doubled the weight of the Fordson, greatly improving traction.

1948 Ford Model 8N with Bombardier tracks

Above: *Bombardier, the Canadian aircraft and snowmobile maker, devised this half-track kit for the famous Ford tractor as well as other brands. The tracks were especially effective when a front end loader was employed. Half-tracked Fords were a favorite of maple-syrup producers because the tracks allowed the tractor to operate in deep snow. This 8N was also equipped with an auxiliary two-speed gearbox. Owner: Palmer Fossum.*

1958 Minneapolis-Moline Jetstar II crawler

Left and below: *Minneapolis-Moline built just fifty-one Jetstar III crawlers. Featured was a 206-ci (3,374-cc), four-cylinder engine; five-speed transmission; foot-controlled shuttle shift; and differential steering. Owner: the Keller family. It was restored by M-M expert Rex Dale.*

Holt, Best, and Caterpillar: The Industry Standard

Benjamin Holt's steam Caterpillar was the first successful agricultural crawler, although later versions found good use in logging operations. Originally, the Holt Manufacturing Company of Stockton, California, simply converted one of its wheeled steam traction engines to crawler tracks. Holt was quite experienced with link-belts, or flat chain drives, having pioneered their use in both its "traveling combined harvesters" and in the drive chains for its wheeled steam traction engines. Holt reportedly bolted blocks of wood to parallel link belts to make the first tracks for his 1905 experiment.

The first Holt steam Caterpillar was sold in 1906 to a Louisiana company working in the Mississippi Delta. Steam machines sold well, but by 1908, internal-combustion power was in vogue. Holt incorporated the Aurora Engine Company also of Stockton to build gas engines both for his crawlers and for other companies as well.

Development and acceptance of the gas Caterpillar came in large part from their use in building the great Los Angles Aqueduct, begun in 1908 and comparable in scope to the construction of the Panama Canal. Some twenty-eight Caterpillars were pressed into drayage duties along the 233-mile (373-km) aqueduct. Much of the route was across the Mojave Desert, which proved to be a severe test for the machines. Most importantly, the work forced the rapid development and improvement of the Holt machines.

The Daniel Best Agricultural Works and Benjamin Holt had been competitors in the combine and steam-traction-engine businesses since the 1880s, when in 1908 the seventy-year-old Best suddenly retired and sold out to Holt. As part of the deal, Daniel's son, Clarence Leo "C. L." Best, was to invest in the new joint company and hold a responsible management position. C. L. worked for the new firm for about two years, but he never paid for his shares, and his position never satisfied him.

1919 Holt 10-Ton

The 10-Ton weighed just 9.5 tons (8,550 kg) and was rated by the factory at 75 hp. It was powered by a 929-ci (15,217-cc), overhead-valve, four-cylinder engine. This model was developed with the help of the U.S. Army in World War I. It had a unique segmented-track-roller frame, which gave it higher speed capability. It was also possible to "back out" of the tracks when reversing with a heavy load. Owner: the Vouk family.

In 1910, C. L. Best left Holt and started his own C. L. Best Gas Traction Company of Elmhurst, California—with financial help and blessings from his father. It started making gas-engine wheeled tractors and an almost direct copy of the Holt 75 Caterpillar crawler.

The two companies wrangled in and out of court for years. One of the main bones of contention was the basic crawler track patent. In a swift move, Best's attorney made a deal with Alvin Lombard, maker of the famous Lombard Log Hauler, to buy his patent rights which pre-dated Holt's crawler patents. Lombard was willing to sell as he believed Holt had pirated his design in the first place and then had refused to negotiate payment for the rights. Best prevailed in the lawsuit and forced Holt to pay royalties to continue to use the design.

Holt sold many Caterpillars to the Allied governments during World War I and was given credit—possibly more than he deserved—for helping develop the tank. Best did not get in on the government wartime largess, but came out of the war years with two classic crawler models—the Best Sixty and Thirty. These were uniquely designed and balanced machines that worked well and looked good. Best called his machines "Tracklayers" since the name Caterpillar had been trademarked.

Holt came out of the war with the 2-, 5-, and 10-Ton models; the later two bore the War Department's influence in their designs. While these were good

1913 Holt Model 60

This Model 60 was purchased new for $4,205 by the Hahn brothers, who ran a ranch in Colusa, California. It was used on the ranch until it was sold at an estate sale in 1980. The 1,230-ci (20,147-cc), four-cylinder, OHV engine was rated at 50 drawbar and 60 belt hp at 500 rpm. Turns were made by releasing one steering clutch and pivoting the front tiller wheel. No steering brakes were provided, so only wide, sweeping turns could be accomplished. A considerable amount of human effort went into controlling one of these monsters. Owners: Larry Maasdam and Ron Miller.

and rugged tractors, the larger two of the three never seemed to garner the popularity of the Best machines. The Holt 2-Ton was, however, a favorite among both farmers and loggers.

In April 1925, in an effort to stem the endless patent and sales conflicts, Holt and C. L. Best combined forces as the Caterpillar Tractor Company. The financial houses brought this about, since there was not really enough business for both firms, and the endless struggle for patents was sapping too much energy. The Thirty, Sixty, and 2-Ton were continued, but Holt's 5-Ton and 10-Ton models were dropped after a short time. By 1927, the first all-new Caterpillar debuted as the Model Twenty, replacing the 2-Ton. Smaller and larger "Cats" followed, and ancillary equipment was added, such as the graders made by the Russell Grader Manufacturing Company of Stephen, Minnesota.

In 1931, Caterpillar unveiled the first diesel tractor—a seminal event in the history of tractors. After a grueling $1.5-million, two-year effort, the Diesel Sixty was tested successfully at the University of Nebraska. Despite many growing pains, the diesel set new standards for economy and rugged power. Although Caterpillar continued gasoline engines in ever larger sizes into the 1930s, the diesel engine ruled after World War II.

1921 Holt Model 75

The 75 was powered by a 1,400-ci (22,932-cc), four-cylinder engine and two-speed transmission. Bore and stroke was 7.50x8.00 inches (187.50x200 mm), giving 50 drawbar and 75 belt hp at 550 rpm. A K-W magneto provided spark. Besides the front tiller wheel, steering clutches and brakes were provided on the Model 75. The large wheels at the rear contained the clutches for the tracks. The machine weighed about 23,000 pounds (10,350 kg). Owner: Larry Maasdam.

1925 C. L. Best Thirty Orchard

Above: *C. L. Best tractors used the trade name "Tracklayer" to distinguish them from the Holt Caterpillars. Upon introduction, the Thirty was originally called the Model S. It was built by C. L. Best and Caterpillar between 1921 and 1932, during which more than 23,000 were sold. Owner: Jerry Gast.*

1933 Caterpillar Ten

Left: *Caterpillar built almost 5,000 Tens from 1928 to 1932. The Ten was one of the few Caterpillars to use a side-valve engine, rated at 10 drawbar and 15 belt hp. Owner: Marv Fery.*

1935 Caterpillar Twenty-Eight

The Twenty-Eight was an update of the Twenty-Five, more closely reflecting its true power capabilities. On the drawbar, the Twenty-Eight was rated at 30 hp. Owner: Marv Fery.

1947 Caterpillar D4 Orchard

The D4 U Series featured a new 4.50x5.50-inch (112.50x137.50-mm) engine with cross-flow cylinder heads. The 350-ci (5,733-cc) diesel engine produced 421 foot-pounds of torque at 1,000 rpm. It normally used a two-cylinder, horizontally opposed starting motor with a 2.75x3.00-inch (68.75x75-mm) bore and stroke, but this example has direct electric start. Author Robert Pripps is at the controls. Owner: Larry Maasdam.

1930s Caterpillar Model Twenty-Two Orchard

Looking more like a twenty-first-century moon rover than a tractor from the 1930s, this Twenty-Two bears the complete set of factory orchard accouterments. The streamlined fenders were designed to let the tractor slip through low-hanging branches without getting caught. A four-cylinder, OHV engine with a bore and stroke of 4.00x5.00 inches (100x125 mm) powered the crawler. Owner: Larry Maasdam.

Best/Caterpillar Sixty

C. L. Best Gas Traction Company of Elmhurst, California;
Caterpillar Tractor Company of Peoria, Illinois

C. L. Best's Sixty was introduced in 1919 and tested in Nebraska in 1921. Despite being a popular tractor noted for pulling power and durability, Best had considerable trouble getting it through the tests. This was mainly the fault of the engine not living up to its expectations. The four-cylinder, 1,128-ci (18,477-cc) engine just could not be coaxed to make 60 hp. With the air cleaner removed and the engine operated at 656 (rather than 650) rpm, 56 hp was the most it could do.

In 1923, Best was back at Nebraska with the engine improved by cam and valve changes. Now, at 650 rpm and with the air cleaner in place, the Sixty was able to produce 66 hp. Finally, the official test backed what loyal owners had known all along.

The Sixty was equipped with a two-speed transmission, but a three-speed unit was optional. Later, the three-speed box was standard. The Sixty originally weighed 17,500 pounds (7,875 kg), but was increased to more than 20,000 pounds (9,000 kg). Early versions had a low seat set far aft, with the steering levers out to the right side. This was fine for agriculture and construction, but for logging, a seat, which we would now call "conventional," was substituted. This logging, or cruiser, seat finally became standard. Selling price began at about $4,000 and rose to $6,000 by the end of production in 1931. Almost 20,000 were sold.

In 1931, a new, diesel engine was installed in the basic Sixty running gear and 157 Diesel Sixtys were made that year. With it, Caterpillar had the first production diesel tractor and pioneered the use of the pony-motor starter. In 1932, it was modernized as the Diesel Sixty-Five.

1920s Caterpillar Sixty brochure

The cylinder above the fender was the massive fuel tank, which a hard-working Sixty could easily empty in a ten-hour day.

1926 Caterpillar Sixty

In its heyday, the Sixty was considered the industry standard for large crawlers by farmers and loggers. Introduced in 1919 by C. L. Best, the Sixty became the Caterpillar Sixty after the 1925 merger. It overwhelmed the competition because of its reliable, well-balanced design. Owner: Dave Smith.

Cletrac-Oliver: "Geared to the Ground"

The White family of Cleveland, Ohio, was an inventive lot. Thomas White, the father, founded a sewing machine company in 1859 that bears his name to this day. The company ventured into transportation around the 1900s by manufacturing both roller skates and bicycles. Sons Rollin, Windsor, and Walter built the successful White Steamer automobile in 1900 and later converted their car line to use their own gasoline engines. In 1911, they started the Cleveland Motor Plow Company, later called the Cleveland Tractor Company. Their crawler tractors were named Cletracs and bore the slogan "Geared to the Ground."

Cletracs were unique in that they employed what was then known as "differential steering." Simply, on a Cletrac, engine power was delivered to a differential, as is the case with a wheel vehicle. To steer a Cletrac, one of the tracks was braked by means of a steering brake lever. Other brands of crawlers did not have a differential between the tracks, but employed a clutch and brake for each track, in addition to the normal clutch used for disengaging the whole powertrain from the engine. To turn, one track was declutched, and then that track was braked as necessary while the other track powered through the turn. Cletrac claimed the differential feature as a great benefit, although many operators found Cletracs harder to control than other brands.

Originally, Best Tracklayers were built with differential steering. At one point, when C. L. Best was having a hard time of it due to his inability to get materials to build tractors during World War I, Rollin White was able to gain control of the C. L. Best Traction Company by buying the stock of disgruntled stockholders. It was not long before Best was able to regain control, but in the meantime, his patent rights to the differential-steering concept were lost. After that, Best machines used the clutch-steering method.

These days, the term "differential steering" has a whole different meaning. Today, the most advanced crawlers employ a hydrostatic drive (hydraulic pump-motor) to bias the gear differential between the tracks,

1917 Cleveland 20
Founded by the White brothers, the Cleveland Motor Plow Company became the Cleveland Tractor Company in 1917 and then Cletrac in 1918. This diminutive crawler had a 12/20 rating provided by a Weidley four-cylinder engine. Owner: Charles Doble.

1917 Cleveland advertisement

"Geared to the Ground" was Cletrac's famous motto.

1920 Cletrac Model F

This 1,900-pound (855-kg) crawler demonstrated a drawbar pull of 90 percent of its own weight. It rode on an inner track of rollers that gave it a nice, even footprint. It was also one of the first to use the elevated drive sprocket.

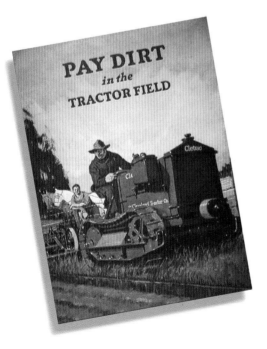

1920s Cletrac brochure

adding speed to one side and subtracting it from the other. By simply moving a hydraulic metering pin, one track can be made to go forward while the other runs in reverse for a pivot turn. Thus, a Caterpillar Challenger, for example, can be spun around in its own length by just an easy movement of the steering wheel.

The pros and cons of differential steering not withstanding, the Cleveland Tractor Company made a credible line of crawlers from 1916 through 1944, when it was sold to the Oliver Corporation. Then, the designs generally continued with little change through the end of the Oliver name. Remarkably, it was the White Motor Corporation that bought Oliver in 1960. In 1965, the crawler line was discontinued.

The smallest Cletrac was the 9-hp, 1,890-pound (850-kg) Model F built from 1920 to 1922. It was characterized by high drive sprockets that resemble modern Caterpillars. During the 1930s, Cletrac went head to head and model for model with Caterpillar. The Cletrac 80 even bested the Cat D8 with 96.73 hp versus the D8's 95.27 hp. The largest Oliver Cletrac was the 130-hp OC-18 of 1952. The OC-18 used a six-cylinder, 895-ci (14,660-cc) Hercules diesel engine.

1936 Cletrac CG
The CG was not a small tractor, weighing almost 6 tons (5,400 kg). It featured a six-cylinder Hercules engine that developed a maximum of 50 hp, and a three-speed transmission. It also offered electric starting.

1952 Oliver HG
The HG had been introduced by Cletrac in 1939. It was powered by an L-head, four-cylinder Hercules engine. It weighed about 2 tons (1,800 kg). Oliver bought Cletrac in 1944 and continued production of the crawler line with Oliver livery. In 1960, a re-organized White—erstwhile founder of Cletrac—bought the Oliver Corporation, proving that what goes around comes around.

Monarch and Allis-Chalmers: Persian Orange Crawlers

The company named after Edwin P. Allis and William J. Chalmers was founded in 1901. Allis was the largest builder of industrial steam engines in the United States. Chalmers was president of Fraser & Chalmers, manufacturers of mining equipment. Allis had died a few years before the merger of the two firms into the Allis-Chalmers Company of Milwaukee, Wisconsin, but he was well represented by his two sons, Will and Charles, and by his nephew Edwin Reynolds, who held the title of chief engineer in the new company.

Almost from the beginning, things did not go well for Allis-Chalmers. The economy was not conducive to the sales of their products, and the board of directors could not pull together to take corrective action. By 1912, the firm went into receivership, with Delmar Call and Otto Falk appointed receivers. The company was then reorganized as the Allis-Chalmers Manufacturing Company. Falk, a general in the Wisconsin National Guard, was named president, a position he would hold until 1932.

Falk saw that the diversification efforts of his predecessors had failed because all eggs were in the same heavy-capital-equipment basket. When the economy was down for one branch, it was down for all. Falk determined that

1939 Allis-Chalmers Model S

This Model S was equipped with a nice cab from its former duties plowing snow. The 10-ton (9,000-kg) S used a 675-ci (11,057-cc), four-cylinder engine developing a maximum of 84 hp. Featured was five-speed transmission giving a top speed of over 6 mph (9.6 kmh).

A-C should go into the agricultural-tractor business with lightweight, inexpensive tractors. Undaunted that his first efforts were not successful, Falk pressed on into larger, more Fordson-like machines by 1918.

The new Allis 15/30 and 18/30 did better, but the tractor business was still loosing money. After a ten-year attempt, Harry Merritt was hired in 1926 as tractor manager, ostensibly to close out the tractor business. Instead, Merritt, a real driver, revitalized the effort, cutting the cost of the tractor line almost in half by re-engineering every part. Then, in 1928, Merritt bought the Monarch Tractor Corporation of Springfield, Illinois. In 1929, he came up with the bright Persian orange paint color. It was the first bright-colored tractor—and essentially became the line's trademark. The addition of Advance-Rumely in 1931, with its dealer and branchhouse network, put Allis-Chalmers in the business for the long haul.

The Monarch line, at the time of the acquisition by A-C, included two crawlers, the Models F and H. Merritt changed the designations to the Models 75 and 50, respectively, to reflect their drawbar horsepower capability. The Monarch label was retained for several more years.

The first original Allis-Chalmers crawler was the Model 35 of 1929. It too was originally called a Monarch, but by 1933, number designations were changed to letters, and the 35 became the K. It was at about that same time that the Monarch moniker was dropped, as was the steering wheel in favor of conventional levers. A-C crawlers had steering clutches and brakes and a hand master clutch.

In the mid-1930s, A-C took a diversionary route into the realm of the semi-diesel for its crawler line. Fuel oil was injected into the engine, but the compression ratio was not high enough to set off the charge. Therefore, a magneto and spark plugs were used. The semi-diesel did not have the fuel consumption advantages of the pure diesel and was never well accepted. It was dropped in 1940 when the HD-14 debuted with a 6-71 two-cycle GM diesel.

A-C used GM diesels in its line of crawlers until 1955 then came out with four-cycle diesels. The HD-21 was the first, with a turbocharged, 844-ci (13,825-cc) six. The largest A-C crawler was the 1970 HD-41, a 50-ton (45,000-kg) monster that had to be assembled on the job. It had a 524-hp engine and could be equipped with a 30-foot-wide (9-m) dozer blade.

In 1974, a merger of Allis-Chalmers and Fiat of Italy created the Fiat-Allis Corporation.

1934 Allis-Chalmers Model K
Originally called the 35, this tractor was later labeled the Model K. Production of the Model K, albeit without the steering wheel, was continued through 1943. A Model K-O version used Allis-Chalmers's semi-diesel engine, a low-compression diesel that used spark plugs to set off the charge. The four-cylinder engine displaced 461 ci (7,551 cc). Owner: Alan Draper.

1969 Allis-Chalmers HD-4
Above and right: *The HD-4 was marketed from 1966 to 1969, with a selling price of $12,000 including the bulldozer blade. The A-C Model 2200 naturally aspirated four-cylinder diesel engine displaced 200 ci (3,276 cc).*

1939 Allis-Chalmers Model L
Facing page, top: *The 22,000-pound (9,900-kg) Model L was powered by a six-cylinder engine of 844 ci (13,825 cc) that delivered more than 90 hp. The twin-carburetor engine featured a split exhaust manifold with twin exhaust pipes. The L was built from 1931 through 1942. Owner: Norm Meinert.*

1941 Allis-Chalmers Model M
Facing page, bottom: *The M was introduced in 1932 and built through 1942. The engine was rated at 32 hp and was the same unit as used in the Allis-Chalmers Model U wheeled tractor.*

1945 John Deere Model BO-Lindeman

John Deere Model BO Orchard tractors were converted to crawler tracks by the Lindeman brothers of Yakima, Washington. The tractor featured the famous John Deere two-cylinder engine of about 25 hp. As converted, the crawler weighed 5,500 pounds (2,475 kg). Individual steering clutches were added. Owner: Harold Schultz.

John Deere Model BO-Lindeman

Lindeman Power Equipment of Yakima, Washington;
Deere & Company of Moline, Illinois

Deere got into the crawler market almost by accident. It all started in 1923 in Yakima, Washington—far afield from Deere's headquarters in Illinois—where Jesse and Harry Lindeman bought the implement business where Jesse had been working. They became a Holt Caterpillar dealer and sold crawlers to their orchard customers. In 1925, when Holt and Best merged, the local Best dealership had seniority, and the Lindemans were out. They then sold the Cletrac and John Deere lines.

Neither the Cletrac crawlers nor Deere's Model D or new Model GP wheeled tractors were really suited for orchard work as they were too high to fit under the trees and had vertical protrusions, such as exhaust pipes and air inlet pipes, that would be knocked off by low-hanging limbs. The brothers modified a GP for orchard work by cleaning up the protrusions and making special castings to lower it. The folks at Deere were impressed. They adopted the Lindeman's ideas, and the first Deere orchard tractor was born—the Model GPO.

In 1932, the brothers again told Deere they had something new to show them. They had adapted the tracks from a Best Thirty to a Deere Model D. Thorough testing proved the concept, but a decision was made to discontinue the D crawler and build a crawler version of the GPO, which was receiving acclaim from orchard owners.

The GPO-Lindeman was built from 1933 until 1935. At first, the usual individual brakes were used for differential steering. Later, the differential was removed and steering clutches incorporated for improved control. In 1935, production of the Model GP was halted in favor of the new Model B. An orchard version, the Model BO, was included in the line. The Lindeman brothers went right on receiving partially completed tractors from Deere and finishing them with tracks, creating the Model BO-Lindeman of 1939–1947.

Deere was so impressed by the Lindeman brothers' work that it bought their operation on January 1, 1947. Later in the year, the Model M replaced the Model B, and Lindeman continued with the conversions in Yakima, creating the MC (M Crawler). In 1953, the updated 40C replaced the MC.

In 1954, Deere moved the crawler operations and many of its employees from Yakima to Deere's Dubuque, Iowa, factory that had been producing the basic tractors that supplied the Yakima plant, a means of consolidating operations for future expansion. Deere planned to get into construction/industrial machinery in a big way. Since then, Deere has produced a full line of thoroughly modern crawlers, including rubber-track versions specifically for agriculture.

1940s Lindeman Model BO-L leaflet

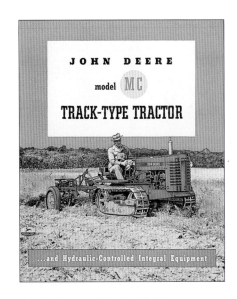

1950 Deere Model MC brochure

The MC replaced the BO crawler. Tractor base units were shipped from Deere to Lindeman in Yakima to have tracking fitted for the West Coast market, and track units were shipped to Iowa for the rest of the United States and export. The new model soon found favor not only with fruit farmers in the hilly Northwest but also with housing and other small contractors. The last MC was built in 1952.

Orphan Crawlers

1915 Bullock Creeping Grip and Neverslip advertisement

The Bullock Tractor Company of Chicago termed its machine the "Flat Wheel Tractor" and promised that every ounce of power was utilized. Even with its evocatively named machines, Bullock suffered several bankruptcies before finally exiting the field in the 1920s.

As with the tractor industry as a whole, it was survival of the fittest in the specialized world of the crawler tractor. Numerous small firms attempted to build their own crawlers in the pioneering years of the gasoline tractor, and many of these machines ended their days as orphan crawlers, wiped out by the economic recession following World War I or the Great Depression of the 1930s.

1917 Bates Steel Mule Model D and C advertisement

"A Tractor Now for All Conditions," announced this ad from the Joliet Oil Tractor Company. The colorfully named Bates Steel Mule went through numerous permutations over the years, from the lightweight 15/22 Model D to the massive Model 80. Joliet merged in 1919 with the Bates Tractor Company of Lansing, Michigan, creating the Bates Machine & Tractor Company. The Great Depression forced production to end in 1937.

Yuba Ball Tread 12/20, 1916

Rather than bogie wheels, the miniature Yuba 12/20's track system rode on large ball bearings between the track and track frame. The Yuba Construction Company of Marysville, California, bought rights to the tractor in 1914 from the Ball Tread Company of Detroit. Ball Treads were made in sizes up to 40/70, always with a tiller wheel. The name was changed to Yuba Manufacturing Company in 1918, but the firm disappeared during the Great Depression.

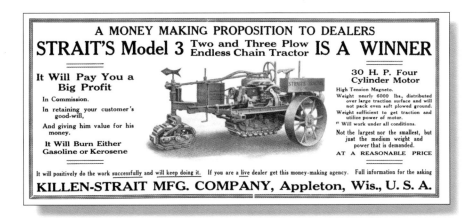

1916 Strait's Model 3 advertisement

The Killen-Strait Manufacturing Company of Appleton, Wisconsin, offered its "Endless Chain Tractor" in the 1910s. Oddly enough, the Strait's Model 3 featured a single wheel to offset the tracks.

1919 Pan Tank-Tread advertisement

The Pan Motor Company of St. Cloud, Minnesota, began to build automobiles in 1916 before introducing its crawler tractor in 1917. The Pan firm's founders were better at raising money than building and selling cars or crawlers, however, and questionable business practices and legal wrangling quickly sank the company.

Caterpillar D8

Caterpillar Tractor Company of Peoria, Illinois

1936 Caterpillar RD8

The RD8 was "big iron" in its day as it featured a six-cylinder engine of 103 hp. The Diesel Seventy-Five became the RD8 in 1936, and the "RD" designation was carried through 1938; the designation was simply "D8" thereafter. The RD8 was a big machine, weighing almost 34,000 pounds (15,300 kg). Owner: Larry Maasdam.

When push comes to shove, Caterpillar's D8 was almost everybody's favorite crawler. It was the Boeing B-52 Stratofortress of tractors until the D9 came out in 1954. By then, the term "D8" was, like the B-52, a synonym for overkill. Nobody really needed more power than the D8 offered—although buyers of the D9, D10, and D11 seemed to think they did.

The D8 was an outgrowth of the Diesel 70 of 1933. In late 1933, Caterpillar created a standard engine with a bore-and-stroke configuration of 5.25x8.00 inches (131.25x200 mm) but using three, four, and six cylinders. When the standard six-cylinder engine was put in the Diesel Seventy chassis, it became the new Diesel Seventy-Five. In 1936, Caterpillar changed its model designators that tended to signify horsepower to a new letters-and-number system that had no such connotation. The Diesel Seventy-Five became the RD8. Later, "R" designators were used for gasoline tractors and a "D" indicated diesel, hence, the D8.

The most famous of the classic D8s was the U Series of 1947–1955. The standard engine was now 5.75x8.00 inches (143.75x200 mm), and power in 1955 was up to 155 hp. The D8 weighed 37,000 pounds (16,650 kg). A five-speed transmission was used.

Stories abound of the legendary feats of the D8. Some come from the author's uncle, Norman Pripps, a World War II Seabee in the South Pacific. His outfit had Allis-Chalmers and International crawlers in addition to D8s. They left the others behind at the end of each island campaign, but kept the same D8s throughout the war. The others required a push to fill a LeTourneau scraper; the D8 could fill the same scraper to overflowing without assistance. When pushing over trees with the D8, the bulldozer blade could cave in if the tree was stubborn.

The D8 had the right balance, power, and a pleasing exhaust note. There is a story of a driver on a logging job that was given an International to operate in place of his aging D8. When asked why he had ripped off the muffler, he responded, "If I can't drive a Caterpillar, at least I can drive something that sounds like one."

1934 Caterpillar Diesel Seventy-Five

The Diesel Seventy-Five was made from 1933 to 1935 and boasted 93 hp from its 5.25x8.00-inch (131.25x200-mm), six-cylinder engine. Owners: the Skirvin Brothers; Carl Skirvin is at the controls.

"No one can see far ahead in these days, but of this we can be certain:
Mechanical devices for winning battles will be the predominant factor. Brave men will
still be essential to the proper handling of war machines, but it will be a war of
machinery, rather than a war of flesh."
—French World War I army commander Marshall Ferdinand Foch, 1926

Farmer Leo Steiner, owner of a large agricultural estate in Hungary, read reports of the large-scale mechanized farms in the United States. Because much of his estate had wet soil, Steiner decided to order a Holt Caterpillar Model 60. He liked the machine so much that he applied to be a Holt dealer, and in 1912, he was awarded the dealership for the countries of Hungary, Austria, and Germany.

Steiner then challenged all competitors throughout his territory to pulling and plowing contests. The prowess of the Caterpillars in these contests soon caught the attention of the Austrian military. The Austrians asked for further demonstrations and invited their German military counterparts to witness them as well. The German representatives were not convinced of the Holt's military significance, but their opinion changed in 1913, and Steiner was ordered to import all the Caterpillars he could get, and to look into manufacturing rights. Fortunately for the Allies, the Germans had delayed their decision long enough for World War I to break out, and all trade with the Central Powers came to a halt before more than a few Caterpillars were delivered.

On June 28, 1914, the Crown Prince of Austria was assassinated in the city of Sarajevo, Serbia, and war broke out between Austria and Serbia. Due to their mutual defense treaties, Germany, France, and England were dragged into the conflict on both sides, sparking World War I. The United States was drawn in to the conflict on April 6, 1917.

Orders for Holt Caterpillar 75s quickly followed from several of the Allies. After Britain, France, and Russia had ordered more than 1,000 Caterpillars, the U.S. War Department finally consented to tests in 1915. The War Department still held to the old philosophy that only animal power was reliable enough for war use, but in 1916, the U.S. Army finally purchased twenty-seven Holt Caterpillars.

The Army Caterpillars were soon pressed into service when President Woodrow Wilson ordered General John "Blackjack" Pershing into Mexico in a punitive foray against Mexican revolutionary Pancho Villa. While Pershing's expedition failed to capture Villa, Caterpillar tractors were instrumental in conveying troops and supplies some 350 miles (560 km) into then-roadless Mexico. Resounding praise by Pershing for the Caterpillars gave them credibility with the army.

Meanwhile, British Army Colonel Earnest D. Swinton heard reports of the performance of the Holt Caterpillars at the front in Belgium: The big crawlers were virtually unstoppable in even adverse conditions. He had the British Foster Company build a completely armored tracked vehicle—soon known as a "tank"—using the Hornsby-Akroid-Roberts track technology previously sold to Holt. These tanks were first used in September 1916 in the Battle of the Somme in France with great effectiveness, putting an end to the concept of trench warfare.

While Holt had nothing to do with the tank, Caterpillar techniques were employed. At the same time, Caterpillars were being armor-plated by the Allied countries to enable them to pull big guns into firing positions. As a result, American newspapers gave credit to Holt for the development of the tank. After the war, Swinton lavished praise on Holt, calling the Holt works in Stockton "the cradle of the tank."

1940s Caterpillar advertisement
From its role as the forefather of the tank in World War I, the crawler served patriotically in World War II in all theaters. Caterpillars did everything from helping to build the Alcan Highway to clearing beachheads with the Navy Seabees.

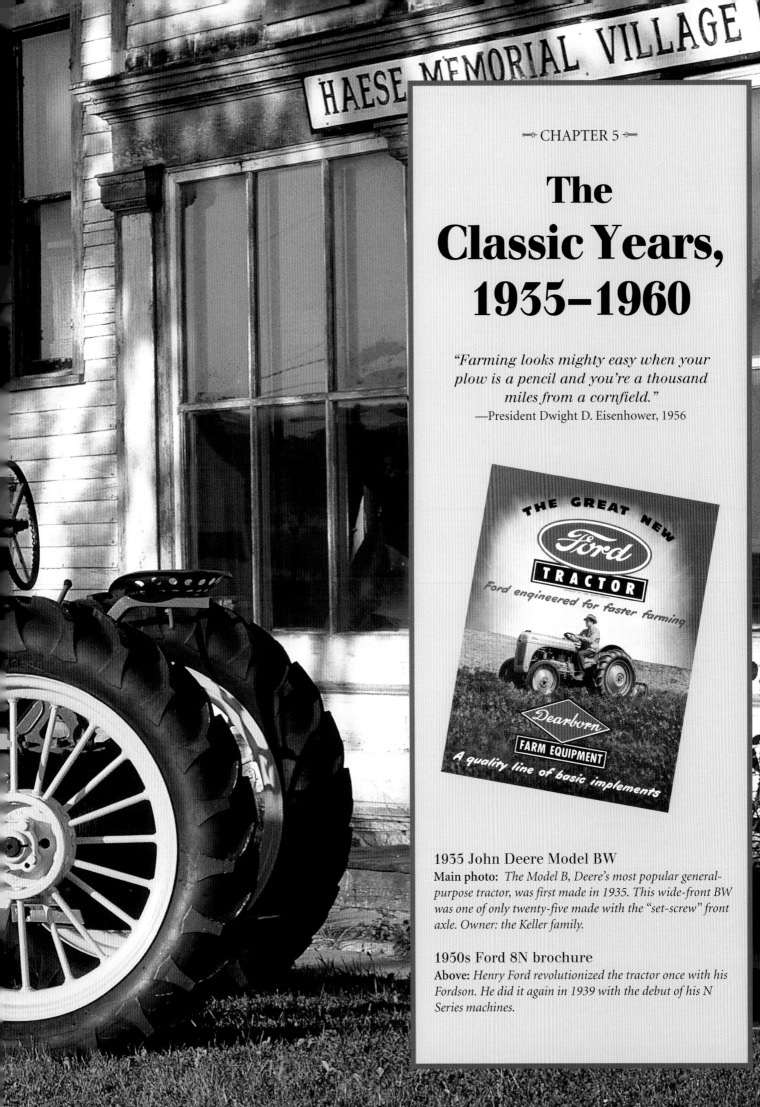

⇒ CHAPTER 5 ⇐

The Classic Years, 1935–1960

"Farming looks mighty easy when your plow is a pencil and you're a thousand miles from a cornfield."
—President Dwight D. Eisenhower, 1956

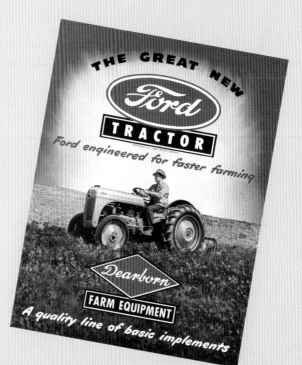

1935 John Deere Model BW

Main photo: *The Model B, Deere's most popular general-purpose tractor, was first made in 1935. This wide-front BW was one of only twenty-five made with the "set-screw" front axle. Owner: the Keller family.*

1950s Ford 8N brochure

Above: *Henry Ford revolutionized the tractor once with his Fordson. He did it again in 1939 with the debut of his N Series machines.*

The Best of Times and the Worst of Times

By 1935, the United States had passed through the worst of the Great Depression. Tractor sales were rising, and the devastating drought of the first few years of the 1930s was over. While things were still tough both on the farm and in the city, President Franklin Delano Roosevelt's New Deal policies were at last having some of the desired effects. Roosevelt's programs had helped increase farm income. In some rural areas, electricity was available; some even had telephone service. Things were looking up for the farmer.

The growling Fordson had been banished to England by the new, general-purpose, row-crop machines. Steam was all but gone from the scene. Tractor sales for 1934 were up 40 percent over 1933, and the surviving tractor makers were offering new, modern models.

Dark specters were lurking on the horizon, however. Minatory dictatorships had risen from the ashes of World War I, which had ended a mere eighteen years earlier. Adolph Hitler's National Socialism threatened to engulf Europe, drawing the globe into its second world war. The farm crawler's military sibling, the tank, became one of the key strategic weapons on both sides of the battle. Afterwards, the remaining tensions of World War II sparked the Cold War.

The 1940s and 1950s were the best of times and the worst of times for the farm tractor. The market for tractors grew steadily and dramatically until 1954, when another industry shakeout similar to that of the 1920s resulted in a market consolidated in the hands of just a few manufacturers.

Throughout these decades the basic shape of the tractor changed little from the general-purpose machine personified by International Harvester's Farmall. Developments were more evolutionary than revolutionary, however, including the rise of live hydraulics, new fuels, and independent PTOs. Tractor makers continued to build a better tractor, thanks in large part to engineering lessons learned during World War II.

Timeline

1937: Dirigible Hindenburg crashes in New Jersey

1939: Germany invades Poland; WWII begins

1939: First American TV broadcast

1941: Japan bombs Pearl Harbor; United States enters World War II

1944: Allies invade France on D-Day

1945: V-E Day May 7; V-J Day August 15, after two nuclear bombs dropped on Japan

1946: U.S. Air Force Captain Chuck Yeager is first man to exceed the speed of sound

1950: Korean War begins

1951: First hydrogen bomb exploded

1954: *Nautilus*, the first nuclear submarine, launched

1959: First computer chip patented

1937 Massey-Harris Challenger
Above and facing page: *The Challenger was a modernized row-crop version of the Wallis 10/20 and was built from 1936 to 1938. Owner: Howard Dobbins.*

1942 Ford-Ferguson 2N
What every tractor collector hopes to find: a forgotten classic hiding in the woods and available for sale.

During the early stages of World War II, many changes took place to get the entire civilian population on a wartime footing. Men too old or physically unfit for the service, as well as women of all ages, were urged to get employment in "defense" plants, on farms, or in construction for the war effort. Gasoline, butter, meat, shoes, and many other items were rationed. Each family member got a ration book with tear-out coupons, and a gas ration book was issued for each vehicle.

At the same time, the Boy Scouts, Girl Scouts, churches, VFW posts, and junk dealers held scrap-metal drives. Anyone who had an old or disabled tractor or other vehicle was encouraged to donate it to the war effort. Both of the author's grandfathers donated to the war scrap metal drive—one a fine old Case steam engine, the other a Cleveland-made 1918 JT crawler. An untold number of the oldest tractors met their fate in that way.

1940 Oliver 80 Diesel

Left and below: *The 80 was an out-growth of the Oliver Hart-Parr 18/27 and 18/28 tractors of 1930–1937. The diesel version was introduced in 1940 with a Buda-Lanova engine. Later, Oliver replaced the engine with one of its own design.*

1935 Allis-Chalmers Model UC

Right: *The UC was A-C's first row-crop tractor and was otherwise the same as the Model U. It was built from 1930 to 1941. Originally equipped with a Continental engine like the Model U, later versions had an Allis engine.*

1941 Case Model VC
Case's Model VC replaced the Model RC in 1940 and was replaced by the VAC in 1942. The four-cylinder L-head engine of the VC was supplied by Continental.

1955 Ferguson TO-35
After the split with Ford, Harry Ferguson's TO-35 was built in Detroit. It had a 134-ci (2,195-cc) Continental engine, six-speed transmission, and weighed about 3,000 pounds (1,350 kg). Owner: Palmer Fossum.

Scrap metal drive
During World Wars I and II, scrap metal drives melted down many a classic farm tractor, turning plowshares into swords for the patriotic war effort. This 1940s ad from Minneapolis-Moline warned farmers that liberty—in the form of the Statue of Liberty—was in danger if they didn't harvest their old tractors for the war. Unstated, naturally, was that farmers would then need a new tractor, preferably a Prairie Gold Minne-Mo.

Deere Model B

Deere & Company of Moline, Illinois

John Deere's Model B probably introduced more farmers to power farming than any other tractor since the venerable Fordson. From its introduction in 1935 until its retirement in 1952, well over 300,000 Model B tractors were delivered.

The B was designed more or less simultaneously with the larger John Deere Model A, which made its debut in 1934. Both had a hydraulic implement lift, adjustable rear-wheel tread width, and one-piece rear-axle housings—new features in 1934–1935. The 2,800-pound (1,260-kg) Model B was designed to compete with a team of horses and cost not much more. In fact, since horses tired and had to be rested, the original B could do the work of two teams. Later-year models became more powerful and heavier, eventually supplanting the original A.

The original Model B two-cylinder engine displaced 149 ci (2,441 cc) and produced about 15 hp on kerosene via a four-speed transmission.

1930s John Deere Models A and B brochure

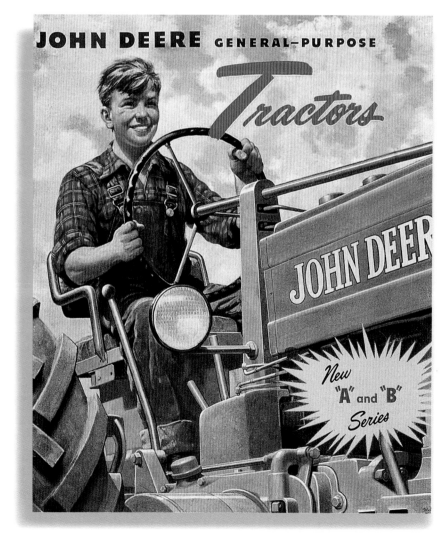

1935 John Deere Model B-Garden

This B, serial number 1798, was built on December 12, 1934. After April 1935, production front pedestals were changed from four to eight bolts, and the designation changed to BN (narrow) indicating the single front wheel. As acquired by Walter Keller in Helena, California, this tractor had the wrong front end. Keller found the right parts and disassembled the front, propping it up on blocks. While working on it, he decided to change the leaking flywheel seal at the same time. In the process, he rolled the flywheel a quarter turn, and the engine fired up. Needless to say, there was a scramble to shut it off.

In 1938, the B received Henry Dreyfuss's styling treatment and a 19-hp engine of 175 ci (2,867 cc). In 1947, the B was restyled yet again by the Dreyfuss studio. Engine displacement for these "late-styled" B's was increased to 190 ci (3,112 cc), producing some 28 hp in the gasoline version with a six-speed gearbox.

The Models B and A were the first of Deere's new general-purpose tractors. Dual narrow front wheels were the conventional configuration, but single-front-wheel and wide-front versions were available, along with standard-tread, industrial, and orchard models. Later, high-crop and special narrow adaptations of the basic B were offered, as was the Lindeman crawler version of the orchard B.

1935 John Deere Model BW

Below: *On the right is the B's owner, Walter Keller. On the left is eighty-three-year-old Ruben Schaeffer, owner of the barn behind the tractor.*

1935 John Deere Model Bs

Above: *Two rare Deere Model B tractors with two famous collector-restorers at the controls. On the left is the BW with Walter Keller. On the right is a B-Garden with Walter's son Bruce.*

1935 John Deere Model BW
This wide-front BW has the optional F&H wheels and rubber tires. Early Model B tractors, such as this one, used a 149-ci (2,441-cc), two-cylinder engine.

1943 John Deere Model BN Styled

This wartime Model BN (narrow, single front wheel) was delivered on steel. Road gear was not included by Deere when tractors were not shipped on rubber tires. From 1941 to mid-1947, the B was equipped with a 175-ci (2,867-cc) engine; after that, a 190-ci (3,112-cc) engine was used. Owner: Larry Maasdam.

Streamlined Styling Comes to the Farmyard

In the middle of the twentieth century, manufacturers suddenly came to the startling realization that visible product differentiation had a positive effect on sales. Dramatic colors and stylish lines flourished on everything from household appliances to food packaging to home radios. Cars, which had been pretty much alike, now began to sport individualistic radiator grilles, sweeping and skirted fenders, raked windshields, and engines with as many as sixteen cylinders.

The radiator grille and the louvered hood side panels were the hallmarks of automotive styling in the early 1930s, so it was little wonder that these items found their way to the tractor. The first volume-produced American tractor to get this treatment was the famous Oliver Hart-Parr 70. It was billed as being so "car-like" that "Bud" and "Sister" could take their turns at the wheel.

The word "streamlined" was soon being used to describe new tractors from a variety of manufacturers. The 1936 orchard version of the Model J from the Minneapolis-Moline Company of Minneapolis looked like it could take its place at the starting grid of the Indianapolis 500 race. In 1937, stylish new sheet metal graced Huber's Model B, Massey-Harris's Pacemaker, Minneapolis-Moline's Z, and the glorious Graham-Bradley from the Graham-Paige Motors Corporation of Detroit, Michigan.

In 1938, the big players in the league reacted. Deere hired noted New York industrial designer Henry Dreyfuss to style its entire line of tractors. The Dreyfuss firm has left its mark on the design of Deere tractors ever since. International Harvester hired the famous automobile stylist Raymond Loewy. The first of the beautiful red Internationals was the long-lived TD-18. These were more than just sheet metal coverings over old machinery: These two design experts analyzed everything from a proper seat to adequate visibility for cultivating, making real and lasting improvements.

The zenith of avant-garde styling came in 1938 on the Minneapolis-Moline Comfortractor Model UDLX. Equipped with the first "factory cab," the UDLX had all the amenities of a sports coupe of the day. It was promoted as a tractor that could be

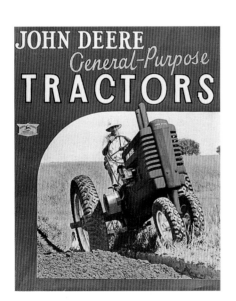

1940s John Deere Models A and B Styled brochure

worked all day and driven to town in the evening at its top speed of 40 mph (64 kmh).

The influence of automotive styling and engineering on tractors reached a peak in 1938 when Henry Ford began work on what was to become the Ford-Ferguson 9N tractor. Ford assigned his Ford Motor Company styling department to come up with the layout. The look of the new tractor complemented the rest of the Ford, Mercury, and Lincoln car and Ford truck lines, which were then classics of art deco. Most of all, the design was functional, could be produced economically, and was sized so that tractors would fit crosswise in a boxcar for maximum shipping economy.

Tractor styling lasted ten to twelve years before refreshing was required. Color became an identifiable trademark for tractor makers, and few changed colors after the 1940s. Toward the end of the 1950s, ergonomics—the science of human convenience—began to be considered. Such things as handholds and safety shields were added, along with better mufflers, lights, and convenient controls. Finally, towards the end of the 1950s, factories began experimenting with insulated, soundproofed, and air-conditioned cabs.

1947 John Deere Model G Styled

The G was introduced in 1937 as the row-crop equivalent of the standard-tread Model D. Power was about the same, although the engines were different. The G was also about 1,000 pounds (450 kg) lighter than the D. The 1942 version received streamlined sheet metal crafted by famed industrial designer Henry Dreyfuss. The 1947 model saw the G in its final form with the backrest seat and electric starting.

1940s Oliver Model 66

Oliver's stylish 66 debuted in 1947 as a 1948 model. Gasoline, diesel, and LPG engines of 129 ci (2,113 cc) were offered, as well as a 144-ci (2,359-cc), distillate-burning engine. All were four-cylinders and produced around 20 hp. Standard-tread and row-crops, both wide and narrow front, were offered. This 66 was a wide-front row-crop diesel.

1941 Farmall M

Above, both photos: *The big M was the top of the Farmall line from 1939 to 1954, replacing the F-30. The M used a 247.7-ci (4,057-cc), four-cylinder engine and could handle a three-bottom plow. It was available in distillate, gasoline, or diesel versions. Sales of the M averaged more than 22,000 units annually.*

1937 Minneapolis-Moline YT

Minneapolis-Moline wanted a small tractor to compete with the Farmall F-14 and the Deere H, and believed the YT to be the answer. The YTs made were prototypes that never went into production, and this rare M-M tractor was one of only twenty-five made. It was unique in that it has a vertical two-cylinder engine of 93 ci (1,523 cc); the engine was basically the back half of a Z engine. Owner: Walter Keller.

Minneapolis-Moline Model UDLX Comfortractor

Minneapolis-Moline Company of Minneapolis

The most famous of the U Series was the UDLX, also known as the U-Deluxe and Comfortractor. This was designed to be a tractor that farmers could drive to town after it had spent the day working in the field, and top speed was a blazing 40 mph (64 km/h). The UDLX featured items like a shift-on-the-fly five-speed transmission, windshield wipers, high- and low-beam headlights, taillights, cigarette lighter, heater, speedometer, and seating for three.

Under the skin, the tractor was basically a Model UTS. While the enclosed cab was comfortable, the lack of hydraulics meant the back door had to be kept open in order to reach implement levers. The tractor was not practical for other than pulling jobs, as there was no belt pulley or PTO. The UDLX was less than optimum on the highway as well, since it did not have sprung axles. Even at low speeds, it tended to waddle like a duck. Where the UDLX really shone was in the service of the custom combiner. The long-distant pulls between jobs could be made in relative comfort and at reasonably high speeds.

The UDLX used the UTS's four-cylinder, overhead-valve engine of 284 ci (4,652 cc) and about 40 hp. It weighed about 4,500 pounds (2,025 kg).

On the downside, without hydraulics the implements had to be hand lifted through the back door, there was no provision for a belt pulley or a PTO, and the lack of springs made the ride barely tolerable at higher speeds. It has been said that the best use given the UDLX was in transporting M-M field men around to dealers. Needless to say, the UDLX attracted a lot of attention then as now.

In the end, only about 150 of these stylish, but not really practical, tractors were built. Today they are one of the most admired collectible vintage tractors of all time.

1930s Minneapolis-Moline UDLX brochure

Minneapolis-Moline UDLX at work, 1930s

A Comfortractor pulls a Minneapolis-Moline corn harvester through a bumper crop.

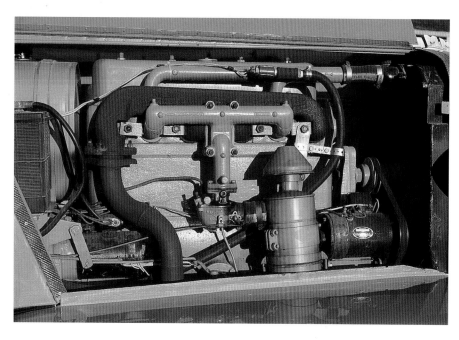

1938 Minneapolis-Moline UDLX

One of the first tractors to have a fully enclosed factory cab, the UDLX was designed to allow a farmer to work all day and then drive the tractor to town in the evening. It had seating for three, wind-up windows, windshield wipers, a speedometer with an odometer, cigarette lighter, and a shift-on-the-fly five-speed transmission. Owner: the Keller family.

Hydraulic Power: A Revolution in Utility

"To Lift the burden of farming from flesh and blood and place it on steel and motors."
—Henry Ford

Probably the greatest step forward for tractor utility came from the addition of hydraulic power. Today, with hydraulic power as common as dust on a windowsill, it is hard to imagine why it was so long in coming. There are two reasons: High-pressure pumps were not available, and high-pressure cylinders did not have adequate life in dirty conditions.

The first tractor hydraulics appeared in 1934 as an implement lift on the John Deere Model A. It was fairly low pressure and was enclosed in the final-drive housing to keep it out of the dirt. Other manufacturers followed with similar systems, culminating in the famous Ford-Ferguson three-point hitch of 1939.

Ferguson's patented system was different from Deere's in that it had a feedback control system. Control-lever movement created an error signal in the valve pack, and the hydraulics moved the implement to correct the error. The secret of Ferguson's system was that implement overload could also create the error signal. Thus, if the plow hit harder soil, it would raise automatically until the draft load was the same as had previously been set by the operator. This raising and lowering to maintain the set draft load happened instantly without operator input. It made tractor plowing a job even the inexperienced could do. To prove the point, Henry Ford had an eight-year-old boy demonstrate plowing with his new 9N at the press introduction in 1939.

1959 Ford 961 Diesel

The 901 Series tractors were 50-hp row-crop machines offered by Ford from 1958 through 1961. The 961 had a live PTO and five-speed transmission. It used the 172-ci (2,817-cc), four-cylinder engine of the 801 Series. Owner Floyd Dominique is at the wheel.

1959 Case 300B Tripl-Range

Above, both photos: *The 300B replaced the Rock Island–built 300, which in turn had replaced the VA. Both the 300 and 300B used a Case 148-ci (2,424-cc) gasoline engine or a Continental 157-ci (2,572-cc) diesel. Tripl-Range drive consisted of a four-speed transmission plus a three-speed auxiliary, for twelve forward speeds and three in reverse.*

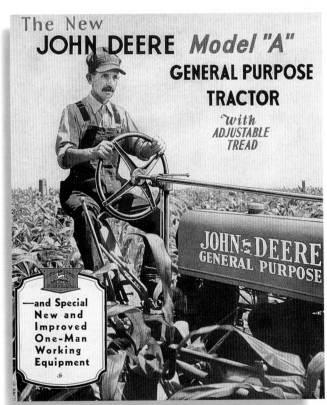

1945 Allis-Chalmers Model C
Above, both photos: *This Model C has a Northfield loader conversion. The C was essentially the same as the Model B, but with a tricycle front end. The C was offered from 1939 to 1949. It was followed by a Model CA, built from 1949 to 1958 with a more powerful engine and adjustable wheel spacing. Owner: Kenneth Anderson.*

1930s John Deere Model A brochure
The Model A was first offered in 1934 and was the first tractor with a hydraulic implement lift.

1952 John Deere Model AWH

Although 1952 was the last year for the Model A general-purpose line, some AO Orchard and AR standard-tread versions were built in 1953. This rare wide-front Hi-Crop was one of the last of its type. The A was at first unstyled, then in 1938 it received styled sheet metal. In 1947, it was restyled into what is known as the "late-styled" configuration. Owner: Larry Maasdam.

Ford-Ferguson 9N

Ford Motor Company of Dearborn, Michigan

The Ford-Ferguson was one of the greatest and most significant tractors of the twentieth century. It heralded the change from the row-crop configuration to the now-standard utility configuration, and introduced the load-compensating three-point hitch. Although small—weighing just 2,300 pounds (1,035 kg) with a 120-ci (1,966-cc) engine—it could plow 12 acres (4.8 hectares) a day with two 14-inch (35-cm) plows. This was a plowing rate that only a much larger and more expensive John Deere Model G or Farmall Model M could equal. More than 840,000 Ford N Series were sold over twelve years at a price starting at less than $600, eventually raising to about $1,200. At the peak of their popularity, 9,000 tractors were being delivered per month.

The Ford-Ferguson 9N was introduced in 1939; the "9" in the model designation stood for the year. Irishman Harry Ferguson had given up trying to build tractors with gear-maker David Brown in England and had made a deal with auto magnate Henry Ford. Ferguson had been working on his system since the 1920s, first applying it to the original Fordson tractor, then to a tractor of his own design, the Ferguson-Brown, and finally, the highly successful Ford-Ferguson. In 1942, a 2N wartime version was introduced, which was

Ford N Series engineer Harold L. Brock, 1990s
Harold L. Brock displays Harry Ferguson's spring-wound tractor model that showed the basic workings of the three-point hitch system. This model was first shown by Ferguson to Henry Ford at the meeting that formed the famous Handshake Agreement. (Photograph © Robert N. Pripps)

1941 Ford-Ferguson 9N
The 1941 version of the famous 9N can be identified by the liberal use of chrome, such as on the radiator cap and shift knob. Owner: Jack Crane.

157

1939 Ford-Ferguson 9N

This 9N was probably built during the first week of production and still sports its cast-aluminum hood. Because of their propensity for damage, such hoods are rare today. Owners, such as Palmer Fossum who owns this one (serial number 364), often polish them to shine like chrome.

essentially the same as the 9N, but was originally built without an electrical system or rubber tires. These items later found their way back onto the 2N, but the designation stayed the same, since it allowed a wartime price increase as well.

In 1948, the modernized 8N arrived, but Ferguson was excluded from the deal by Ford Motor Company's new president, Henry Ford II. Young Henry, grandson of the auto magnate, discovered that the company had already lost $25 million selling tractors to Ferguson, who re-sold them through his tractor and implement dealerships. Young Henry's interpretation of the famous Hand-shake Agreement between his grandfather and Ferguson was that either party

1930s Ford-Ferguson 9N brochure

could break it at any time without cause. While Ferguson agreed with that part of it, he didn't agree that the 8N could incorporate his patented Ferguson System. A rancorous and expensive lawsuit followed.

In the end, Ford settled by paying Ferguson $12 million—a fraction of the original suit—and by producing the all-new NAA Jubilee tractor, which had a different hydraulic system. The basic patents on Ferguson's three-point hitch had run out by then, and all manufacturers were jumping aboard. Ferguson went on with his own version of the tractor, the TE-20 built in England and the TO-20 built in Detroit. Ferguson later sold out to Massey-Harris, which then became Massey-Ferguson.

1945 Ford-Ferguson 2N

This 2N has a two-bottom disk plow mounted on the three-point hitch. The 2N used a 120-ci (1,966-cc), L-head, four-cylinder engine, which gave a belt rating of 23 hp. Owner: Dean Simmons, Frederickstown, Ohio.

1946 Ford-Ferguson 2N

Built from 1942 through most of 1947, the 2N began life as a wartime version without starter, generator, or rubber tires. Later, as these items were removed from the list of critical war effort parts, they found their way back into production. 2Ns were painted a solid deep gray at the factory. This one, owned by Doug Marcum, is painted in 8N colors.

1952 Ford 8N and 1960 Ford 601 Workmaster

These two tractors have been "zero-timed" by N-Complete of Wilkinson, Indiana. More than a restoration, they have been remanufactured to completely new standards and carry a new-tractor warranty.

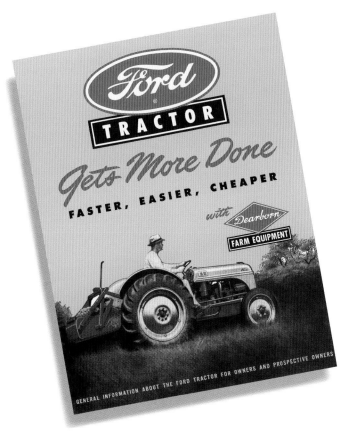

1952 Ford Model 8N

Above: *This was the final version of the venerable 8N, the largest-selling Ford tractor after the Fordson Model F—more than 520,000 8Ns and 750,000 Fordson Fs were built. Collector Palmer Fossum is at the controls.*

Left: 1950s Ford 8N brochure

THE HARRY FERGUSON GENIUS

"You haven't got enough money to buy my patents."
—Harry Ferguson to Henry Ford at the time of the Handshake Agreement, 1938

Henry George "Harry" Ferguson was born in Growell, Northern Ireland, in 1884. He was the fourth of eleven children, which was more than the family farm could support, so he followed his older brother into town and into the budding automobile business. To promote his brother's garage, Harry became a race-car driver, chalking up several victories. He next turned to airplanes, and in 1909, just six years after the Wright brothers flew, Ferguson took to the air in a monoplane of his own design. In fact, he won a £100 prize for being the first to make a three-mile (4.8-kmh) flight in the Irish town of Newcastle.

Racing and flying had made Ferguson quite famous. With his fame and winnings, he opened his own automobile business. He then hired twenty-year-old Willie Sands as a mechanic. Sands, as it turned out, had a natural aptitude for engineering. He would continue to be Ferguson's right-hand man into the 1950s, and his contributions to Ferguson's success were immense.

In 1914, Ferguson became a dealer for the Overtime tractor, the overseas version of the Waterloo Boy. When World War I broke out, the British government made every effort to gather all available tractors to produce food. When domestic tractors were not available in sufficient quantities, the government acquired all available imports from the United States. Ferguson was employed to keep records of government-owned tractors in Northern Ireland. He and Sands traveled the country, gaining experience with the good and bad features of several brands.

There were by that time a considerable number of Ford Model T cars in Britain, and several companies were offering kits to convert the Ford into a tractor. Ferguson and Sands devised a plow for one of these kits in which the draft load was reflected to the underside of the Ford ahead of the rear wheels. Increased draft loads pulled down on all four wheels, increasing traction and eliminating any tendency to rearing.

By 1918, there were some 6,000 of Ford's own new lightweight tractor plowing in England. Before the end of the year, the first government driver had been killed in a backflip accident. The tractor, subsequently to be called the Fordson, was notorious for this fault. When the plow struck an obstacle, the lightweight tractor would rotate around its own rear axle, pinning the hapless driver to the ground. Ferguson, Sands, and their team—which now included Archie Greer and John Williams—applied their experience with the Model T plow to the Fordson.

The result was a plow called the Duplex Hitch Plow. It was semi-rigid in the vertical plane, preventing back-flips, but free in the lateral plane, to allow steering. To counter the tendency for the plow to come out of the ground when the front wheel dropped into a hole, an ingenious linkage system to a skid at the rear made the plow move counter to the front of the tractor. This patented feature was called a floating skid. The team then harnessed the new field of tractor hydraulics to the Duplex Hitch Plow.

When U.S. Fordson production was discontinued and production was slow to begin in Ireland, Ferguson's team bought components of their own design and made a tractor known simply as the Black Tractor, because of its paint color. It was about 8/10-scale version of a Fordson, but it had built-in hydraulics and used a three-point hitch. Ferguson demonstrated the tractor around the country and won many accolades. He finally persuaded David Brown to join him in building the tractor, which was then known as the Ferguson-Brown.

Sadly, the Ferguson-Brown did not sell well. Brown would not build in sufficient quantities to get the price down, and the little tractor would not sell at the price required to cover the costs of small lots. It was at that time that Ferguson and Brown parted ways, and Ferguson joined with auto magnate Henry Ford to make the Ford-Ferguson 9N.

1933 Ferguson-Brown "Black Tractor"
The "Black Tractor" created by Harry Ferguson and British gear maker David Brown bore a suspicious resemblance to the Fordson. It used a Hercules engine with a David Brown transmission and differential.

1955 Ferguson TED-20
The TED-20 was the version of the basic English-built "Fergie" designed for distillate, or Tractor Vaporizing Oil (TVO).

While Ferguson had undeniable mechanical talent, he was primarily a feisty promoter. His enthusiasm for the task was so infectious that he was able to surround himself with all the other talents he needed. With shameless chutzpah, he talked Ford into advancing him $50,000 to get started. When the Ford-Ferguson deal dissolved in 1947, Ferguson was a millionaire, and Ford had lost $25 million in selling tractors to Ferguson.

In retrospect, there is disagreement as to whether Ferguson should get the lion's share of the credit for the 9N and the three-point hitch. Engineers involved with the project also heap praise on Sands, Williams, and Greer—as well as the superb engineering and manufacturing capability of the Ford Motor Company and its N Series design engineer Harold L. Brock. In any case, it was Ferguson who pulled it off.

It was also Ferguson who built his own Ferguson version of the N Series tractor on both sides of the Atlantic when the famous Handshake Agreement was dissolved—and he out-sold Ford at Ford's own game. It was Ferguson who marketed a line of extremely clever implements for the three-point hitch. And it was Ferguson who caused his name to grace the finest farm machinery, both as Ford-Ferguson and Massey-Ferguson, to this day.

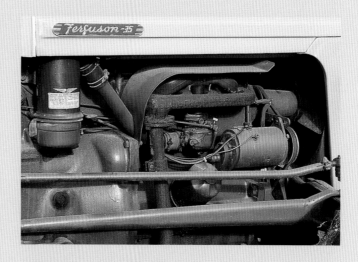

1955 Ferguson TO-35
A 134-ci (2,195-cc), four-cylinder, OHV Continental engine powered the TO-35.

Allis-Chalmers Model B

Allis-Chalmers Company of Milwaukee, Wisconsin

1938 Allis-Chalmers Model B

The B was introduced in late 1937 as a 1938 model. It weighed just a ton (900 kg) and originally cost $495. Until mid-1940, standard equipment did not include an electrical system. A variety of custom implements were offered, making the B a handy tractor for the small farm. Drawbar power was about 10 hp.

In response to the success of the Farmall, Allis-Chalmers introduced its small, inexpensive Model B in 1938. It was a one-plow machine weighing less than one ton (90 kg) and featuring a wide front arched axle.

It was designed as a replacement for a team of horses, which still provided most of the motive power for pre–World War II farms. Front and rear tread was adjustable by reversing wheels and by changing wheel clamps; a fully adjustable front axle was available later. With rubber tires and an electrical system, the Allis B, as it was affectionately called, sold for less than $600.

1939 Allis-Chalmers Model B
Above left: *A Model B mounted with a one-row cultivator. Owner: Keith McCaffree.*

1951 Allis-Chalmers Model IB
Above right: *The IB was a low, compact version of the B built for industrial uses. It had foot controls like a car—including a gas pedal—for easier operation by people not used to tractors. Owner: Gaylord De Jong.*

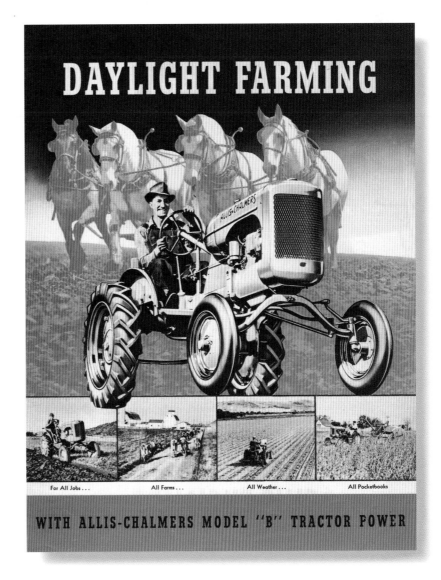

1940s Allis-Chalmers Model B brochure

Orchard Tractors: Streamlined Form and Function

In the late 1920s, modified versions of standard tractor models were first offered for specialized agricultural chores. The innovative John Deere offered some of the first of these machines, which included high-clearance tractors and wide and narrow front ends. Deere soon released a streamlined orchard machine, with rear fenders that enclosed the wheels and other cowling designed to aid the tractor in slipping through the low branches of orchard without harming the valuable trees.

1937 McCormick-Deering O-12
The O-12 was the orchard version of the standard-tread W-12. The row-crop version was much more widely known—the F-12 Farmall. Only 4,000 O-12 machines were built between 1932 and 1940. Owner: Dan Schmidt.

1947 Case VAO

Above, all photos: *The orchard version of the popular Case VA Series, the VAO was built from 1942 to 1955. The engine was a 124-ci (2,031-cc), OHV four, giving about 20 belt hp on gasoline; a distillate manifold was an extra-cost option. The VAO weighed about 2,700 pounds (1,215 kg). The Eagle Hitch and hydraulics came out on the VAO in 1949, but older tractors could be retrofitted. Owner: Larry Maasdam.*

1950s Oliver 70 Orchard brochure

The Fuel Revolution: From Diesel to "Greased Air"

Kerosene was the undisputed tractor fuel of choice until the late 1930s. It was cheap, stored well, and generally provided satisfactory operation. The quality of gasoline varied greatly, and engine designers had to engineer for the lowest expected gasoline grade, losing much of gasoline's power advantage over kerosene. Still, a small quantity of gasoline was required for kerosene-engine starting, and engines typically needed to be shut off on gasoline as well, or the kerosene in the carburetor would make starting difficult next time.

With the advent of octane ratings and standards for gasoline in the mid-1930s, gasoline gained in popularity. Gasoline's benefits came in large part from higher compression, so the same size engine could generate more horsepower. Side benefits came from easier starting, easier vaporization, and lower fuel consumption.

Gasoline was still in the process of supplanting kerosene and its variations such as distillate, or tractor vaporizing oil (TVO) when the diesel engine arrived on the scene. Caterpillar was first with a diesel tractor, the Diesel Sixty of 1931. International Harvester followed with the first diesel wheeled tractor, the WD-40 of 1934.

The diesel engine depended on a variable-displacement, high-pressure injector pump. Making such a pump to survive the low-lubricity diesel fuel, which was a close relative to kerosene, was a difficult problem that had to be solved before the diesel was ready for everyday use. Also, the diesel's 16:1 compression ratio made the engine extremely large and heavy until better steel castings became available.

The diesel's high compression ratio and restriction-free inlet contributed to low fuel consumption per horsepower hour. Another big economy factor was the fact that diesels run on the lean side of stoichiometric combustion,

1955 Ferguson TEF-20

Ferguson's TEF-20 was similar in size and shape to the Ford 9N/2N, as Ferguson used Ford tooling in setting up production in Coventry, England. The 20 had an indirect-injection diesel engine from the Standard Motor Company, a British car maker. The four-cylinder engine developed 26 hp.

rather than on the rich side as do gasoline and kerosene engines. Diesel entirely supplanted other tractor fuels by the late 1970s.

Another fuel revolution was hailed in the 1940s with liquefied petroleum gas (LPG)—nicknamed "greased air" in the early days. Minneapolis-Moline first equipped tractors to run on LPG in 1941, but it was not until 1949 that the Minneapolis-Moline U LPG was the first tractor tested on LPG at the University of Nebraska. LPG gained popularity slowly before reaching its peak of use.

When the engine compression ratio is raised to about 9:1, LPG provides more horsepower than the same gasoline engine at 6:1 compression. Because of its clean burning, LPG engines ran better without tune-ups for longer periods of time, and oil stayed cleaner and did not need to be changed as often. The cost of operation was also less than for an equivalent gasoline engine. On the down side, LPG was more difficult to store and refuel than gasoline or diesel fuel. Ultimately, its economy was not as great as that of diesel.

Popularity of LPG peaked in the 1960s and then faded. The University of Nebraska's test in June 1968 of a Minneapolis-Moline G-900 (LPG) was the last LPG-fueled tractor test.

1957 Massey-Harris 333 Diesel

The Massey 333 was the final version of the line that started in 1939 with the Model 81. Beginning with the Model 30 of 1946, the line was considered to be capable of pulling a three-bottom plow in most soils. This is one of only 150 made between 1956 and 1958. Power came from a 201-ci (3,292-cc) Continental. A five-speed transmission with high-low range and a three-point hitch were provided. Weight was about 6,000 pounds (2,700 kg). Owner: Ken Peterman.

1950s Massey-Harris 44 Diesel Standard

Both photos: *The 44 was possibly the best tractor ever built by Massey-Harris. It was available with a Massey four, Continental six, or Massey diesel four. All produced about 46 hp, giving the tractor a three-plow rating. Owner: Dan Peterman.*

1950s Massey-Harris brochure

1954 Minneapolis-Moline GBD

Above and right: *The GB-Diesel had a 426-ci (6,978-cc) Minneapolis-Moline diesel with Lanova-type combustion chambers and produced 63 hp. The tractor weighed about 8,200 pounds (3,690 kg). Owner: Keith and Adam Bruder.*

1950s Massey-Harris 44 Vineyard Special

Left: *The Vineyard version of Massey's famed 44. Owner: Larry Maasdam.*

1960 John Deere 830 Rice Special

The 830 was the last of the big two-cylinders from Deere. It featured a 472-ci (7,731-cc) diesel turning a rated 1,125 rpm and putting out 75 hp through a six-speed transmission. Weight was a little over 8,000 pounds (3,600 kg) without ballast. The 830 was rated for a six-bottom plow or a 20-ft (6-m) disk. The Rice Special version had a wider axle with mud shields and mud covers on the brakes. This one also has the 24-volt electric-start option. Owner: Ken Peterman.

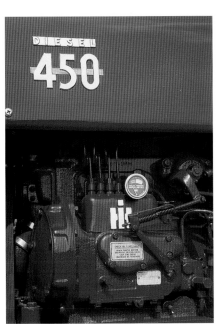

1958 Farmall 450 Diesel

The Farmall 450 was built from 1956 to 1958 in regular and high-clearance as well as LPG, diesel, and gasoline versions. The 281-ci (4,603-cc) engine gave the 450 four-bottom capability. Owner: Norm Seveik.

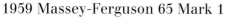

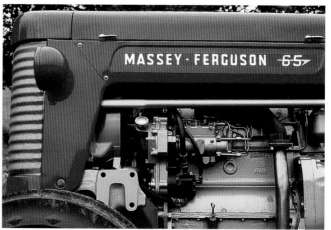

1959 Massey-Ferguson 65 Mark 1

The 1958–1965 British 65 was basically the U.S. 40 with a 50-hp Perkins indirect-injection diesel. From 1961 on, a direct-injection diesel was used. Final-drive gear reduction was made within the hubs to compensate for the larger tires required by the increased power. Owner: Mike Thorne.

1960 John Deere 520 LPG

Left and below: *The 520 LPG had a two-cylinder engine rated at 38 PTO hp. Owner: Melanie Maasdam.*

1960 Oliver XO-121

Left: *The XO-121 was an experimental tractor powered by a 199-ci (3,260-cc) engine with a 12:1 compression ratio for high-octane gasoline. The engine produced 57.5 brake hp at a specific fuel consumption of 0.385 pounds per hp hour—a rate comparable to diesel engines. The tractor now resides in the Floyd County Historical Society Museum in Charles City, Iowa.*

Oliver Hart-Parr 70
Oliver Farm Equipment Corporation of Chicago

Oliver set the industry standard in 1935 with its new, streamlined, six-cylinder Oliver Hart-Parr 70. The "70" model designation indicated a high-compression engine designed to run on the newly defined 70 octane automobile gasoline. There was also a low-compression-engine option for use with kerosene or distillate fuels. The 70 reflected the increasing influence of the automobile on tractor design, and considering the times, the new model was a strong statement of confidence in the future.

Four configurations of the 70 were available: row-crop, high-crop, orchard, and standard-tread. Optional equipment included a starter and lights. The tractor was marketed in Canada by the Cockshutt Farm Equipment Company of Brantford, Ontario, as its Cockshutt 70.

In 1937, the Hart-Parr name was dropped completely, and the 70, along with other Oliver/Cockshutt tractors were restyled. Under the new Fleetline styling, the 70 remained much the same as before. Rubber tires and a six-speed transmission became standard equipment in 1939.

1935 Oliver Hart-Parr 70
With its six-cylinder engine, the Oliver 70 of 1935 was a remarkable leap forward in tractor technology. It was one of the first to use stylish sheet metal to lure buyers. With a self-starter and convenient hand controls, it was also one of the first to cater to the needs of women and young people as tractor operators. The tractor was also one of the first designed to run on the new 70-octane gasoline, hence the designation "70." A low-compression version was available for those not ready to give up their low-cost kerosene fuel.

Orphan Tractors: The Second Industry Debacle

The tractor makers who had survived the economic recessions and depressions leading up to World War II, looked forward to the postwar years as a new, golden dawn when power farming would make them rich. These newfound halcyon days were short lived, however. In 1954, yet another economic recession struck farm-equipment manufacturers, and more makers fell by the wayside. In 1930, there had been some forty-seven tractor builders in North America. By 1960, there were but twelve.

1937–1938 Co-op Duplex No. 2
The Duplex No. 2 was built by the Co-operative Manufacturing Company of Battle Creek, Michigan. It was powered by a 201-ci (3,292-cc), six-cylinder Chrysler engine and used a four-speed transmission. Owner: Don Wolf.

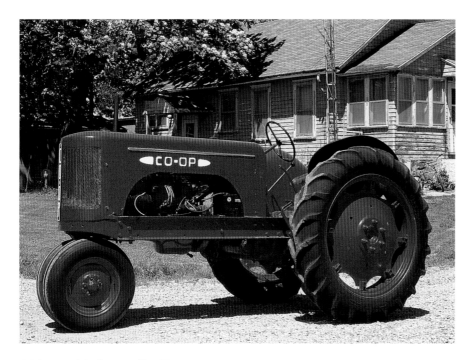

1940–1941 Co-op B2JR

Built by the Arthurdale Farm Equipment Corporation of West Virginia, the B2JR was built from 1940 through 1941. It featured a 201-ci (3,292-cc), Chrysler industrial engine and four-speed transmission. Governed to 1,500 rpm, the engine produced 33 hp. Owner: Larry Maasdam.

1936 Eagle 6B

The Eagle Manufacturing Company of Appleton, Wisconsin, made a long line of innovative tractors beginning in 1906. In 1930, the modern Eagle 6A standard-tread was introduced using a 358-ci (5,864-cc), six-cylinder Hercules motor. It was followed by the 6B row-crop in 1936 with a smaller Hercules six. A 6C that debuted in 1938 was the standard-tread version of the 6B. Production ended in 1940. Owner: Richard Grimm.

1938 Avery Ro-Trak

Made in Peoria, Illinois, by the Avery Farm Equipment Company, the Ro-Trak was convertible from a narrow to a wide front configuration. Since there was no axle pivot as on conventional tractor front ends, the vertical tubes contained soft springs to allow the front wheels to go over bumps without undue frame twist. An unusual feature was that when the brakes were applied, the front dipped like a soft-sprung car. A 212-ci (3,473-cc), L-head, six-cylinder Hercules engine was used. No power rating was given, but the Ro-Trak was called a two-to-three-plow tractor. It had a three-speed transmission giving a road speed of 16 mph (25 kmh). Production ended in 1941.

High-Clearance Tractors: Standing Tall

The row-crop tractor was born to allow cultivation of tall crops, such as corn. It soon became evident, however, that the normal row-crop machine still did not provide adequate clearance for late-growth tilling. To meet this new demand, most manufacturers developed high-clearance versions of their row-crop tractors. These only sold in limited numbers and are thus now among the most sought after of tractors by collectors.

1956 Case 400 HC

Right: *This Case 400 High-Clearance is one of only 150 made. It had the Eagle Hitch. The Case 400 was available in gasoline or diesel versions; this one is gasoline. Owner: Jay Foxworthy. This 400 HC came from the sugar cane fields of Louisiana.*

1948 Case VAH

The high-clearance member of the Case VA Series, the VAH was built from 1948 to 1955. The engine was a 124-ci (2,031-cc), OHV four, giving about 20 belt hp on gasoline; a distillate manifold was an extra-cost option. The Eagle Hitch and hydraulics were available for the VAH in 1949. Owner: Norm Seveik.

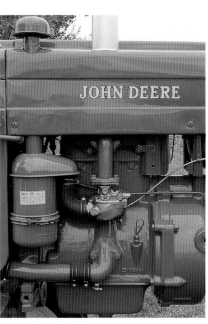

1955 John Deere 40V
Only 310 of the rare 40V were built, all in 1955. Higher than the standard 40, the 40V gave 26 inches (65 cm) of crop clearance. The 40 had a vertical two-cylinder engine of 100.5 ci (1,646 cc), which gave it 25 belt hp. Owners: Ken and Dan Peterman.

1950s Massey-Harris 44 Diesel Special High-Crop

Below, both photos: *Only two examples of the Massey 44 Diesel High-Crop are known to exist. The engine was built by Massey-Harris and rated 45 hp. Owner: Larry Maasdam.*

1955 Farmall 400 HC

Above and right: *The 400 was the successor to the mighty Farmall M and Super M, but was only built in 1955 and 1956. It was then replaced by the 450. This rare 400 High-Clearance was equipped with the Torque-Amplifier dual-range power-shift gearbox. Owner: the Keller family.*

The Evolution of Live PTO and Hydraulics

1940s Case Model SC

The Case Model SC was announced in November 1940 and was all-new from top to bottom. The "plain" S was the standard-tread version; there were also Orchard (SO), Industrial (SI), and the SC-4 versions. The SC-4 was only built in 1953–1954 and had a fixed-tread wide front axle.

Tractors had power takeoffs in the form of belt pulleys from the earliest days of steam. In the true sense of the word, however, the term "power takeoff" implied an output for supplying tractor engine power to an implement while the tractor is in motion, which would not apply to a belt-pulley drive. The McCormick-Deering 15/30 of 1921 was the first tractor to be equipped with a true PTO. This PTO, and most others until the mid-1950s, was driven by gears downstream of the clutch; when the clutch was disengaged, the PTO no longer received power from the engine.

There were several early examples of "live" PTOs, or PTOs that either had their own clutch or were continuously connected to the engine. An example of the former is the 1924 Hart-Parr 12/24 E: It had an optional PTO driven from the clutch end of the engine by means of a separate clutch. A series of shafts and universal joints carried the power back across the operator's platform, terminating by the drawbar. Another example of the live PTO is the cable winch drives used by Caterpillar and others to control trailed earthmover scrapers.

The traditional live PTO as known today with a two-stage clutch pedal (one stage disconnects the engine from the transmission, the second stage disconnects the PTO) first debuted on the Cockshutt Model 30 of 1946.

The situation with hydraulic power was similar. Initially, pumps were mounted near the transmission/differential and driven by gears downstream of the clutch. Often, the same powertrain was used for the pump as for the PTO.

Later, as efficient high-speed hydraulic pumps became available, pumps were driven directly by the engine, thereby allowing for "live" hydraulics. Deere offered an optional live hydraulic pump on its 1948 Model B. It was not until the early 1950s that others followed suit.

1930s Cockshutt Model 30

The Cockshutt Plow Company of Brantford, Ontario, dated back to 1877. For years, it marketed tractors made by others, mostly Oliver, with the firm's own colors. In 1946, however, Cockshutt released the first tractor of its own design, the Model 30. It was the first production tractor to have a live PTO of the type used today. The engine was a 30-hp, four-cylinder Buda.

Farmall MD

International Harvester Company of Chicago

Beginning with the 1924 Regular, IHC's McCormick-Deering Farmalls were the first volume-production all-purpose tractors. Representing the top of the line, the Model M, was launched in 1939. The big, three-plow M was also the best-selling Farmall. It later evolved into the Super M-TA with the first power-shift underdrive. It was available in engine configurations for distillate, gasoline, and LPG fuels, but the diesel version, which came out in 1941, revolutionized farm power and normalized the use of the diesel engine.

The first diesel tractor was the Caterpillar Diesel Sixty of 1931, followed in 1934 by McCormick-Deering's WD-40. The WD never gained the popularity of the MD, however. Sales of the MD averaged 22,000 units per year, even though the MD cost 50 percent more than a gasoline version. Fuel consumption was about one-third to one-half that of the gasoline engine.

McCormick-Deering diesels had a unique starting system. The engine was equipped with a spark-ignition setup as well as the diesel-fuel system. A compression-release lever enlarged the combustion chamber, diverted intake air through the carburetor and activated the carburetor float. Once running on gasoline, the compression lever was thrown, which also engaged the diesel injectors. The engine was then running on diesel.

The MD was a big tractor for its time, weighing in at 5,300 pounds (2,385 kg) in 1941 and growing to

1941 Farmall MD

A diesel-powered version of the great Farmall M debuted in 1941 as the MD and won many converts. The MD was upgraded with M-W aftermarket auxiliary gearbox, power steering, live hydraulics, and live PTO. Owner: Alan Smith.

5,900 pounds (2,655 kg) by 1952. An additional 3,000 pounds (1,350 kg) of ballast was not unusual. Originally, the four-cylinder, 248-ci (4,062-cc) engine produced a maximum of 35 hp on the belt pulley. By the end of production, internal improvements resulted in the availability of almost 40 belt hp.

A Super MD debuted in 1952 with a four-cylinder, 264-ci (4,324-cc) engine and about a third more power. Weight was up to 6,000 pounds (2,700 kg), without ballast. Farmers claimed a 2.5-acre (1-hectare) per hour plowing rate for the Super MD with fuel consumption of a gallon (3.3 liters) per hour.

1954 Farmall Super MD-TA

The MD-TA was the diesel version of the famous M with the lever-controlled Torque Amplifier. Super M Farmalls were built from 1952 to 1954. The 264-ci (4,324-cc) engine gave the Super a 32 percent power boost over the previous MD. In addition to the MD, gas and LPG versions of the Super M, with and without the Torque Amplifier, were also available. Owner: Donald Schaeffer.

Allis-Chalmers Model WC and WF

Allis-Chalmers Company of Milwaukee, Wisconsin

Allis-Chalmers introduced its two-plow WC in 1933, the first tractor to be offered with rubber tires as standard equipment; steel wheels were optional. A channel frame was employed, which was lighter and less expensive than the castings used on the Model U, and the WC weighed only 3,200 pounds (1,440 kg). The 201-ci (3,292-cc) engine featured a 4.00x4.00-inch (100x100-mm) bore and stroke, and was rated at 1,300 rpm. Both kerosene and gasoline versions were available. The WC was a row-crop tractor; its standard-tread running mate, the WF, was introduced in 1940 and was produced through 1951.

Allis-Chalmers built more than 186,000 WC and WF tractors.

The popular WC was succeeded by the WD in 1948. The WD boasted the first power-adjustable rear wheel tread and was also one of the first tractors available with a live power takeoff (PTO). The same engine was used as in the WC, but its rated speed was upped to 1,400 rpm. The WD was available in dual tricycle, single, and adjustable wide front ends.

The WD was followed in 1953 by the WD-45, built along the same lines. The engine of the WD-45 had a 4.50-inch (112.5-mm) stroke, giving it substantially more power. It could be had in gasoline, dual-fuel, or LPG versions. In 1955, the WD-45D six-cylinder diesel was offered.

1941 Allis-Chalmers WF
The WF was the standard-tread version of the famed WC row-crop and was built from 1940 to 1951. They were both two-plow tractors and featured the first "square" engine in the industry, with bore and stroke being equal at 4 inches (100 mm).

1940s Allis-Chalmers WC brochure

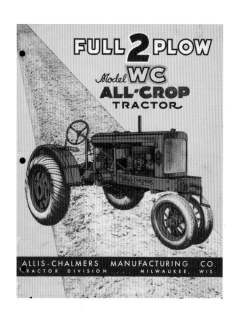

1930s Allis-Chalmers WC brochure

Above: *The two-plow WC was introduced in 1933. It was the first tractor to be offered with rubber tires as standard equipment; steel wheels were optional. A channel frame was employed, and the WC weighed only 3,200 pounds (1,440 kg). The 201-ci (3,292-cc) engine was rated at 1,300 rpm.*

1947 Allis-Chalmers WF

Right, both photos: *The WF featured a four-speed transmission and 201-ci (3,292-cc), four-cylinder, OHV engine of 28 hp. It sold for about $1,200 in 1947. Weight was about 3,500 pounds (1,575 kg). Owner: Paul Mihalovich.*

Tractors of Many Colors

From the 1930s through the 1950s, tractor makers began to settle on distinctive colors and paint schemes to set their machines apart from the competition. These trademark colors became famous in the industry—and tractors of a brand's "color" became easily identifiable in the field.

1946 Farmall H

The Farmall H was introduced in 1939 and used a 152-ci (2,490-cc), OHV four-cylinder engine. Most were equipped for gasoline, but a distillate option was available. Owner Leon E. Geiss bought this H new in May 1946. It still has the original wartime S-3 tires.

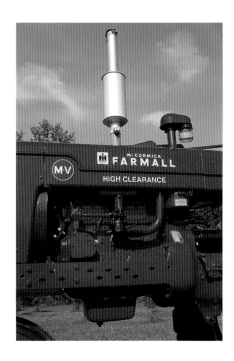

1948 Farmall MV

Above, both photos: *This unusual Farmall high-clearance model was ordered with a single front wheel. The MV could be had with either the wide front end or the single front wheel. The rear wheels were driven by drop boxes at the end of each axle, which raised the axle to provide more clearance. Owner: Norm Seveik.*

1948 Farmall HV

The HV was some 10 inches (25 cm) taller than the standard H, allowing the cultivation of taller crops such as corn and sugar cane. IHC made a cotton picker based on the HV, and some have been converted to the much-sought-after HV. This came from the factory as a single-front-wheel HV. Owner: Larry Maasdam.

1948 Oliver 60 Standard

Above and left: *To compete with small tractors from the other makers, Oliver offered its 60 in 1940, and production continued through part of 1948. The 60 was a scaled-down 70, offering a four-cylinder engine rather than the six. Belt power was about 18 hp. Gasoline and distillate fuels were options, as were row-crop or standard-tread versions.*

1950s Oliver advertising poster

1950s Oliver Super 55

Above: *Built from 1954 to 1958, the Super 55 was Oliver's answer to the Ford 9N, 2N, 8N, and NAA tractors with three-point hitch. Of the same basic configuration as the Ford N-Series, the Super 55 didn't leave anything to chance. Oliver offered a six-speed transmission (instead of three or four), gasoline or diesel engines (Ford only offered gasoline), and a 144-ci (2,359-cc) engine (Ford's largest was the 134-ci/2,195-cc in the NAA). Oliver may have thought it had roused the sleeping giant, however: In 1955, Ford's models began to proliferate in all directions.*

1950s Oliver 77 brochure
This cutaway drawing showed the heart of the 77: Oliver's six-cylinder powerplant.

1959–1960 Oliver 440

Built in 1959 and 1960, the 440 was the culmination of the line that began with the Super 44 of 1957–1958. The two models were the same, except for the paint. The 2,000-pound (900-kg) tractor used a 20-hp Continental engine. The offset configuration, with the engine set to the left and the steering wheel and driver's seat to the right, ostensibly enhanced the visibility when using an under-belly cultivator.

1960s Oliver 660

Introduced in 1959, the 660 was an improved and restyled Super 66. Gasoline or diesel engines of 155 ci (2,539 cc) were offered. Disk brakes were standard, but power steering was an option. Production continued through 1964.

1960s Oliver 880

Above and right: *The 880 was the last of the line that began with the 18/27 of 1930. It went through the 80, 88, and Super 88 before reaching its final version. The 880 was built from 1958 to 1963. It featured improvements such as a power-shift torque amplifier, standard power steering, and load-biased three-point hitch. Gasoline, diesel, or LPG, the 880 was in the 60-hp class.*

1950 Case Model D
The three-plow Model D replaced the Case C and was basically a styled version of its predecessor. It was the best-selling Flambeau Red tractor with around 100,000 sold from 1939 to 1953.

1958 Case 400B Case-O-Matic

Except for the Case-O-Matic torque converter drive, the 400B was much the same as the old 300C. The tractor featured a 148-ci (2,424-cc), four-cylinder engine and sixteen gear ratios plus the torque converter. With ballast, it weighed just over 8,000 pounds (3,600 kg). Owner: Norm Seveik.

1965 Case 830 CK

The 830 was a five-plow tractor with a 284-ci (4,652-cc), four-cylinder engine. A dual-range conventional transmission was available, but the Case-O-Matic torque converter drive was available. Besides gasoline, LPG and diesel versions were also offered.

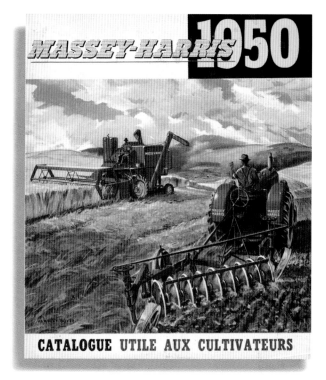

1950 Massey-Harris brochure

1940s Case brochure

1940 Massey-Harris Super 101

Left: *Massey-Harris's flagship Super 101 was powered by a 218-ci (3,571-cc) Chrysler six. Owner: Wayne Svoboda. (Photograph © Robert N. Pripps)*

1960 Allis-Chalmers D-12

Allis-Chalmers D-10 and D-12 tractors were built simultaneously from 1960 to 1967—and were essentially the same. The D-10 was a single-row machine, while the D-12 was made for two rows and had adjustable wheel-tread spacing. Originally, an engine of 139 ci (2,277 cc) was used, but in 1961, a 149-ci (2,441-cc) engine was substituted. From 1964, the tractor had a 12-volt electrical system and a draft-load compensating three-point hitch. Owner: Helle Farm Equipment.

1953 Minneapolis-Moline BF

Above and right: *Minneapolis-Moline's BF tractor began life in 1939 as the Cletrac-General CC, made for Cletrac by B. F. Avery Company of Louisville, Kentucky. In 1951, this tractor became the M-M BF. By that time, its four-cylinder engine displaced 133 ci (2,179 cc). Owner: Vernon Parizek, president of the M-M Collector's Club.*

1941 Minneapolis-Moline ZTU

Above: *The Z Series was built from 1937 to 1956. Originally, the Z used a 186-ci (3,047-cc) engine, but by 1950, it had been increased to 206 ci (3,374 cc). Owners: Don and Betty Zwicky.*

1950 Minneapolis-Moline U

Right: *The U was powered by a 284-ci (4,652-cc), four-cylinder engine of 40 hp along with a five-speed transmission. Owner: James Taylor. Taylor's father, Russell Taylor, bought this U new. James first drove it when he was fifteen years old. He still uses it around the farm, so it isn't retired yet.*

1939 Minneapolis-Moline R

Left: *The R was the smallest tractor in the M-M line, but used the same basic engine as the Z. The displacement was reduced to 165 ci (2,703 cc), and the rated rpm was also cut, giving the R 26 hp, about 10 less hp than the Z. The R could be equipped with a Comfortractor-type cab, as on this machine.*

1958 Minneapolis-Moline 5 Star

Left and below: *The 5 Star was made from 1957 to 1961, although standard-tread gasoline and LPG versions were only made in 1958. A 283-ci (4,636-cc) engine gave it 55 hp. Owner: Walter Keller.*

Ford's World Tractor

1953 Ford Jubilee Model NAA

The NAA was the first all-new Ford tractor in fourteen years and was a result of the settlement of the lawsuit with Harry Ferguson over patent infringements. Because of the settlement, an all-new hydraulic system was used. Other improvements over the 8N, which it replaced, made it heavier and more powerful. Owner: the Sparks family. This NAA had just been remanufactured by N-Complete of Wilkinson, Indiana. N-Complete owner Tom Armstrong is at the controls.

For decades, Ford was a one-tractor company. The Fordson in its heyday and the 8N at its peak each sold more than 100,000 units in a single year in the United States. These were far and away the largest-selling models in North America. The Fordson claimed 70 percent of the tractor market; the 8N out-sold the entire Deere line and was second only to the entire IHC line. In England, Ford remained loyal to its Fordson E27N Major, which was built from 1945 to 1952. But then the market—and Ford—began to change.

In 1955, the Ford Motor Company went public, and Henry II had stockholders that were not interested in the altruistic motives of Old Henry. Then, in 1956, British Ford sold more tractors than the original American firm. Rather than be further embarrassed, Detroit expanded the domestic line to two engine sizes with a variety of transmission and other options, including diesel and LPG.

But sales still slumped, so the concept of the "World Tractor" came into being in 1961. By 1964, a new line of tractors was being made in new plants in Highland Park, Michigan; Basildon, England; and Antwerp, Belgium.

The World Tractor concept was successful, and by 1966, Ford was again number two in sales, just behind Massey-Ferguson of Toronto, Ontario.

1955 Ford 800
Above, both photos: *The 800, like the later 801, used Ford's 172-ci (2,817-cc) engine. The 800 was built from 1955 through 1957. Owners: Jim and Jerriann Endries.*

1960 Ford 601 Workmaster
Left: *Built from 1958 through 1961, the Workmaster used a 134-ci (2,195-cc), four-cylinder engine.*

1958 Ford 861 Powermaster
Below, both photos: *The 861 used a 172-ci (2,817-cc), four-cylinder engine and five-speed transmission. It had live hydraulics and live PTO. Power was in the 50-hp range. LPG and diesel versions were also available, as was a ten-speed Select-O-Speed power-shift transmission.*

The End of the Reign of Johnny Popper

"A New Generation of Power"
—Deere advertising slogan, 1960

The side-by-side, transverse-mounted, two-cylinder engine was common engine architecture from the earliest times. Henry Ford's first home-built gasoline engine was a two-cylinder. Early Hart-Parrs were two-cylinders, as were most International Harvester Titans and Rumely OilPulls. In some designs the pistons moved in unison; in others, in opposition.

In the case of the famed Deere two-cylinder engine, which came to Deere with its purchase of Waterloo Boy in 1917, the pistons moved in opposite directions. Being a four-cycle engine meant that the firing sequence was not evenly spaced: It was like a double-barreled shotgun where the barrels fired sequentially, reloaded, and fired again. There was something intriguing about the exhaust note of a laboring John Deere two-cylinder, which seemed to account for much of their popularity, as well as sobriquets such as "Poppin' Johnny" and "Johnny Popper."

Variations of Deere's venerable two-cylinder engine powered the smallest tractors and the largest diesels. Originally, the configuration was popular because the close proximity of the exhaust gases to the intake manifold made a good arrangement for burning of kerosene, the cheapest fuel at the time. Also, the transverse mounting eliminated the need for bevel gears. As time went on, only Deere stuck with the two-cylinder approach. It was the focus of much of Deere's advertising, stressing that fewer parts meant a more reliable tractor.

As the 1950s waned and the power race topped 75 hp, the engineers at Deere knew the two-cylinder was at

1957 John Deere 620
The 620 arrived in 1956, the successor to the famous Deere Model A and subsequent 60. It featured the draft-control three-point hitch called Custom-Powr-Trol. A 20 percent power increase came mostly through an increase in engine rpm from 975 to 1,125. Owner: Bruce Copper.

the end of its line. It was no longer practical to increase displacement and still get the engine under the hood of a reasonably sized tractor. Further, the large-displacement two-cylinders, such as those in the Deere 820 and 830 were rated at 1,125 rpm, which was fast for an engine with an 8.00-inch (200-mm) stroke. An equivalent short-stroke, four-cylinder engine would produce the same horsepower at 2,600 rpm and half the displacement.

With secrecy rivaling the World War II Manhattan Project that created the atomic bomb, Deere management detailed selected engineers to a converted grocery-store building. Sworn to secrecy, the engineers began designing a whole new line of completely modern multi-cylinder tractors. They knew they would have just one chance to convince their loyal customers that these new three-, four-, and six-cylinder machines were worthy to bear the name of John Deere. Marketing did its part too. A gigantic hoopla was planned and carried off on August 30, 1960, at the Dallas, Texas, Coliseum. The event was known as Deere Day in Dallas. The firm flew in dealers and press people from all over the country to introduce what they called the New Generation of tractors. Besides the tractors, there were big-name entertainers, fireworks, and barbecues.

The New Generation consisted of four lines: the 30-hp 1010, 40-hp 2010, 55-hp 3010, and 80-hp 4010. Most were available in gasoline, diesel, or LPG versions and in all the configurations that were previously offered, from utility to row-crop. The 1010 was also available as a crawler.

The new tractors were nimble, well balanced, and thoroughly up to date. They were also nicely styled by famed industrial designer Henry Dreyfuss. The dealers liked them and farmers bought them. Deere had created a new generation of tractors that upheld the reputation built by the beloved Johnny Poppers.

1960 John Deere 630S

The standard-tread version of the powerful 630 was quite rare. The 630 was available with gasoline, "all-fuel," or LPG engines; a diesel was not offered. The 630 was offered by Deere from 1958 through 1960 to replace the 620 Series. It could handle a four-bottom plow with its 321-ci (5,258-cc), two-cylinder engine and six-speed transmission. The fenders and a big oval "low-tone" muffler were new on the 630. Owner: Larry Maasdam.

1959 John Deere 730

Above and left: *Still working after forty-two years, this gas 730 with power steering used a 360.5-ci (5,905-cc), two-cylinder engine rated at 1,125 rpm and 60 hp. Not restored, this 730 is in original finish. Owner: Ken Kass.*

1959 John Deere 530

The final version of the series that started with the venerable Model B, the 530 was a thoroughly modern general-purpose tractor. Owner: Kent Bates. It is shown in front of a 1926 Gordon Van Tyne kit-built barn. These kits included everything except the gravel and water for the cement.

1960 Deere New Generation brochure

Deere's new generation of three-, four-, and six-cylinder tractors officially arrived on August 30, 1960, when they were launched to dealers at the Dallas, Texas, Coliseum. It was the end of an era—and the beginning of a new one.

Classic Tractor Replicas: A Labor of Love

The restoration of a vintage tractor is daunting work, but some tractor enthusiasts choose to go even a step further. The creation of working, scale replicas of classic tractor requires dedication and skill that is often rewarded by the respect of other tractor buffs at vintage tractor shows and meets.

½-Scale Rumely OilPull
Built by Glen Braun, this replica uses a two-cylinder Continental engine. Engine rotation, however, had to be reversed. Braun also made a six-bottom Rumely plow for it using bottoms from garden tractor plows. Braun also has a full-scale Rumely 20/40 Type G built in 1923.

½-Scale John Deere 3020
Ken Peterman constructed this one radio-controlled replica. The radio even controls the clutch, steering, engine start and stop, and the three-bottom plow. It is powered by a Yanmar diesel engine and has a Farmall Cub transmission. Peterman spent 2,400 hours on the project.

½-Scale Massey-Harris 44 Diesel
Above: *Powered by a three-cylinder Dakota engine, this replica was built by Ken Peterman. Peterman also built a ½-scale Massey combine to go with it.*

½-Scale Allis-Chalmers IB
Left: *Powered by a 3½-hp Tecumseh engine, this replica has a three-speed transmission that uses gears from lawn mowers. Everything is hand built, and even the belt pulley works! Builder: Gaylord De Jong, who also has a full-size IB.*

Hot-Rodded Farm Tractors

The search for more power began as soon as a tractor got stuck in a muddy field or a larger plow was available to till new acreage. Neighborhood mechanics or farmers handy with a wrench sometimes created their own "hot-rod tractors" by swapping engines or pairing two tractors into a jury-rigged machine that could do double the work.

During World War II, Ford built some pickups and small vans with four-cylinder Ford tractor engines instead of the normal sixes and V-8s. Enterprising businessmen soon realized that the switch could be made the other way around, and 9N, 2N, 8N, and NAA Jubilees were converted to Ford six and V-8 power. Converted as such, they became the most powerful tractors in their days.

These hot-rodded machines sometimes became local legends, winning their builder renown—and often a telephone call at an inopportune time when someone was stuck in the mud. In the larger history of tractors, they served as a stepping stone toward the creation of more-powerful factory-built machines and eventually, the articulated, four-wheel-drive tractor that rules the field today.

1950s Funk-Ford 8N V-8

Below and right: *The Funk brothers, foundrymen from Coffeeville, Kansas, produced adaptation kits in the early 1950s to convert Ford tractors from the standard four-cylinder engine to the 239-ci (3,915-cc) Ford flathead V-8 or 226-ci (3,702-cc) Ford six. The six produced 182 foot-pounds of torque at 1,200 rpm; the V-8 created 187 foot-pounds at 1,600 rpm. Most Funk-Ford V-8s use the dual vertical straight exhaust pipes that gives the operator unbeatable stereo exhaust music. Less than 100 Funk-Ford V-8s were believed to have been built. Owner: Robert Meyer.*

1950s Funk-Ford 8N V-8
Left: *The main reason the hoods of Funk-Ford tractors were higher than standard was due to the need for a larger radiator, and Ford radiators were supplied with the engine kits. Because exhaust gasses passed through the water jacket of the flathead V-8, it required an exceptionally large radiator. Owner: Palmer Fossum.*

1950s Farmall M V-8 Special
This Farmall M was custom built by Norm Sevick and his son Jeremy and is propelled by an International truck V-8.

1964 Fordson Power Major V-8 Special

Builder Richard Vincent mounted a 200-hp, 510-ci (8,354-cc), Perkins V-8 diesel in this Fordson Power Major in search of more plowing power.

The Development of Articulated Four-Wheel-Drive Tractors

Articulated four-wheel-drive tractors were almost unheard of in 1959. The first such machine, the TR-14A Diesel from Wagner Tractor of Portland, Oregon, was tested at the University of Nebraska in June 1959. The TR-14A was a descendant of the earlier, non-articulated Wagner TR-9. These big, heavy, powerful movers stemmed originally from aircraft tugs. Powered by a six-cylinder, 148-hp Cummins engine, the TR-14A weighed a massive 21,050 pounds (9,473 kg) but could pull 10,749 pounds (4,837 kg).

At about the same time, articulated wheel loaders came on the scene. A firm named Scoopmobile made the first in 1952. Not many of these were delivered until later in the decade due to problems with the hinge. It is likely that this type of loader was related to the two-wheel tractor/scraper developed by LeTourneau of Peoria, Illinois, in the late 1930s, which incorporated hydraulic articulated steering and a heavy-duty center hinge.

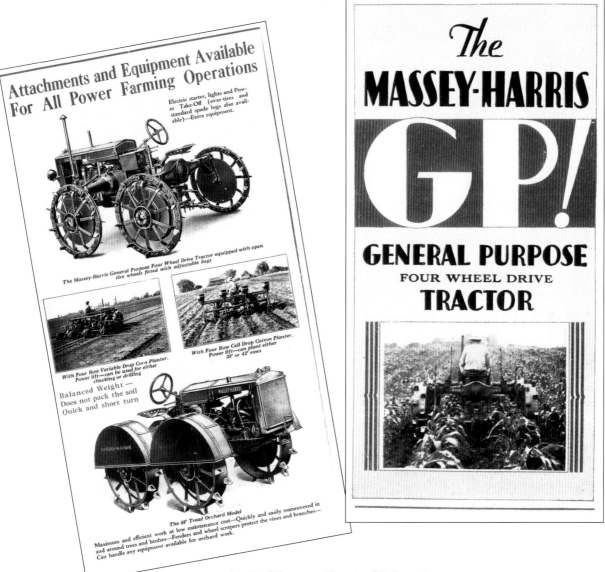

1930s Massey-Harris GP brochure
Launched in 1936, Massey-Harris's 15/22 GP had "Four Wheel Drive! Balanced Traction! Flexibility!" according to this brochure. Sadly, the GP wasted too much of its four-cylinder Hercules engine's power getting power to the ground, and the machine never lived up to its promise.

1920s Allis-Chalmers Duplex

The amazing Duplex combined two 6/12 tractors mounted back to back, offering farmers a pioneering tandem tractor for heavy-duty chores. The transmission controls of the two tractors were joined together, giving the machine a crude form of four-wheel drive. The Duplex was years ahead of its time—too far ahead, in fact, and few were built or sold.

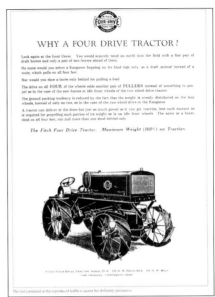

1920s Fitch Four Drive brochure

The Four Drive Tractor Company of Big Rapids, Michigan, was one of several firms to pioneer four-wheel drive. As this brochure noted, "The drive on all FOUR of the wheels adds another pair of PULLERS instead of something to propel." The Fitch Four Drive debuted in 1916 and was built into the 1930s. It was powered by a Climax four and rated at 20/36 hp.

1968 Deere-Wagner WA-17

In 1968–1969, Deere marketed the 225-hp WA-14 and 280-hp turbo WA-17 four-wheel-drive articulated tractors made by the Wagner Tractor Company of Portland, Oregon. The WA-14 was powered by a 178-drawbar-hp Cummins N 855; the WA-17 by a 220-drawbar-hp Cummins NT 855.

1960s Fordson Major Doe Triple D Conversion

In the quest for more power in the 1950s and 1960s, some handy farmers and intrepid firms combined two tractors into one. Two Fordson Majors were joined to make this articulated four-wheel-drive tractor before the days when production machines available. Owner: Jon Hooper.

John Deere Model 8010/8020
Deere & Company of Moline, Illinois

John Deere's Model 8010 sparked amazement when it was introduced at Deere & Company's field day in Marshalltown, Iowa, in 1959. The 8010 was huge: 20 feet long, 8 feet wide, and 8 feet tall (600x240x240 cm). It weighed 20,000 pounds (9,000 kg) without ballast and 24,000 pounds (10,800 kg) with liquid in tires that were nearly 6 feet (180 cm) high. And it was the first Deere in forty years to have more than two cylinders in its engine.

The 8010 boasted a six-cylinder GM 6-71 engine of 215 hp at a time when no other Deere tractor had yet exceeded 80 hp. It also had a nine-speed transmission while the most any other Deere had was a six-speed. Instead of mechanical brakes like every other Deere, the 8010 had air brakes.

1959 Deere 8010 brochure

Besides seeing what was being done with four-wheel-drive aircraft movers and end loaders, Deere was prompted to experiment with the 8010 when some northern Quebec farmers replaced the tracks on their John Deere Model B-Lindeman crawlers with balloon tires to provide increased floatation over muskeg soil. The converted B-Lindemans were steered like present-day skid-steer machines. Previously, Deere engineers experimented with a Model R tractor with a 108-hp GM diesel. This tractor was shown to a limited number of Great Plains farmers who loved the doubled horsepower, suggesting to Deere that big power would sell.

Unfortunately, the 8010 did not sell as expected. A total of 100 production models were built between 1960 and 1961. Only one 8010 was sold in 1960; it took until 1965 to sell the rest. The 8010 had some problems with the engine and transmission, and almost all of the 100 production models were recalled and rebuilt into the Model 8020, after which they were returned to their owners. Deere does not have records on about 15 of the 100 production 8010s, so they may not have been rebuilt.

The question is why such an advanced tractor sold so poorly? Did not the farmers that tried the 108-hp R ask for more power? Was not the reception at the Marshalltown unveiling of the 8010 positive? Even with the rebuilding into 8020s, one big problem remained: price. The cost for an 8020 with three-point hitch was $30,000—a chunk of change in the early 1960s considering that the 4020, Deere's next largest tractor, cost a mere $10,000.

Some of those who did farm with the 8010/8020 liked them and put them to good use. Others said the tractor was a dog; its power didn't live up to claims. Probably due in large part to the peculiarities of the two-cycle GM engine, farmers used to the pleasant exhaust note of the new Deere four- and six-cylinder engines didn't run the "Jimmy" hard enough. One owner reported that to operate an 8010/8020 properly, you had to slam your hand in the cab door about three times. Then, when good and mad, you were in the proper frame of mind to operate the engine.

1959 John Deere 8010

While other tractor makers were breaking the 100-hp barrier, Deere was breaking the 200-hp line. The big 8010 was one of the first articulated four-wheel-drive tractors and the first Deere in forty years to have more than two cylinders. The 10-ton (9,000-kg) 8010 had six cylinders in its GM 6-71 supercharged, two-cycle diesel rated at 215 hp. The 8010 shown here is the first one made, serial number 1000. It was never sold as a new tractor, but was used by Deere for tests and demonstrations. All of the 99 other 8010s were converted by Deere to 8020s. The Marshalltown, Iowa, dealer sold this 8010 for Deere to Walter Keller. At the time, it had a cracked head and a broken gear in the transmission. Repairs have been made, and the tractor is restored to new condition. Walter Keller is in the cockpit.

=+ CHAPTER 6 +=

The Modern Era, 1960–Present

"Only one in twenty Americans lived on a farm in 1980 as opposed to 1940 when one in four was a member of a farm family."
—Implement & Tractor, 1980

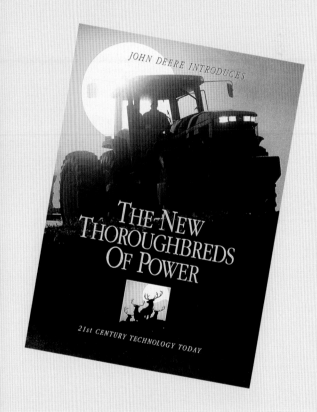

1990s John Deere 6900

Main photo: *Deere launched its new 6000 Series in 1992, adding the six-cylinder 6900 in 1994. This thoroughly modern tractor boasted 130 hp.*

1994 John Deere 8000 Series brochure

Above: *"The New Thoroughbreds of Power" brochure announced Deere's 8000 Series in 1994.*

Where Have All the Tractors Gone?

Timeline

1960: John F. Kennedy becomes U.S. President

1962: John Glenn becomes the first American to orbit the earth

1963: John F. Kennedy assassinated in Dallas

1965: Civil rights unrest reaches a peak in Selma, Alabama

1969: Richard M. Nixon becomes U.S. President

1969: Concorde Supersonic Transport (SST) makes first flight

1969: Neil Armstrong is the first man to walk on the moon

1973: Arab oil embargo causes fuel shortages with far-reaching effects

1973: Last U.S. troops leave Vietnam

1974: Nixon resigns the presidency

1980: Ronald Reagan becomes U.S. President

1987: Dow-Jones Industrial Average drops 508 points in one day for the worst stock market crash in history

1989: Berlin Wall falls signifying the end of Soviet communism

1991: Persian Gulf War

2000: Dawn of the new millenium

At its peak in the twentieth century, the farm tractor industry offered as many as 200 unique tractor brands. At the start of the twenty-first century, there were four tractor companies with American names: AGCO, CNH Global (Case–New Holland), Caterpillar, and Deere. Not all of these were American-owned, and a great number of the tractors from these manufacturers were made overseas.

Change has always been the rule in the tractor industry: mechanical evolutions and revolutions; corporate mergers, consolidations, and failures. But as with the ever-increasing pace of life, the changes today seem to be accelerated and more earth shattering than any that have come before.

1969 Ford 9000 and 1953 Ford Model NAA Jubilee
Two generations of tractors separated by only a decade—but oh, what changes and improvements! The 9000's six-cylinder, 401-ci (6,568-cc), turbocharged diesel produced 131 hp. Its transmission offered sixteen speeds forward with partial range power-shifting. Owner: Dean Simmons.

1962 Fordson Super Major
Left: *Until 1964, Ford of England made a separate line of tractors under the Fordson banner. The Super Major was a 5,500-pound (2,475-kg) tractor in the 60-hp class. The transmission was a three-speed with a high-low auxiliary. It had a three-point hitch with draft control. Owner: Dean Simmons.*

1964 John Deere 1010 Grove-Orchard
The 35-hp 1010 was the smallest of the New Generation Deere tractors. This is one of seventy-two Orchard 1010s made and one of only sixty-three with a gas engine. Owner: the Keller family.

John Deere 4020
Deere & Company of Moline, Illinois

John Deere's 4020 is one of the most significant tractors since the Ford-Ferguson 9N. It has been called the most copied tractor in history and was Deere's largest seller since the two-cylinder B.

The 4020 was actually an improved version of the original 4010. Introduced in late 1960, the 4010 was at the time the largest of Deere's New Generation tractors. The 4010's major features were an ergonomic operator platform with a seat designed by an orthopedic doctor, a lower-link draft-control three-point hitch, and a central hydraulic system.

The hydraulic system had the greatest influence on the design of future tractors. The system's heart was a variable-displacement pump driven from the front of the crankshaft. The pump supplied pressure for raising implements, both three-point and remote cylinders, the power steering (there was no mechanical connection to the front wheels), power brakes, and the differential lock.

Built from 1963 to 1972, the 4020 offered an optional eight-speed power-shift transmission with four reverse ratios. The tractor was made in row-crop, high-crop, and standard-tread versions. It was available with gasoline, LPG, and diesel engines, although the diesel was the most popular.

The diesel version featured a six-cylinder, 404-ci (6,618-cc) engine. The gasoline and LPG engines displaced 340 ci (5,569 cc). Rated engine speed was 2,200 rpm for all versions. The diesel version developed 91 hp in its Nebraska test. The gasoline version produced 88 hp whereas the LPG version made 90 hp.

The 4020 was significant for another reason as well: It was the first John Deere two-wheel-drive tractor to bear a price tag of more than $10,000.

1971 John Deere 4000 Low Profile

The 4000 was a lower-priced version of the 4020. Only forty-six were made. Owner: the Keller family.

1962 John Deere 4010 HC LP

This was one of only twenty-three Hi-Crop 4010s powered by LPG; most were delivered to sugar-cane country in Louisiana. The 4010 had a 380-ci (6,224-cc), six-cylinder engine. It was also available as a diesel or a gas tractor, and in standard-tread, tricycle, or Hi-Crop configurations. Owner: the Keller family.

1969 John Deere 4020 brochure

Right: *Deere's 4020 was one of the most significant tractors in history. Introduced in late 1960, the 4020 was an improved version of the 4010. The 91-hp diesel version featured a six-cylinder, 404-ci (6,618-cc) engine. The 88-hp gasoline and 90-hp LPG engines displaced 340 ci (5,569 cc).*

1972 John Deere 4030

Below: *The 4030 used a 329-ci (5,389-cc), six-cylinder engine of 80 hp. This working tractor is owned by Glen Braun. "Lady" guards the tractor.*

Farmall 806

International Harvester Company of Chicago

International Harvester's answer to the Deere 4020 was the row-crop Farmall 806 and standard-tread International 806. The 806 featured a central hydraulic system similar to that pioneered by Deere, although the I-H system had separate circuits for steering, brakes, and implements.

The Farmall 806 was billed at the time as the world's most powerful all-purpose tractor at more than 90 hp. It recorded 94.93 PTO hp during its Nebraska test compared to the Deere 4020's 91.17 hp. The 806 used a six-cylinder engine displacing 361 ci (5,913 cc) for the diesel version and 301 ci (4,930 cc) for the gasoline and LPG models. Rated engine speed was 2,400 rpm as opposed to 2,200 rpm for the 4020.

The 806 sported an eight-speed transmission with a two-speed Torque Amplifier for sixteen forward ratios and two in reverse. Front wheel assist was an option.

The 806 was built between 1963 and 1967. It was replaced by the 100-hp 856, which remained in production through 1971.

1967 International 806

Billed as the most powerful all-purpose tractor of its day, the 806 recorded just under 95 hp in its Nebraska test with it's six-cylinder diesel engine of 361 ci (5,913 cc). Gas and a 301-ci (4,930-cc) LPG version were also available, as were both narrow and wide front ends. An eight-speed transmission was used by all. A central hydraulic system, after the fashion of the Deere 4010/4020, powered the steering, lift, and brakes. The 806, one of the most popular Internationals, was produced from 1963 to 1967.

The 100-Plus Horsepower Magic

Horsepower is simply the rate of doing work. Since farm work seems to always need to be done at once, there is no substitute for horsepower. One can only wonder at the patience of the farmer of the 1920s with hundreds of acres to till with a one-bottom plow!

In 1960, the average farm tractor had 40 to 50 hp. Today, that is the average for compact tractors. The largest of the two-wheel-drive tractors today has more horsepower than some four-wheel drives of the 1960s. Toward the end of the century, however, tillage practices and high costs have led to a decline in horsepower from the peak in the late 1970s.

With its RD-8 crawler, Caterpillar was the first to break the 100-hp barrier, as recorded by the University of Nebraska in 1936. The 34,000-pound (15,300-kg) tractor featured a six-cylinder, 1,246-ci (20,409-cc) engine. Cletrac soon followed with both its FD diesel and FG gasoline crawlers.

The first two-wheel-drive, wheel-type tractor to exceed 100 brake hp was the 1962 Deere 5010. Its six-cylinder, 531-ci (8,698-cc) diesel made 121 PTO hp. To harness this two-wheel-drive power without excessive slippage, 24.5x32 rear tires were used with a burdened weight of more than 17,000 pounds (7,650 kg). Allis-Chalmers also entered a two-wheel-drive machine in 1963 at 103 horsepower, the Model D-21.

Once the 100-hp genie was out of the bottle, everyone wanted part of the magic. All the manufacturers jumped on the bandwagon. Turbochargers, intercoolers, and after-coolers became commonplace in the horsepower race. The Case 1031 and Minneapolis-Moline G-1000 entered in 1966 as two-wheel-drive models. Four-wheel drives came into the picture in 1959 with the Deere 8010, 1962 International 4300, and 1964 Case 1200. Deere's 8010 was also the first farm tractor to exceed 200 hp.

The horsepower race was led by the Big Bud firm of Havre, Montana, which started constructing tractors in 1968. Big Bud's 1976 KT-450 had a 450-hp Cummins engine. The Big Bud 1978 model used on some California and other Western farms boasted a sixteen-cylinder, 760-hp engine. The current champion, however, is the giant, 800-plus-hp, $1-million Caterpillar D11, although it is not much used on farms except for deep sub-soiling.

"When you drop your implement and hit the throttle, you expect instant power and fast acceleration."
—Steiger Tractors brochure, 1980s

1974 Oliver 1655 Diesel
The horsepower race was on! Both the gasoline and diesel versions of the six-cylinder Model 1655 were rated at 70 hp. The diesel displaced 283 ci (4,635 cc) while the gasoline type displaced 265 ci (4,341 cc).

1974 Massey-Ferguson 1080

Right: *Using a Perkins 381-ci (6,241-cc) diesel, the 1080 was in the 80-hp class. Operating weight was about 12,000 pounds (5,400 kg). A six-speed transmission with partial-range power-shift gave twelve forward speeds. Owner: Maurice Burston.*

1963 Minneapolis-Moline M-504

Above, both photos: *This diesel M-504 with four-wheel drive was one of only twenty-one made. The M-504 was only built in 1962 and 1963. Owner: the Keller family.*

1966 Case 1030 Comfort King

The 1030 was available as a general-purpose model as shown, or in a standard-tread (Western) model. It featured the 451-ci (7,387-cc) six and was Case's first tractor to exceed 100 hp. Owner: Jay Foxworthy.

1971 Minneapolis-Moline G-1050 LPG

The G-1050 has a 504-ci (8,255-cc) six-cylinder engine producing 110 hp. Owner: Roger Mohr.

Massey-Ferguson trio

Above: *Massey-Ferguson's 9240, 6150, and 65 grace a sunny hillside.*

1975 International 966 Hydro

Left: *The '66 Series International tractors were built from 1971 to 1976. The 966 was a 100-hp example; this one had the optional full Hydrostatic transmission. A 414-ci (6,781-cc), six-cylinder diesel was used. Turbocharging was optional.*

1973 Ford 8600

Using the naturally aspirated Ford 401-ci (6,568-cc) diesel, the 8600 was the successor to the 8000. Internal improvements brought power up to 110 hp, and a partial range power-shift gave sixteen forward speeds.

1984 Ford TW-35 FWD Diesel

This 171-hp tractor featured a 401-ci (6,568-cc) engine with turbocharger and intercooler. It had a working weight of about 10 tons (9,000 kg). Owner: the Bissen family.

Allis-Chalmers D-19
Allis-Chalmers Company of Milwaukee, Wisconsin

1965 Allis-Chalmers ED-40
Above: *Similar to Allis's D-12, the ED-40 was built at A-C's factory in Essendine, England, for the British and Canadian market starting in 1963. It featured a 138-ci (2,260-cc), four-cylinder diesel engine and a four-speed transmission with a two-range auxiliary.*

1963 Allis-Chalmers D-19
Right: *The D-19 was built in Milwaukee, Wisconsin, from 1961 to 1964, with a few more than 10,000 constructed. They were available in gasoline, LPG, and diesel variations, but the diesel was noted for being the first production farm tractor to use a turbocharger. All engines were the A-C 262-ci (4,292-cc) six. Power was in the 65-hp class. Allis-Chalmers was one of the largest producers of turbochargers for aircraft during World War II. Owner: the Karg family.*

Despite working with outdated manufacturing facilities, Allis-Chalmers continued to produce creditable and competitive products, and the D-19 was no exception. The D-19 was the first production tractor to use a turbocharger, which has since become almost standard fare among the larger tractors.

A turbocharger consists of a centrifugal compressor on one end of a shaft with a radial inflow turbine on the other. Exhaust gas from the engine cylinders, which still has considerable heat and pressure when the exhaust valves open, drives the turbine to high speed. The turbine in turn powers the compressor via the common shaft. The compressor forces air into the intake manifold at two to three times atmospheric pressure. The harder the engine works, the more power there is in the exhaust to drive the compressor, which gives the engine more power to pull the load. Unlike superchargers, such as were used in the GM two-cycle diesels, the turbocharger consumes only power that would otherwise have been wasted in the exhaust. With a turbocharger, a small engine acts like one with a larger displacement, but consumes fuel like the smaller unit it is.

Swiss engineer Dr. Alfred J. Buchi invented the turbocharger in 1909. Nothing much came of it until World War II, however. General Electric, who had experience with water and steam turbines for driving generators, made turbochargers for most of the high-performance U.S. military aircraft, allowing them to retain their power as they went higher in altitude.

Production of Allis-Chalmers's turbo D-19 ran from 1961 to 1964, and only about 10,000 were built. It was available with LPG and gasoline engines, but only the diesel incorporated the turbocharger. All of the engines were six-cylinders displacing 262 ci (4,292 cc) and creating 65 PTO hp.

Following the D-19's successful application of the turbocharger, other tractors followed suit. Companies like M&W Gear Company sold aftermarket kits. By the end of the 1960s, all of the big U.S. tractor makers were offering turbocharged tractors.

1963 Allis-Chalmers D-21

Left: *The first Allis with more than 100 hp, the D-21 was rated at 119 hp. It was powered by a 426-ci (6,978-cc), six-cylinder diesel. After 1965, a turbo-charged version was available with 127 hp. Owner: the Karg family.*

Factory Cabs: Comfort Comes to the Tractor

"Just as the city man needs a comfortable closed car to pursue his activities, so the farmer who spends a big share of his time on a tractor needs and wants greater comfort on the job."
—Minneapolis-Moline UDLX brochure, 1938

Although pioneered by Minneapolis-Moline with its UDLX of 1938, the factory-provided tractor cab did not become popular until the 1970s. In the original tractor designs, the operator sat as far back as possible in order to reach the implement controls. With the advent of hydraulic controls, the operator's seat was moved forward for a better, safer ride. Although the operator no longer had to reach external controls, many farmers did not like the idea of being inside when cultivating: They wanted to see the shovels going past the corn. As rear-mounted, three-point cultivators became more and more accepted, there was no way to actually watch the shovels. Looking backwards had to be done carefully, if at all, so the last resistance to the cab disappeared.

In the 1960s, aftermarket companies supplied cabs for the most popular tractor models. Many of these were only marginally satisfactory. Some actually increased the intensity of the noise and dust.

Cabs provided by the tractor companies were engineered for better results. Along with heating, air conditioning, and a nice radio came a comfortable seat—more like an office chair—with adjustments to fit the operator. Controls and displays were arranged for convenience. Positive-pressure fans kept the dust out and noise was so low that the radio could actually be used. In 1971, the University of Nebraska began reporting interior noise levels for all tractors tested.

1972 John Deere 4430
Above, both photos: *With a six-cylinder turbocharged engine of 404 ci (6,617 cc), the 4430 was a 126-hp tractor.*

1971 Allis-Chalmers One-Ninety XT Series III
Above and left: *The One-Ninety and One-Ninety XT were identical, except for the engine. The regular version used a 265-ci (4,341-cc) engine, while a 301-ci (4,930-cc) unit powered the XT. The One-Ninety was built from 1964 through 1973. A version of the XT Diesel used a turbocharger and made 93 drawbar hp. Owner: the Karg family.*

1973 Oliver 2255

Left: *Powered by a 573-ci (9,386-cc) Caterpillar V-8, this 17,000-pound (7,650-kg) tractor rated 147 hp, backed by an eighteen-speed transmission. Owner: Lee Miller.*

1988 Case-IH 956XL

Left: *The XL version of Case-IH's 956XL had a deluxe cab with air conditioning available.*

1980s Massey-Ferguson 3095

Below, both photos: *A Massey-Ferguson 3095 pulls a New Holland 865 baler.*

Transmissions: The Ratio Race

By 1960, multi-ratio transmissions were standard, and half-step power downshifts, like those pioneered by International Harvester's Torque Amplifier, were common. In 1957, Case introduced its Case-O-Matic torque-converter transmission, which had excellent load-starting ability. Oliver came out with a similar arrangement in 1958 with its Model 995 GM Lugmatic. In 1981, Steiger began using five-speed Allison (then a division of GM) torque-converter/power-shift transmissions with a two-speed auxiliary.

In 1959, Ford introduced the first all-power-shift transmission—the ten-speed Select-O-Speed. Deere offered a similar arrangement in 1963. Today, power-shift transmissions with up to eighteen speeds are available. The Caterpillar Challenger, for example, features a sixteen-speed forward unit (with nine reverse speeds) providing five shift modes, such as pulse shifting one gear at a time, continuous sequential shifting, preselected gear shifting, programmable up- and downshifting, or automatic shifting through gears ten through sixteen. In 1990, Ford offered a similar eighteen-speed unit called

1964 Minneapolis-Moline M-5
The famous M-5 was available in this LPG-powered high-crop version. Produced from 1960 to 1964, it was powered by a 336-ci (5,504-cc), four-cylinder engine with a five-speed transmission plus a two-speed power shift. The M-5 was also available in gasoline and diesel versions. Owner: the Keller family.

Ultra-Command. With it, the shift lever was moved forward and backward for forward and reverse in any gear selected. Gears were chosen by moving the shift lever left for lower gears, or right for higher speeds.

International Harvester introduced hydrostatic drives in 1969 on its 826 and 1026 models. These tractors also were equipped with manual high/low range shifters, but within either range, ground speed was infinitely variable at a constant engine speed. Versatile Manufacturing of Winnipeg, Manitoba, also offered a hydrostatic drive in 1977 on the Versatile Model 150.

In 1972, Oliver topped the ratio chart with eighteen forward speeds. This was accomplished with a six-speed conventional transmission and a three-speed power-shift auxiliary with under-, direct-, and overdrive. Allis-Chalmers took away those honors in 1973 with a twenty-speed arrangement on it 7030 and 7050. Massey-Ferguson offered a twenty-four-speed arrangement in 1978. Steiger boasted a twenty-four speed on the Tiger IV in 1984. Case-IH also had a twenty-four-speed unit in 1986, consisting of four gears and a six-speed power-shift. Deere offered a twenty-four-speed unit in 1989.

The 1987 Massey-Ferguson 3050 and 3060 came with thirty-two speeds accomplished with a four-speed power-shift, a gearbox with four synchronized gears plus a high/low range and a shuttle shift. In 1995, White also boasted of thirty-two speeds, but with an eight-speed manual gearbox and four-speed power-shift auxiliary. The all-time ratio champ, however, was the 1992 AGCO-Allis 8630 with forty-eight speeds: a sixteen-speed gearbox and a three-speed power-shift auxiliary.

1973 Ford 4000 Diesel
The 4000 was equipped with a three-cylinder, 201-ci (3,292-cc) engine, putting it in the 50-hp class. Weight was just under 5,000 pounds (2,250 kg), but that could be doubled with ballast. The eight-speed fixed-ratio transmission gave speeds from 1.5 to 17 mph (2.4–27 kmh). Owner: Dennis Burstin.

Technology Left Behind

Since the 1960s, the tractor industry left behind distillate fuels and LPG. June 1968 saw the last LPG tractor test at the University of Nebraska.

The industry has also left behind gasoline. The International 284 was the last gasoline-powered tractor tested at the University of Nebraska, in 1978. Since that time, only diesel tractors have been available on the American market, with the exception of small lawn tractors. One exception is the "new" N Series Ford manufactured by N-Complete of Wilkinson, Indiana. According to N-Complete's Tom Armstrong, the Fords are re-manufactured using parts that meet new tractor specifications. The tractors also carry a warranty the same as a new machine.

One of the most profound changes went almost unnoticed, however: the disappearance of the tricycle front end. While the narrow, or tricycle front, remained in the catalogs for a time, they were rarely sold after 1973. Two things accounted for the demise of the narrow front: The use of chemicals largely eliminated the need for the cultivation of tall crops, and the advent of the front-end loader, which seemed to work so much better on a wide-front machine.

1966 Case 1030
This working 1030 was powering a grain auger filling rail cars for Farmer's Feed and Grain in Charles City, Iowa, in the summer of 1999. Wayne Bottloson was the operator.

1964 Minneapolis-Moline M-670
This early version of the M-670 was LPG powered and was one of the last with narrow-front. The M-670 was built from 1964 to 1970. Owner: Matt Ross.

The Proliferation of Articulated Four-Wheel-Drive Tractors

The trend toward larger, more powerful tractors continued in the 1960s. Steering limitations of powered front wheels led manufacturers to try both the skid-steer concept and the articulated four-wheel drive. Skid-steer soon lost out, and articulation became the chosen road.

1979 International 4586

Left: *The 4586 featured an 800-ci (13,104-cc) diesel and nine-speed transmission. It was built from 1976 through 1980.*

1980 John Deere 8440

Below: *The 8440 was powered by a 466-ci (7,633-cc) turbocharged and aftercooled diesel of 180 hp. Owner: Don Bray.*

1984 John Deere 8850

Above and right: *Powered by a turbocharged and aftercooled V-8 of 955 ci (15,643 cc), the 8850 was the top of Deere's line. Six headlights lit up the fields, so that the $120,000 machine could work day and night. Maximum power was 304 PTO hp. The big 8850 had a drawbar pull of 94 percent of its own weight. Owner: Ruth Schaefer.*

1982 John Deere 8450

Weighing nearly 15 tons (13,500 kg), the 8450 was a big four-wheel-drive articulated tractor. Its turbocharged and aftercooled six-cylinder engine developed 187 hp.

1964 Case 1200 Traction King

Case's first venture into four-wheel drive, the Traction King used four-wheel steering as well. Power was from a 461-ci (7,551-cc) diesel. Owner: John Thierer.

1979 Ford FW-30

Above and left: *Powered by a 903-ci (14,791-cc) Cummins V-8 diesel, the 32,000-pound (14,400-kg) FW-30 was a big machine for its time. Steiger made the FW Series tractors for Ford. Owner Dale Bissen added a turbocharger, upping power from 205 to 270 hp.*

1980 International 3588

The last of the new tractors from International Harvester before the merger with Case, the 2+2 Series tractors were the ultimate in their day. The 3588 had a 150-hp diesel.

1983 White Field Boss 4-225

Powered by a 636-ci (10,418-cc) turbocharged Caterpillar V-8, the 4-225 had a closed-center hydraulic system and eighteen-speed transmission. The cab featured a fourteen-channel digital monitor and air conditioning.

1971 White Plainsman A4T-1600

The articulated Plainsman began life under the Minneapolis-Moline banner. It was also sold as the Oliver 2655 before becoming the White Plainsman in 1970. The engine was an M-M 585-ci (9,582-cc) diesel of 143 hp. A ten-speed selective fixed-ratio transmission was used. It weighed 20,000 pounds (9,000 kg).

1982 International 6588

The International Harvester 2+2 design was introduced in January 1979. It was a unique approach to articulated four-wheel-drive tractors with the operator's cab behind the articulation point and the engine ahead. In fact, the engine was ahead of the front axle for weight distribution purposes. The large fuel tank was behind the front axle and acted as a sound shield between the engine and cab. Two sizes were available: the 130-hp 3388 and the 150-hp 3588. These were replaced by the 6388 and 6588 in the 1982 model year with transmission improvements, but with the same power. Two larger versions were in the works, the 210-hp 7288 and 235-hp 7488 when IH financial difficulties became insurmountable, and the Tenneco buyout was imminent. The buyout occurred in 1984 and the 2+2 tractors were dropped.

Versatile
Versatile Manufacturing Ltd. of Winnipeg, Manitoba

As a lad on his family's farm in Canora, Canada, Peter Pakosh was always fascinated by machinery. During the tough times of the Great Depression, he was forced to leave the farm and seek a job at Massey-Harris. When he was refused a transfer to Massey's design department in 1945, Pakosh began crafting his own machinery in his Toronto basement, building a grain auger that had fewer moving parts than existing models and would be less expensive to manufacture.

With the aid of his machinist brother-in-law, Roy Robinson, Pakosh started the Hydraulic Engineering Company in 1947, mortgaging everything the two owned and borrowing the egg money Pakosh's wife was saving for a fur coat. They branded their auger and new field sprayer the "Versatile," and incorporated in 1963 as Versatile Manufacturing Ltd.

In 1966, Pakosh launched his first four-wheel-drive tractor, which was the first mass-produced four-wheel drive, but it sold for about the same price as major makers' smaller two-wheel drives. Pakosh had earned a reputation for designing simple, straightforward machines that small farmers could afford to buy and could often maintain and repair themselves. Versatiles were mostly sold in Canada as well as in Minnesota, Montana, and South and North Dakota.

Pakosh sold Versatile in 1976 to Cornat Industries of Vancouver. In 1987, New Holland purchased the firm, but in 1999, Versatile was excluded from the CNH Global NV deal and is once again independent.

1977 Versatile 150
Introduced in 1977, the Model 150 was Versatile's revolutionary bi-directional tractor.

1980 Versatile 895
With an 855-ci (14,005-cc), supercharged and intercooled Cummins six-cylinder engine, Versatile's articulated 895 tractor produced 251 drawbar hp.

Steiger

Steiger Tractor Company of Fargo, North Dakota

**STEIGER TRACTORS
CAT DIESEL ENGINES**

**A HIGH-POWERED COMBINATION
FOR HIGH-PRODUCTION FARMS**

1980s Steiger brochure
*By the 1980s, Steiger's lineup included
the Cat-powered Bearcat III, Cougar III,
Panther III, Panther 1000, and Tiger III.*

Necessity was the mother of invention for brothers Maurice and Douglass Steiger. The duo who wanted a powerful four-wheel-drive tractor for their farm near Red Lake Falls, Minnesota, but no existing machine came close to meeting their needs. Starting with a Euclid earthmover, the brothers built their own tractor in the family dairy barn during the winter of 1957–1958.

The Steiger's 15,000-pound (6,750-kg) home-built machine was constructed from salvaged parts and powered by a 238-hp Detroit Diesel engine. Neighboring farmers liked the tractor and put down cash for a "Steiger" of their own. Some 125 tractors were eventually built on the farm.

Steiger Tractor was incorporated in 1969, with a factory in Fargo, North Dakota. That same year, Steiger's Series I Wildcat, Super Wildcat, Bearcat, Cougar, and Tiger machines hit the market. The firm was eventually contracted to build machines for a variety of the major makers, including Allis-Chalmers, Ford, and International Harvester.

By 1986, however, the ailing farm economy pushed Steiger into bankruptcy, and it was acquired by Tenneco. Steiger continued to build machines that were now painted Case red instead of Steiger green. By 2000, the firm was part of CNH Global NV and had built more than 50,000 four-wheel-drive tractors.

1982 Steiger Panther CP-1360
The 334-hp Panther was powered by a six-cylinder Caterpillar engine and built by the Steiger Tractor Company of Fargo, North Dakota. It boasted sixteen forward speeds. Weight was 35,000 pounds (15,750 kg).

1991 Case-IH 9280

In 1986, Tenneco took over the failing Steiger, folding it into its Case-IH line. By 1991, the 9280 was the largest tractor produced by the company. It used an 855-ci (14,005-cc) engine producing 344 hp with turbocharging and aftercooling.

1999 Case-IH Steiger 9330

AGCO: A Proud Heritage

On November 1, 1960, just before John F. Kennedy was elected president, the White Motor Corporation of Cleveland, Ohio, bought out the Oliver Corporation. The next year, the Canadian Cockshutt outfit was added to the White family, and Minneapolis-Moline was added in 1963. These brand names continued until 1969 when all were dropped in favor of the name White Field Boss.

In 1985, Allis-Chalmers was folded into Klockner-Humboldt-Deutz (KHD) of Germany and became Deutz-Allis. In 1990, Allis-Gleaner Company (AGCO) bought Deutz-Allis; in 1993, it acquired the White line. In 1993 and 1994, AGCO purchased the worldwide holdings of Massey-Ferguson, which by that time also included McConnell Tractors. Tractors produced under the AGCO banner now include AGCO Allis, AGCOSTAR, Massey-Ferguson, White, and Landini.

The heritage of these modern tractors goes all the way back to Hart-Parr. Many firsts were included in the designs that have led up to the present time: the first tractor factory; first production tractor model; first tractor advertising; first production kerosene-burning tractor; first multi-speed tractor transmission; first overhead-valve tractor engine; first production cultivating tractor; first articulated tractor; first tractor with starter and lights; first live PTO; first differential lock; first tractor to offer rubber tires as standard equipment; first LPG tractor engine; first tractor disk brakes; first tractor cab with radio; first four-valve-per-cylinder tractor engine.

It's a proud heritage.

1968 Minneapolis-Moline M-670

Available configured for gasoline, diesel, or LPG fuels, the M-670 used the M-M 336-ci (5,504-cc) engine block. All three versions were in the 70-hp class.

1963 Oliver 1600
Left, both photos: *Built in 1962 and 1963, the 1600 was available in LPG, gasoline, or diesel versions. This one was gasoline powered. Owner: Eldon Oleson, who worked at Oliver/White in Charles City, Iowa, for thirty-nine years.*

1960 Oliver 770
The 770 came out in 1958 and was an improvement over the previous Super 77. The six-cylinder engine gave about 55 hp in gasoline, diesel, or LPG versions. The gasoline engine is shown.

1970 Oliver 1755
The diesel engine in the 1755 offered 86 "certified" hp from 310 ci (5,078 cc). The gasoline version was slightly smaller at 283 ci (4,636 cc), but also gave 86 hp.

1975 Oliver 1755

This 1755 had the 310-ci (5,078-cc) diesel and the "Over-Under" power-shift along with the six-speed gearbox. Owner: David Preuhs.

1978 White 2-180 Series 3

Above and right: *The Field Boss 2-180 pulls a Model 605F Vermeer baler. The big White was powered by a Caterpillar V-8. Owner: Bruce Copper.*

1999 White 6124

The new White 6124 was in the 125-hp class.

1995 AGCO-Allis 8630

Above and left: 1992 Deutz-Allis 9130 FPA

1970 Case 1070 Agri King
Above and left: *The 451-ci (7,387-cc) Case 1070 was in the 100-hp category. The Model 1070 was sold from 1970 to 1978 with a six-cylinder engine and either an eight-speed manual or six-speed transmission with partial-range power-shift for twelve forward speeds.*

1976 Case 1570 Spirit of '76

Case built the 180-hp turbocharged 1570 in 1976 and 1977. During the U.S. Bicentennial year of 1976, special commemorative paint jobs were available. Owner: J. R. Gyger.

1960 Case 830 HC Comfort King

This high-clearance 830 had the Case-O-Matic transmission. The 830 was a 60-hp tractor. Owner: J. R. Gyger.

1973 International 1466 Turbo

Produced from 1971 to 1975, the 145-hp 1466 used a 436-ci (7,142-cc), six-cylinder diesel engine.

1973 International 1066

Built from 1971 to 1975, the 1066 was available with turbocharging and the fully hydrostatic transmission. Power, with the turbo, was 125 hp.

1979 International 784

The 784 featured a 65-hp, four-cylinder diesel of 246 ci (4,029 cc). The 84 Series tractors were built in IH's Doncaster, England, factory.

1993 Case-IH 7130

Built from 1988 to 1993, the 7130 featured a 505-ci (8,272-cc), six-cylinder diesel of 175 hp and an eighteen-speed power-shift transmission.

1982 International 5488

With its 466-ci (7,633-cc), six-cylinder diesel, the 5488 was the first International two-wheel drive in the 180-hp class, with a rating of 187 hp. Front wheel assist was later made available.

CNH Global NV: A Conglomerate Rich With History

The November 1999 merger of the Case Corporation and New Holland NV produced the world's leading maker of farm equipment. The company, which is expected to have sales of $12 billion, will be headquartered in Racine, Wisconsin. In 1844, when J. I. Case began manufacturing threshing machines in Rochester, Wisconsin, Rochester city fathers denied him water rights to the Fox River millrace. Case moved his operation twenty-five miles (40 km) east to Lake Michigan and the town of Racine. It was Rochester's loss.

Throughout its history, Case's management bounced from being either conservative or flamboyant. Despite this, the firm arrived in the 1960s in good shape, having just acquired the American Tractor Corporation in 1957, which put Case solidly into the crawler and construction-equipment businesses. By 1970, however, cash shortages forced Case to sell out to the giant conglomerate Tenneco of Houston, Texas. A bevy of technologically advanced tractors then issued from the Case factories. To expand its European foothold, Case acquired David Brown Tractors of England in 1972.

Meanwhile, the fierce competition in the tractor business was causing International Harvester insurmountable financial woes. IHC had been number one in tractor production until 1963, after which John Deere took the lead. IHC countered with thoroughly modern tractor designs, including new articulated four-wheel-drive models with the Control Center cab aft of the articulation point. In order to keep stockholders happy, however, IHC management failed to plow enough profits back into plants and technology. Even at that, stockholder unrest caused several management shakeups as dividends fell. Then, the United Auto Workers union struck for higher wages and increased benefits. The strike lasted six months, and IHC never recovered.

In 1985, Tenneco acquired IHC's Tractor and Implement Division, which was then folded into Case. The

1961 Fordson Dexta Diesel
A British-built tractor in the 30-hp class, the Dexta had a three-cylinder, 144-ci (2,359-cc), Perkins engine. The 1962 Super Dexta boasted a 152-ci (2,490-cc) engine. It was imported and sold in North America as the Ford 2000 Diesel. Owner: Dean Simmons.

1962 Ford 5000 Diesel
The 5000 Diesel was really a British Fordson Super Major in cream and blue paint and with different decals that was imported for sale in North America. Like the Super Major, it used a 220-ci (3,604-cc), four-cylinder Ford engine. Owner: Fred Bissen.

consolidation put Case-IH on a firm foundation for the future, and allowed the purchase of the ailing Steiger Tractor Company.

At the same time, Ford had acquired New Holland in 1986, and the Ford Tractor Division became Ford–New Holland. Ford also bought the Canadian Versatile Company. In 1994, Italy's Fiat Agri began a buyout of Ford–New Holland, which was completed in 1995. Since 1997, the line of tractors has been marketed worldwide under the New Holland brand. After eighty years of Ford tractors, the name disappeared from the field.

The new CNH Global NV company is 71 percent owned by Italian automaking conglomerate Fiat. The U.S. Justice Department required some divestitures before approving the merger. Case must sell its ownership in Hay & Forage Industries, which was jointly held with AGCO. New Holland must sell off its Winnipeg, Manitoba, plant along with its Versatile and Genesis tractor lines. New Holland was allowed to keep its TV-140 bi-directional tractor, however. Its production is being moved to another facility.

1967 Ford 6000
Built from 1961 to 1967, the 6000 used the ten-speed power-shift Select-O-Speed transmission. Early models, painted red, had troubles with the transmission and were recalled. When reissued, the paint was changed to this blue and white. The 6000 was a 10,000-lb (4,500-kg), 60-hp tractor.

1972 Ford 8000
The 8000 was a 105-hp tractor with a 401-ci (6,568-cc), six-cylinder diesel. Working weight is about 15,000 pounds (6,750-kg). Owner: Floyd Dominique.

1972 Ford 7000
The 85-hp 7000 was equipped with a 256-ci (4,193-cc), four-cylinder diesel with turbocharger. Owner: Frank Bissen.

1976 Massey-Ferguson 1135
Above: *The 1135 had a 120-hp, 354-ci (5,799-cc) Perkins diesel with turbo-charger. The tractor was two-wheel drive, but the reversed-tread front tires prevented sliding on wet ground. Owner: Rich Hollicky.*

1992 Ford 7840 Powerstar SL
Above, right: *One of a series of new Powerstar tractors for 1992, the 7840 used a 90-hp, 401-ci (6,568-cc) Genesis engine.*

1990s Massey-Ferguson 3655
An M-F 3655 works with a New Holland combine to harvest a wheatfield.

1990s Massey-Ferguson 8160

Deere and Caterpillar: Steering the Straight Course

Deere and Caterpillar have gone through this period virtually unscathed. They have neither acquired, nor have they been acquired. Both have had exemplary managements and outstanding products since early times.

The two Illinois-based companies have demonstrated an affinity for each other over the years. In 1928, as Deere was developing a combine for the market, Caterpillar offered to sell Deere its Western Harvester Division with its line of successful combines. The asking price of $1.25 million was more than Deere could handle after funding the development of the in-house design.

Seven years later, Caterpillar again approached Deere with an idea. Cat dealers were suffering in competition with Allis-Chalmers and International Harvester because they only had track-type tractors. Caterpillar purposed a joint dealer arrangement where both Deere wheeled tractors and Caterpillar crawlers would be sold. For further enticement, Caterpillar offered to *give* their combine line to Deere. Deere accepted and, in doing so, also obtained access to Caterpillar's foreign dealerships. The arrangement was maintained into the 1960s, but was substantially diminished after Deere began marketing its own crawlers.

Although Caterpillar had steered more into the heavy construction side of the business over the years, its management has always remembered the firm's agricultural roots. Special Ag versions of Cat's small- and mid-sized crawlers have been available. Then in 1987, the rubber-tracked Challengers made the scene, combining the advantages of both rubber-tired and track-type tractors with good highway transport speeds and high floatation over soft ground.

Both Deere and Caterpillar appear ready to tackle the new century and continue their long lineages.

1960 John Deere 3010

The 3010 sported a four-cylinder engine of 254 ci (4,161 cc). This one was gasoline-fueled, but diesel and LP were options.

1980 John Deere 2640

The Dubuque-built 2640 was a 70-hp, four-cylinder tractor. Displacement was 276 ci (4,521 cc).

1999 John Deere 8300T

Announced in 1996, production of the 8000T Series rubber-track models started in June 1997. For the first time since the 1960s, it was possible to purchase either a wheeled or tracked version of the same Deere tractor. This time, however, the tracks were rubber instead of steel link. The 8300T was rated at 205 hp.

1996 John Deere 6900

A John Deere 6900 pulls a Klaas Quadrant 1150 baler and sledge.

1996 John Deere 6400

The 6400 was the top-of-the-line four-cylinder Deere tractor. The 276-ci (4,521-cc) diesel produced 100 hp.

Caterpillar Challenger
Caterpillar Inc. of Peoria, Illinois

The first production farm tractor to combine the speed and mobility of a wheeled tractor with the floatation and traction of a crawler was the Caterpillar Challenger Model 65, introduced in 1987. From this single model, the rubber-tracked Challenger has grown into a full-line series covering a range of horsepowers and including three sizes of row-crop machines with adjustable track widths.

For 1999, conventional (non-row-crop) Challengers were in their fifth generation following the original Model 65. Included were the 310-hp 65E, 340-hp 75E, 370-hp 85E, and 410-hp 95E. The full power-shift transmission had ten speeds forward and two in reverse.

Row-crop models included the 175-hp 35, 200-hp 45, and 225-hp 55. The row-crop transmission had sixteen speeds forward with a shuttle reverse in nine speeds. All Challengers had hydrostatic differential steering controlled by a conventional steering wheel. All featured state-of-the-art cabs and electronics.

By 2000, both Case-IH and Deere had also entered the rubber-track market, and Claas KgaA of Germany began marketing Caterpillar's Challengers in Europe. Implements, such as spreaders and even combines, are now being made with rubber tracks. Watch for both smaller and larger tractors in the future to sport these new-technology treads.

1996 Caterpillar Challenger 45
The row-crop version of the rubber-tracked Challenger had 200 hp and a sixteen-speed transmission. Owner: John Yotter.

251

1992 Caterpillar Challenger 65B

Powered by Cat's 3306 turbocharged engine with 285 hp, the 65B had a ten-speed power-shift transmission and full hydro-static steering. It is shown with a DMI 44.5-ft (13.4-m) field cultivator with which it can cover 30 acres (12 hectares) per hour. It is also equipped with a 500-gallon (1,650-l) chemical tank. Owner: Rich Hollicky. Hollicky's son, Scott, is an ag engineering student at the University of Illinois. Scott reported the Challenger was easy to drive, stayed straight on hillsides, and was comfortable for long days and nights in the field. They have had few repairs to the machine. When the alternator went out one spring Saturday night at 11:30, their dealer, Ziegler of Minneapolis, opened up at 1:30 Sunday morning to provide a new alternator, and the Challenger was back in the field by daybreak.

Index

A. Harris, Son & Co., Ltd., *42*

A. M. Archambault & Co., *15*

Advance Thresher Co., *27*
  Advance steamer, *27*

Advance-Rumely Thresher Co., *27, 45, 56–59, 125*
  Rumely OilPull, *4, 27, 56–59, 207*

Allis, Edwin P., *124*

Allis-Chalmers Co., *27, 45, 124*

Allis-Chalmers Mfg. Co., *104, 124–125, 164–165, 189–190, 226–227, 240*
  6/12, *64, 67*
  D-12, *199*
  D-19, *226*
  D-21, *223, 227*
  Duplex, *213*
  ED-40, *226*
  HD-14, *125*
  HD-4, *127*
  HD-41, *125*
  Model B, *155, 164–165*
  Model C, *155*
  Model E, *45*
  Model IB, *165, 207*
  Model K, *125*
  Model L, *127*
  Model M, *127*
  Model S, *124*
  Model U, *104–105, 127, 189*
  Model UC, *138*
  Model WC, *189–190*
  Model WF, *189–190*
  One-Ninety XT, *228*

Allis-Gleaner Co. (AGCO), *240*
  AGCO-Allis 8630, *231, 243*

American-Abell Engine & Thresher Co., *27*

Appleby Automatic Knotter, *10–11*

Appleby, John F., *10–11*

Arthurdale Farm Equipment Corp., *178*
  Co-op B2JR, *178*

Aultman & Taylor Machinery Co., *27, 45*

Avery Co., *26, 29, 35, 89, 179*
  Avery steamer, *26*
  12/25, *29*
  40/65, *35*
  40/80, *35, 62*
  Model C, *89*
  Ro-Trak, *26, 179*

Avery, Cyrus, *26*

Avery, Robert, *26*

B. F. Avery Co., *200*

Ball Tread Co., *131*

Bartholomew, John, *26*

Bates Steel Mule, *see* Joliet Oil Tractor Co.

Best, Clarence Leo "C. L.," *112, 114, 120*

Best, Daniel, *22–23, 112*

Big Bud, *223*

Big Four tractor, *see* Gas Traction Co.

Brock, Harold L., *157, 163*

Bull, Stephen, *33*

Bull Tractor Co., *50, 62–64*
  Big Bull, *63*
  Little Bull, *50, 62, 63*

Bullock Tractor Co., *130*

Butterworth, William, *50*

C. L. Best Gas Traction Co., *112, 118–119*
  Sixty, *112, 114*
  Thirty, *112, 114, 115, 129*

Canadian Waterloo Mfg. Co., *24*

Case, Jerome Increase, *17*

Caterpillar Tractor Co., *114, 118–119, 132, 249, 251–252*
  Challenger, *122, 230, 251–252*
  Challenger 45, *251*
  Challenger 65B, *65, 251, 252*
  D4, *116*
  D8, *122, 132*
  Diesel Forty, *9*
  Diesel Sixty, *114, 118–119, 168, 186*
  Diesel Sixty-Five, *118*
  RD-8, *132, 223*
  Sixty, *118–119*
  Ten, *115*
  Thirty, *115*
  Twenty, *114*
  Twenty-Eight, *116*
  Twenty-Two, *109, 117*

Chalmers, William J., *124*

Charter Gas Engine Co., *30*
  Charter tractor, *30*

Charter, John, *30*

Chase, L. W., *84*

Cleveland Motor Plow Co., *120–121*
  20, *120*

Cleveland Tractor Co. (Cletrac), *120–123*
  80, *122*
  CG, *123*
  Model F, *122*

CNH Global NV, *237, 238, 247*

Cockshutt Farm Equipment Co., *176, 240*
  70, *176*
  Model 30, *184, 185*

Cockshutt Plow Co., *185*

Co-operative Mfg. Co., *177*
  Co-op Duplex No. 2, *177*

Crozier, Wilmot, *84, 85*

Dahl, John, *37*

Dain, Joseph Sr., *50*

Daniel Best Agricultural Works, *16, 22–23, 112*
  Daniel Best steamer, *22–23*

David Brown, *157, 162, 246*
  Ferguson-Brown "Black Tractor," *157, 162*

Deere & Co., *33, 42, 50–51, 52, 87, 94–97, 129, 140–145, 166, 204–205, 214–215, 220–221, 230, 249*
  1010 Grove-Orchard, *219*
  2640, *250*

3010, *205, 249*

4000 Low Profile, *220*

4010 HC LP, *220*

4020, *220–221, 222*

4030, *221*

40V, *181*

4430, *228*

520 LPG, *175*

530, *206*

620, *204, 205*

630S, *205*

6400, *250*

6900, *217, 250*

730, *206*

8010/8020, *214–215, 223*

830 Rice Special, *173*

8300T, *250*

8440, *233*

8450, *233*

8850, *234*

Dain All-Wheel-Drive, *50–51*

Deere-Wagner WA-17, *213*

Model A, *140, 142, 146, 154, 155, 204*

Model AWH, *156*

Model B, *129, 135, 140–145, 146, 184, 206*

Model B-Garden, *141, 143*

Model BN, *141, 145*

Model BO-Lindeman, *128, 129*

Model BW, *135, 143, 144*

Model D, *52, 94–96, 129, 147*

Model G, *147, 157*

Model GP, *97, 129*

Model GPO, *129*

Model GPO-Lindeman, *129*

Model MC, *129*

Waterloo Boy tractor, *39, 51, 52, 87, 94–95, 204*

Deutz-Allis, *240*
  9130 FPA, *243*

doodlebugs, *73–75*

Dreyfuss, Henry, *142, 146, 147, 205*

E. G. Staude Mfg. Co., *73*

Eagle Mfg. Co., *179*
  Eagle 6B, *179*

Emerson-Brantingham Implmt. Co., *15, 64*
  Model L 12/20, *64*

Empire Agricultural Works, *10*
  Fearless thresher, *10*

Ewing, W. Baer, *84*

Falk, Otto, *124–125*

Farkas, Eugene, *76, 77*

Ferguson, Harry, *157–159, 162–163, 202*
  Ferguson-Brown "Black Tractor," *157, 162*
  see also Harry Ferguson, Inc.

Fiat Agri, *247*

Fiat-Allis Corp., *125*

Ford Motor Co., *30, 76–77, 82–83, 147, 157–161, 194, 202–203, 230*
  4000 Diesel, *231*
  5000 Diesel, *246*
  6000, *247*

601 Workmaster, *161, 203*
7000, *247*
7840 Powerstar SL, *248*
800, *203*
8000, *225, 247*
8600, *225*
861 Powermaster, *203*
8N, *111, 135, 147, 158–159, 161, 194, 202*
9000, *218*
961 Diesel, *154*
Automobile Plow, *76, 83*
Ford-Ferguson 2N, *137, 157–160, 194*
Ford-Ferguson 9N, *157–159, 162–163, 194*
Fordson All-Around, *61, 107*
Fordson Dexta Diesel, *246*
Fordson E27N Major, *79, 202*
Fordson Major Doe Triple D, *213*
Fordson Power Major V-8 Special, *211*
Fordson Super Major, *219, 246*
FW-30, *233*
Jubilee Model NAA, *159, 194, 202, 218*
TW-35 FWD, *225*
Ford–New Holland, *247*
Ford Tractor Co., *84*
Ford Tractor ("Minneapolis" Ford), *84–85*
Ford, Henry, *24, 26, 30, 73, 76–77, 82–83, 84,*
86, 107, 147, 154, 157, 162–163
Ford, Henry II, *82, 158–159, 202*
Ford, Paul B., *84*
Four Drive Tractor Co., *213*
Froelich, John, *30, 39, 52*
Funk Brothers, *208*
Funk-Ford 8N V-8, *208–209*
Gaar, Scott & Co., *15, 27*
Gaar-Scott steamer, *27*
Galamb, Joe, *76*
Gas Traction Co., *33, 34*
Big Four tractor, *33, 34*
General Motors, *77*
Graham-Paige Motors Corp., *146*
Graham-Bradley, *146*
Gray Tractor Co., *36*
Gray 18/36, *36*
Groundhog thresher, *10*
Hadfield-Penfield Steel Co., *110*
Handshake Agreement, *159, 163*
Happy Farmer Tractor Co., *65*
Harry Ferguson, Inc.,
TE-20, *159*
TED-20, *163*
TEF-20, *168*
TO-20, *159*
TO-35, *139, 163*
Hart, Charles, *33–34*
Hart-Parr Gasoline Engine Co., *33–34, 40–41*
30/60 "Old Reliable," *40–41*
30A 15/30, *37, 61*
Little Devil, *64, 68*
Model 40 20/40, *32*
Henry Ford & Son, *34, 76–81, 82, 84, 87*
Fordson, *76–77, 78–79, 82, 92, 98, 99*

Fordson Model F, *79–81, 87, 161*
Fordson Model N, *79, 101, 107*
Hoard & Bradford, *15*
Holt Mfg. Co., *22, 112*
Holt steamer, *22*
Model 60, *113*
Model 75, *112, 114, 133*
10-Ton, *6, 112, 114*
2-Ton, *112, 114*
Holt, Benjamin, *22, 110, 112, 114*
Huber Mfg. Co., *64, 91*
25/50, *5*
Light Four, *64*
Super Four, *91*
Hussey, Obed, *10*
Indiana Silo & Tractor Co., *64*
International Harvester Co., *11, 42, 46–49, 50,*
87, 92–93, 98–99, 100–103, 146, 186–188,
222, 246–247
1066, *244*
1466, *244*
3588, *235*
4586, *233*
5488, *245*
6588, *236*
784, *245*
8/16, *49, 64, 87*
806, *222*
966 Hydro, *225*
Farmall, *87, 97, 98–99, 100–103*
Farmall 400 HC, *182*
Farmall 450 Diesel, *173*
Farmall 806, *222*
Farmall F-12, *100, 166*
Farmall H, *191*
Farmall HV, *192*
Farmall M, *150, 157, 182, 186*
Farmall M V-8 Special, *210*
Farmall MD, *186–188*
Farmall MV, *192*
Farmall Regular, *101–102, 186*
Farmall Super MD-TA, *188*
McCormick-Deering 10/20, *49, 93*
McCormick-Deering 15/30, *92–93, 95,*
184
McCormick-Deering 22/36, *92*
McCormick-Deering O-12, *166*
Mogul, *46–49, 92*
Titan, *46–49, 52, 62, 64, 73, 78, 87, 92*
Interstate Engine & Tractor Co., *88*
J. I. Case Plow Works, *68*
J. I. Case Threshing Machine Co., *15, 17–21,*
31, 33, 42, 246–247
10/18 Crossmotor, *87*
10/20, *64, 67*
1030 Comfort King, *224, 232*
1070 Agri King, *243*
1200 Traction King, *234*
1570 Spirit of '76, *244*
300B, *154*
400 HC, *180*

400B, *198*
830 CK, *198*
830 HC Comfort King, *244*
Case steamer, *17–21, 24*
Model CC-3, *106*
Model D, *197*
Model SC, *184*
Model VAH, *180*
Model VAO, *4, 167*
Model VC, *139*
Johnston, Edward A., *98, 101*
Joliet Oil Tractor Co., *109, 130*
Bates Steel Mule 12/20, *109, 130*
Kardell Tractor & Truck Co., *37*
Keck-Gonnerman, *13*
Killen-Strait Mfg. Co., *131*
Kinnard-Haines Co. *88*
Flour City tractor, *88*
Klockner-Humboldt-Deutz (KHD), *240*
La Crosse Tractor Co., *64, 65*
Happy Farmer, *64, 65*
Legge, Alexander, *86, 98*
Lindeman Power Equipment, *129*
Lindeman, Harry, *129*
Lindeman, Jesse, *129*
Little Giant Co., *91*
Loewy, Raymond, *100, 146*
Lombard Log Hauler, *110, 112*
Lombard, Alvin Oliver, *110, 112*
M. Rumely Co., *15*
Massey Mfg. Co., *42*
Massey-Ferguson, *159, 163, 202, 231, 240*
1080, *224*
1135, *248*
3095, *229*
3655, *248*
6150, *225*
65, *174, 225*
8160, *248*
9240, *225*
Massey-Harris Co., *42, 64, 69, 159*
333 Diesel, *170*
44 Diesel, *171, 182, 207*
44 Diesel Special High-Crop, *182*
44 Vineyard Special, *172*
Challenger, *136*
GP, *212*
Parrett No. 2, *69*
Super 101, *198*
McCormick Harvesting Co., *34*
McCormick reaper, *10*
McCormick, Cyrus Hall, *10–11*
McCormick, Cyrus III, *86–87*
McVicker, Walter, *50, 51*
Melvin, C. H., *50*
Merritt, Harry, *125*
Minneapolis Steel & Machinery Co., *33, 34,*
42, 107
Twin City 16/30, *43*
Twin City 21/32, *42, 107*
Twin City Model 40, *33, 34*

Minneapolis Threshing Machine Co., *45*
    17/30 Type A, *38*
    22/44, *45*
    27/44, *7, 38*
Minneapolis-Moline Power Implmt. Co., *42,*
    151–153, 228, 240
    5 Star, *201*
    BF, *200*
    FT-A, *107*
    G-1050 LPG, *224*
    GBD, *172*
    Jetstar II, *111*
    M-504, *224*
    M-5, *230*
    M-670, *232, 240*
    R, *201*
    U, *169, 200*
    UDLX, *7, 9, 146–147, 151–153*
    YT, *150*
    ZTU, *200*
Minnis Steam traction engine, *110*
Mogg, Peter, *74*
Mogg Tractor, *74*
Moline Implmt. Co., *42*
Moline Plow Co., *64, 66–67, 70–72*
    Universal, *64, 66–67, 70–72*
Monarch Tractor Corp., *125*
Morris, George, *18*
New Deal Tractor Co., *75*
New Holland NV, *246, 247*
Nichols & Shepard, *13*
Nilson 22/45, *89*
Northwest Thresher Co., *14, 27*
Oliver Farm Equip. Corp., *122, 123, 176, 231,*
    240
    1600, *241*
    1655 Diesel, *223*
    1755, *241, 242*
    2255, *229*
    440, *195*
    60, *193*
    66, *148*
    660, *196*
    70 Orchard, *167*
    77, *194*
    770, *241*
    80 Diesel, *138*
    880, *196*
    Cletrac, OC-18, *122*
    HG, *123*
    Super 55, *194*
    XO-121, *175*
    Oliver Hart-Parr 18/28, *138*
    Oliver Hart-Parr 70, *146, 176*
orphan tractors, *88–91, 130, 131, 177–179*
Pakosh, Peter, *237*
Pan Motor Co., *131*
Parkhurst, A. B., *52*
Parr, Charles, *33–34*
Parrett Tractor Co., *69*
Paterson tractor, *31, 33*

Paterson, William, *31, 33*
Pioneer Tractor Mfg. Co., *32*
    Pioneer 30, *32*
Pitts Agricultural Works, *16*
    Buffalo Pitts thresher and cleaner, *10–11,*
    16
    Pitts steamer, *16*
Pitts, Hiram A., *10*
Pope, Jacob, *10*
Reeves Co., *15*
    Reeves Canadian Special steamer, *15*
Remington steam engine, *22–23*
Remington, Marquis DeLaFayette, *22–23*
Reynolds, Edwin, *124*
rubber pneumatic tires, *104–105*
Rumely, Edward, *27, 54*
Rumely, John, *27*
Rumely, Meinrad, *27*
Russell Grader Mfg. Co., *114*
Russell & Co., *15, 35*
    Russell Giant 30/60, *35*
    Russell steamer, *15*
Samson Tractor Co., *77*
    Model M, *77*
Sands, Willie, *162*
Sawyer-Massey Co., Ltd., *25*
Sears, Roebuck Economy Tractor, *75*
Secor, John, *56*
Shedd, Claude, *84*
Short Turn Tractor Co., *37*
Smith Form-A-Tractor Co., *74*
Staude Mak-A-Tractor, *73*
Steiger Tractor Co., *238–239, 247*
    Case-IH Steiger 9330, *7, 239*
    Panther CP-1360, *238*
Steiger, Douglass, *238*
Steiger, Maurice, *238*
Tenneco Inc., *236, 238, 246–247*
    Case-IH 7130, *245*
    Case-IH 9280, *239*
    Case-IH 956XL, *229*
    Case-IH Steiger 9330, *7, 239*
Townsend Mfg. Co., *31*
    Model 30/60, *31*
Twin City, *see* Minneapolis Steel & Machinery
    Co.
United Tractor and Equipment Corp., *105*
Universal Tractor Co., *64, 66, 70–72*
University of Nebraska Tractor Tests, *84–85*
Van Duzen Gasoline Engine Co., *39*
Versatile Mfg. Ltd., *231, 237, 247*
    150, *237*
    895, *237*
Wagner Tractor Co., *212, 213*
Wallis Tractor Co., *34, 68*
    Cub, *64*
    Model K, *4, 6, 68*
Walrath, Jessee, *17–18*
Waterloo Gasoline Engine Co., *39, 51, 52–55*
    Waterloo Boy tractor, *30, 39, 51, 52–55,*
    64, 73, 78, 84, 85

Waterloo Gasoline Traction Engine Co., *30,*
    33, 39, 52
    Froelich tractor, *30, 39, 52, 62*
Waterville Iron Works, *110*
Wheat tractor, *91*
White Motor Corp., *122, 240*
    2-180 Series 3, *242*
    6124, *242*
    Field Boss 4-225, *235*
    Plainsman A4T-1600, *236*
White, Rollin, *120*
Williams, W. H., *34, 41*
Wm. Deering & Co., *34*
Wood Brothers Inc., *26*
    Wood Brothers steamer, *26*
Wood, F. J., *26*
Wood, R. L., *26*
Yuba Construction Co., *131*

About
the Authors

Robert N. Pripps was born in 1932 on a small farm in northern Wisconsin. Besides farming, his father did local road building and maintenance with a JT crawler and Russell grader. Hard times during the Great Depression put an end to both the farming and road construction, and Bob's dad went to work as a Wisconsin Conservation Department Forest Ranger, a job that he held for the next thirty-five years. Living at the Ranger Station, Bob was always exposed to trucks and tractors. His first driving experience came at age nine when he disked a fire lane with an Allis-Chalmers crawler. During summers throughout World War II, Bob worked on neighboring farms, earning the opportunity to drive one farmer's new Farmall H at age eleven.

Bob's curiousity with things mechanical almost cost him his life at age twelve. He got a mitten caught in the power takeoff of a Gallion road grader. He extricated himself from the machine before it killed him, but the encounter cost him his right thumb.

When he was fourteen, another life-changing event occurred: His best friend's father bought the first Ford-Ferguson tractor in the area. Abject envy is not a pretty thing, but that's what reigned in Bob's heart. It was in no way sated until Bob got his own 2N at age fifty.

Bob went to high school in Eagle River, Wisconsin, earning his private pilot's license by the time he graduated in 1950. His missing right thumb kept him from military service, so he attended Parks Air College to study engineering and receive a commercial pilot's license and multi-engine rating. To help support himself, Bob took a night job at McDonnel Aircraft in St. Louis. Marriage and family responsibilities soon made the job a priority and schooling secondary. Bob became a flight test engineer on the RF-101 Voodoo while continuing night and correspondence school. Subsequent jobs in test engineering included Atlas missile base activation for General Dynamics and jet engine starter and constant speed drive testing for the Sundstrand Corporation.

After seventeen years of part-time classes, Bob graduated from college in 1969 with a Bachelor of Science in Marketing. Bob also held a certificate in Aeronautical Engineering by that time. He then served as the marketing manager for Sundstrand's Dayton, Ohio, office, retiring at fifty-five.

Along the way, Bob inherited thirty acres of maple forest that were part of the Wisconsin farm on which he was born. That's when he found justification for the Ford-Ferguson 2N that helps with harvesting sap for maple syrup. He later added a 1948 John Deere Model B, 1958 John Deere 440C, and 1962 Massey-Ferguson 85 to the farm.

After retiring, Bob wrote a book on his favorite tractor, the Ford. The book was published in 1990, teaming Bob with renowned English automotive photographer Andrew Morland. Since then, Bob and Andrew have collaborated on eleven books on classic tractors, and Bob has also authored five other tractor titles on his own.

Bob and his wife Janice now live in northern Wisconsin, almost within sight of the original homestead. Besides steady work on books, Bob and one of his three sons make about 150 gallons of maple syrup each spring.

Andrew Morland was educated in Great Britain. He completed one year at Taunton College of Art in Somerset and then three years at London College of Printing studying photography. He has worked since graduation as a freelance photojournalist, traveling throughout Europe and North America. His work has been published in numerous magazines and books; among his published books is *The Big Book of Caterpillar*, published by Japonica Press. His interests include tractors, machinery, old motorbikes, and cars. He lives in a thatched cottage in Somerset, Great Britain, that was built in the 1680s. He is married and has one daughter.

LUCIEN LELONG

LUCIEN LELONG

Jacqueline Demornex

With 134 illustrations, 48 in colour

Thames & Hudson

Translated from the French *Lucien Lelong: L'Intemporel* by Luisa Nitrato Izzo

Managing Editor: Patrick Mauriès, assisted by Alice Nez

First published in the United Kingdom in 2008 by
Thames & Hudson Ltd, 181A High Holborn, London WC1V 7QX

www.thamesandhudson.com

Original edition © 2007 Éditions Gallimard
This edition © 2008 Thames & Hudson Ltd, London

British Library Cataloguing-in-Publication Data
A catalogue record for this book is available from the British Library

ISBN 978-0-500-51435-1

Printed and bound in China by C&C Offset Printing Co., Ltd

Preface | 7

A Family Business | 8

16, Rue Matignon | 14

The 'Garçonne': The Age of the Flapper | 16

Kinetic Fashion | 20

Perfume from A to N | 28

Portrait of a Marriage | 32

A Return to Harmony | 36

Luxury Prêt-à-Porter: The First Steps | 46

Couture-Sculpture I | 52

A Fashion Icon | 58

The Crisis Years | 60

Portrait of the Artist: A Digression | 68

Couture-Sculpture II | 74

The Coming of War | 80

Elegance: The Secret Weapon | 87

Liberation, Exoneration | 92

The 'Théâtre de la Mode' | 96

The End of the Affair | 104

Lucien Lelong, Perfumer | 118

A Fine Garden Near Biarritz | 128

Lucien Lelong, A Timeless Genius | 132

Chronology of a Life | 135

Select Bibliography | 139

Acknowledgments | 142

To Jean Chalon, without whom I would never have started this book,
and to the stubborn optimism that helped me finish it.

Lucien Lelong represents something of a paradox in the history of fashion. He undoubtedly played a historical role of great significance: it is directly thanks to him that French haute couture remained in Paris during the Second World War, rather than being transferred to Berlin or Vienna as the Nazis would have wished. His commercial flair is legendary: he invented luxury prêt-à-porter in 1934, among many other innovations. And he had an uncanny knack of picking his staff: Pierre Balmain and Christian Dior both trained under him.[1]

Yet Lelong's career as a designer, spanning thirty years from 1918 to 1948, has been largely forgotten. Three decades of his work (some 1,200 collections) have fallen into obscurity. It is as if his business acumen had eclipsed his talent as a fashion designer. But in fact Lucien Lelong was an extraordinary couturier whose sophisticated minimalism enthralled the most demanding clientele. The image of extreme elegance he projected owed much to Princess Natalie Paley, his wife and muse throughout the 1930s, an evanescent beauty who epitomized chic and was frequently photographed for *Vogue* in her husband's designs. For Lelong, elegance went hand-in-hand with movement. He developed a style philosophy dubbed *kinétisme* – kineticism – whereby clothes 'should be as beautiful in motion as they are at rest'. Looking at them now, freeze-framed in the pages of bygone glossy magazines, it is hard for us to imagine them worn by vivacious young women. But Lelong's peers could recognize his garments just from the way they moved. Flowing lines were his signature. Most striking is the incredible modernity of his style. While he sought to capture, as he put it, 'the essence of the era', he also managed to transcend his era with designs that had a timeless quality. The pieces Lelong produced in the 1920s, particularly his coats and jersey garments, look as fresh today as when they were first conceived. And his 1930s evening dresses are breathtakingly contemporary.

His 'hands on' working method was every bit as modern as his designs. He was the creative force behind his couture house and all it produced. Everything he put his name to – dresses, handbags, compacts, jewelry, perfumes, advertising – was chosen, developed and approved by Lelong himself. In short, he assumed the role of creative director played by most couturiers today.

As elegant in person as one of his designs, Lelong is a figure whose importance extends beyond fashion. Saviour of French haute couture, inventor of luxury prêt-à-porter, creator of a whole new concept of fashion based on pure, clean lines: more than a couturier, Lucien Lelong helped shape fashion history.

1   For a brief period in 1946, Hubert de Givenchy also worked for Lelong.

A Family Business

For Lucien Lelong, fashion was always a family affair. His parents owned a small Parisian couture house, A.E. Lelong,[1] which produced exquisite 'dresses, coats, and robes of court' for a highly elite clientele. In 1898, the Lelongs moved from Rue Vignon to 18, Place de la Madeleine. Their business card declared them 'suppliers to foreign courts', and Queen Victoria herself was a client, presumably commissioning garments from the Lelongs' London branch.[2]

A child of the Belle Époque,[3] the young Lucien was initiated into the fashion industry at an early age. From his uncle, a textile merchant, he gained an appreciation of the science and the sensuality of fabrics; from his parents, a love of progress. Arthur and Éléonore were among the first in their Parisian quarter to install a telephone line, and in 1911 they didn't hesitate to join the recently formed Chambre Syndicale de la Couture (the governing body and guild of the French haute couture industry), alongside much larger couture houses such as Poiret, Paquin and Lanvin. By this time the husband and wife team had already made a name for themselves,[4] and the Lelong brand exuded an aura of modernity. In Colette's 1908 novella *Les Vrilles de la vigne* (The Tendrils of the Vine), the chic, hauty heroine Valentine insists on dressing in the label of the moment: Lelong.[5]

By this time, Lucien Lelong had turned twenty and was keen to make his mark on the family business. He began by redecorating the salon, which was much too pretty for his taste. The result was pure drama: a blackout. The fashion journalist Lucien François recalled: 'I must have been about six years old when I first saw Lucien Lelong. He was doing his military service at the time and cut a dashing figure in his red soldier's trousers. He was small, wiry and highly-strung, but brimmed with pride when he talked about the changes he was making at his mother's highly respected couture house.'[6] François went on to describe the new salon: with its black carpets, black walls and ceiling, and black couches, it looked like a jewelry box lined with black.

1 | David Seidner, the 'Théâtre de la Mode', design by Lucien Lelong, 1990. Dress in turquoise muslin with white polka dot print.

Just a few years later, in 1914, Lelong produced his first collection; but he was forced to cancel the show. On 2 August, France mobilized its troops, and Lelong was called up to his regiment. War was declared two days later on 4 August, the very date Lelong's show had been scheduled.

...

Amidst the hell of the trenches, Lelong served on the front line. He was an intelligence officer in the French military attachment to the British army, reporting to a British colonel on the movements of German troops. His reconnaissance missions frequently took him to the most dangerous zones, and on 24 May 1917 he suffered shrapnel wounds to the right of his face, his left hand and right thigh.[7] He was out of action for nine months while he recovered in hospital, and was awarded the French Military Cross for his fortitude and courage.

2 | Invoice from the A.E. Lelong couture house, 1909.

After the war, Lelong returned to the family couture house in Place de la Madeleine. His father had kept the salon open throughout the war, but the tills were empty. Lelong immediately set about redirecting his indomitable fighting spirit into reviving the family business.

From 1921, his collections started attracting the attention of the press. *Femina* magazine featured his ladies' suits, fur-trimmed coats and his beautifully fluid evening gowns. Waistlines were low and skirts cut to reveal the ankle.

Waistlines dropped further in 1922, while at Lelong, necklines rose: the winter collection had a Louis XIII theme, with musketeer cuffs and capes tossed over one shoulder à la d'Artagnan. *Art, Goût, Beauté* magazine published a trio of opulent looks in velvet, silk and fur.

Fashion was still feeling its way in this early post-war period, with few distinct trends coming through: there was much asymmetric draping, and Russian embroidery was popular, but designers were still hesitating over the length and fullness of skirts.

In 1923, however, there was a very definite move towards simplicity. The January issue of *Vogue* put this shift down to the sudden boom in travel and tourism, the scarcity of domestic staff – 'complicated dress designs require a large number of staff' – and by the new body consciousness. 'Ladies with enviable, graceful, svelte or athletic figures will want the focus to be on them rather than their dresses, however sumptuous the latter may be.' The two were not mutually exclusive, as the fashion industry would prove just two years later.

...

Lucien Lelong quickly grasped the importance of wooing the beau monde, and glamorous society women were soon lining up to appear in fashion magazines wearing his designs. In May 1923, Simone de Caillavet (future wife of French author André Maurois) declared that she 'would love'[8] to be photographed by *Femina* in a crystal-studded dress by Lelong. It was certainly worth her while, since Lelong gave her discounts for 'advertising' his creations. As she explained to her husband: 'You know full well why I agreed to pose in Lelong for the fashion magazines. It means that he'll let me buy his *Pluie de jade* dress, which is covered in embroidered beading, for just 600 francs, while other women will have to pay 2,000.' She asked her mother not to tell anybody: 'M. Lelong doesn't want his rich clients to start asking him for two-thirds off the full price in return for modelling his dresses in the press....'

As designer Charles James bluntly put it, 'You don't always make your rich customers pay for the clothes. You give them away as gifts, so that they will attract more rich customers...who will pay for the clothes.'[9] Soon enough this type of discreet arrangement became more commonplace. Other society ladies posed for Lelong, including the Countess of Chabannes and Princess Galitzine.

The photo captions in *Vogue* and *Femina* gave detailed descriptions of Lelong's magnificent, original fabrics: gleaming black lace, gold brocade with sparkling pink flecks, cross-stitched embroidery with lead and steel beading, dresses dripping with crystals and mother-of-pearl, coats of textured silver... Lucien Lelong had clearly inherited the family passion for textiles.

...

By the early 1920s, Lelong was so successful that he was outgrowing the salon in Place de la Madeleine. His clients encouraged him to expand and move to a larger, more elegant property, but he held out for a while. Simon de Caillavet commented, 'Place de la Madeleine is rather cramped, but [Lelong] has a long lease on the premises which means that it is relatively cheap.'[10]

Business was booming: in 1918, Lelong employed fewer than twenty staff; by 1926, there were 1,200 on the payroll.

3 | *Above* Sleeveless dress in pale green silk crêpe with V-neck embroidered with pearls (detail), 1920. Les Arts Décoratifs, Musée de la Mode et du Textile, Paris.

4 | *Opposite* Lucien Lelong choosing fabrics. Photograph by Lee Miller.

1   The initials A.E. stood for Arthur Lelong and his wife Éléonore, née Lambelet.

2   Located at 1, Brook Street, Hanover Square, London

3   Lelong was born in Paris on 11 October 1889.

4   A.E. Lelong won a succession of fashion awards at the international exhibitions of Liège (1905), Milan (1906) and London (1908).

5   Colette, *Les Vrilles de la vigne*, Gallimard, 'Bibliothèque de la Pléiade', Vol. I, p. 1010. Interestingly (as the note on p. 1563 points out), Colette cited a different couturier in an earlier draft of the text: Paquin, who was subsequently replaced by Lelong in the definitive version.

6   Lucien François, *Comment un nom devient une griffe* (How a Name Becomes a Label), Gallimard, 1961, p. 20.

7   'On 24 May 1917 at around 11 o'clock in the frontline trench, near an observation point just before the section following the River Seine, [Lucien Lelong] was injured by shrapnel to the right of his face, his left hand and right thigh.' Paris Archives, 1034/W Vol. 0057. This report also notes that Lelong distinguished himself in the battles of Andreguis, Romeries and the Chemin des Dames.

8   Simone de Caillavert quoted by Michelle Maurois in *Déchirez cette lettre* (Tear Up This Letter), Flammarion, Paris, 1990, p. 369.

9   Charles James in conversation with the author at the Chelsea Hotel, New York, January 1975.

10   Mme de Caillavet, quoted by Michelle Maurois, *op. cit.*, p. 386.

16, RUE MATIGNON

In 1924 Lucien Lelong left Paris's traditional fashion district for the Champs-Élysées, which was rapidly becoming the location of choice for the big couture houses: Poiret reigned supreme at the Roundabout, and Madeleine Vionnet had moved to 40, Avenue Montaigne in 1922. Lelong chose 16, Rue Matignon.[1]

The former residence of the Ducs de Guiche was vast, yet only just big enough to house Lelong's growing empire. For a while, as the premises were being refurbished, the team of seamstresses worked shoulder to shoulder with painters and decorators. The walls still smelled of fresh plaster, and the property shook to the sound of hammering and sawing. The garden was sacrificed to make way for a small three-storey building, which was later extended upwards as the couture house's success grew from collection to collection. Telephones – Lelong's favourite gadget – were eventually installed throughout the premises (including the lifts) for the use of clients and staff alike. The collections were presented in the grand salon in expertly orchestrated shows: before parading past the audience, the models would pose on a stage lit by hidden projectors that could recreate evening or daytime light effects, while uplighters in the glass flooring picked out the embroidered detailing on skirts.

In this brand new setting, Lelong presented a brand new look, characterized by simple, fluid lines. 'I have eliminated the full form,' he proclaimed in 1924. 'I prefer straight pleats which give a sense of volume while retaining a streamlined silhouette.' Movement was always part of Lelong's conception: his love of soft, supple forms would remain his trademark for the rest of his career.

5a | *Opposite left* White suede jacket with four pockets and leather belt, designed to be teamed with sports wear. *Femina,* April 1927.

5b | *Opposite right* Dress in beige and white mouslikasha fabric with narrow suede belt at the waist. *Femina,* April 1927.

1   The address now corresponds to 16, Avenue Matignon; the 'Rue' was subsequently renamed 'Avenue'.

entire new generation of independent women who travelled alone, smoked, drove their own cars, played sports, and went out in the evenings by themselves; in short, confident women who had learned to do without men during the war. But the garçonne was also an ambiguous, complex creature, full of contradiction; one might very well be both a garçonne and her opposite.

By night the garçonne metamorphosed into a dazzling social butterfly who danced the Charleston. In 1926, Lucie Delarue-Mardrus brilliantly described this aspect of the 'new woman' in her book *Embellissez-vous* (Make Yourself Beautiful): 'Oh, the bliss of shortening our dresses, dropping the waistlines, swapping black-stockinged legs for pink and chignons for short hair, the bliss of dressing in silver and pearls, or looking like little men in jackets or pyjama suits, the bliss of being versatile, the bliss of being extravagant...'[3] – and the bliss of being fit and playing sport!

Sport was of primary importance to Jean Patou. For him, as for Chanel, sport was more than just a hobby requiring a few appropriate outfits, it was the very foundation of modern style: it was what gave fashion its dynamism, its personality, and its newfound simplicity. In 1921 Patou created an outfit for tennis champion Suzanne Lenglen which was both practical and photogenic – a short pleated skirt teamed with a man's tank top – and he later opened a sports and leisure wear section in his couture house which appealed both to women who played real sports and to those who simply liked the look. Jean Patou didn't hold the monopoly over sports and leisure wear, however; Lucien Lelong also excelled at it. The chic young women of the 1920s loved Lelong and Patou in equal measure, and while Patou was the more famous of the two thanks to his gift for marketing, Lelong was more consistently successful.[4]

LUCIEN LELONG

7 | *Opposite* Cream silk velvet evening dress with printed floral motif, *c.* 1927. Musée Galliera, Paris.

8 | *Above* Beach outfit in an illustration by Lofer, 1920s.

1   Cecil Beaton, *The Glass of Fashion*, Weidenfeld and Nicolson, London, 1954, p. 162.

2   Colette wrote a number of articles for *Vogue* and *Demain* making fun of the new fashion, which was designed to be worn by women much thinner than herself. See in particular 'Arrière-saison' and 'Logique', republished in the collection of articles and essays entitled *Le Voyage égoïste*, 'Bibliothèque de la Pléiade', 1928 edition, Vol. II, pp. 1163 and 1179.

3   Lucie Delarue-Mardrus, *Embellissez-vous*, Les Éditions de France, Paris, 1926, pp. 159–60.

4   As pointed out by Madeleine Ginsburg in *Les Années folles de la mode*, Celiv, Paris, 1990, p. 87.

KINETIC FASHION

'Sporty', 'simple', 'young': this is how Lucien Lelong defined his style in 1925.[I] He encapsulated the spirit and dynamism of the times with his 'kinétique' line (sometimes referred to in the press as 'cinématique' or 'kinoptique'). According to Lelong, fashion had until then been designed for women who didn't move – who were literally 'mannequins'.

'I wanted my clothes to be constructed in such a way that their true shape would emerge in movement, not at rest,' he would later write. 'I worked on sketches with the same attention to detail as an engineer: they were like blueprints tracing the evolution of my ideas from start to finish. I even exhibited them in my salons, much to the astonishment of my foreign clients.'

Kinetic fashion rejected the convoluted curves and spiralling forms of ruffles, flares, flounces and fussy detailing, favouring narrow pleats which would move with

9 | *Opposite* Blue woollen casual suit over blue and beige jersey pullover, 1920s.

10 | *This page, left* Black and white knit sports sweater over black jersey skirt with side pleats for added volume. *Femina,* April 1928.

11 | *This page, right* Seated woman wears pale yellow picador crêpe dress by Lucien Lelong with decorative paste clasp at neck. *Femina,* April 1928.

Following pages
12 | Afternoon and evening wear modelled by Hélène Bigotte, 1920s.

the garment but fall back in place at rest. Soft, flowing fabrics were also essential.[2] Rodier's cashmere-mix 'kasha' fabric was the ideal choice for day wear: warm, soft and versatile, it came in a range of styles from casual to elegant, including woven, striped and dazzling oriental-style embroidered versions.

The kinetic collection also embraced crêpe in all its varieties: Moroccan, Roman, crêpe de Chine, crêpe Georgette, satin crêpe and crêpella. For the evenings, when women wanted to dance, Lelong used fabrics that would 'dance' with them, notably silk muslin, lace and transparent materials, 'to maintain that mobility and diaphanous fluidity which make movements look so graceful.'[3]

It might have lacked poetry, but the term 'kinétique' proved effective at drawing attention to Lelong and his unique stylistic vision. From 1925 onwards, his look became more defined. *L'Art et la Mode* declared: 'Fashion lovers can recognize a particular couturier's style from fifteen paces: Vionnet's draping, Patou's chic, Lucien Lelong's fluidity.'[4]

'Fluidity' is synonymous in this context with 'movement', and it was during sports and physical activity that this dynamism was most in evidence, and when the body and clothes in motion together acquired a certain timeless quality. Lelong's style blended flowing lines, youthfulness and athleticism, a trinity that we still revere today.

Femina was particularly impressed by the simplicity of the dresses in Lelong's winter 1925 collection, which featured skirts skilfully pleated to create volume at the front. Three sketches published in *Vogue*'s December issue illustrated the 'kinetic' style perfectly: a dress and matching coat in black satin crêpe which lightly skimmed the hips and flared outwards towards the hemline, and another dress in Chantilly lace, again gently flared with pleated frills which looked ready to 'dance' at the slightest movement.

The same year Lelong made his first trip to America, where he was profiled in the October issue of US *Vogue*. The article describes him as a small, slim but broad-shouldered man with dark hair and blue eyes, and impeccably turned-out. He has a rakish air in the accompanying photograph, with his pencil-thin moustache and cigarette between his pursed lips. But above all, he looks confident and determined.

Lelong's interview positively crackles with youthful energy and ambition, and with good reason. He was on the way to employing 3,000 staff, double the number at any of the other major couture houses. He summed up his objectives in a single phrase: his aim was to 'industrialize' the art of haute couture (the idea of 'art' – he was at pains to emphasize – being every bit as crucial as the idea of 'industry'). While he did not actually design the clothes, he was the creative force behind his label, and everything it produced was chosen, developed and approved by him. Lelong's fashion empire was a reflection of his personal taste, which gave his collections a remarkable sense of artistic unity.

His comments about the Paquin couture house revealed a lot about Lelong himself. Mme Paquin's creative talent was a given, but he also admired the commercial flair of her husband, who was the first to see the potential for Parisian couture to expand into the international arena.

When asked about his trip to the United States, his response was simple: 'I'm here to breathe the air of America.' In reality, his journey bore all the hallmarks of a study trip. The French government had tasked him to investigate the working conditions of women in the US fashion industry, not from a social or humanitarian perspective, but to understand how, with what machinery, and by what miracle of technology, it was possible for an item hand-made in Paris to be mass-produced in the millions, and to a higher quality than the original. This was a burning question in the 1920s, and the answer hinged on the fact that simpler designs were simpler to copy. In short, Lelong was asked to produce a report on the American prêt-à-porter industry.

Lelong had his own motives for wanting to visit the US: the next year he planned to launch his first perfumes. All the more reason to get under the skin of the country where his most faithful clients resided, and to make himself known there at the same time.

1   A 1925 advertisement for Lelong couture in *Vogue* read: 'Modern fashion should have a SPORTY feel…Fashion should be SIMPLE. I have created a clean, crisp look which underscores today's more relaxed attitude. Fashion should be YOUNG. With their trim figures and active lifestyles, modern women maintain a youthful appearance.' Quoted by Pierre Faveton in *Les Années 20* (The 1920s), Temps Actuels, Paris, 1982, p. 54.

2   'Kinétisme' had much in common with Modernist writing, as it was defined by Italian Futurist Filippo Tommaso Marinetti in his manifesto *L'immaginazione senza fili e le parole in libertà* (Imagination Without Strings, Words in Freedom), Lacerba, Vol. I, 1913: 'A loathing of curved lines, spirals and tourniquets. A love of straight lines and tunnels. A horror of slowness, minutiae, detailed analyses and explanations. A love of speed, brevity, synopsis and synthesis: "Tell me everything, quickly, quickly in two words."'

3   *Vogue*, February 1926.

4   *L'Art et la Mode,* 16 October 1926.

13 | *Opposite* Lucien Lelong's salon at 16, Rue Matignon. Decor by Chalom. Photograph by Thérèse Bonney. *L'Art et la Mode,* 19 June 1926.

PERFUME FROM A TO N

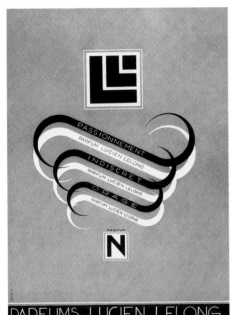

Lucien Lelong was not the first couturier to diversify into perfume. In 1911, Poiret had founded a perfume company called Rosine, named after his eldest daughter. 'What my clothes do for your body, I want my perfumes to do for your soul' he declared, but he never put his own name to the Rosine fragrances, which were only modestly successful. Conversely, Chanel's *No. 5* and Lanvin's *Arpège* (created in 1921 and 1923 respectively) became instant classics, and effectively launched the designer perfume industry.

The traditional perfumers such as Guerlain and Coty were furious: they would never dream of branching out into clothes design, they complained. But the couturiers had a watertight response: since their industry was all about capturing the essence of the times, what better way to do this than with perfume, which was the accessory *par excellence* to an elegant outfit?

In 1926 Lelong launched his *ABC* trio of perfumes collectively named 'Tout Lelong', which lent itself in English to the wordplay 'All Along Lelong'. The fragrances were presented as three variations on a theme: 'My *A* is a regal scent, for the evening [...]. My *B* is a bright, optimistic perfume and an ideal partner for afternoon wear. My *C* is as joyful as the sun it evokes.'[1]

In a press release written for the US market, Lelong even claimed to have discovered the 'science' that enabled him to match his perfumes to colours and scents, A, B and C corresponding to the three primary colours: 'A for red, B for blue, C for yellow'.

The following year, in 1927, the couturier launched two new perfumes with two more initials, *J* and *N*: *J* for Jasmine and *N* for Natalie.

14 | *Opposite* Young woman powdering her face, 1920s. Outfit and compact by Lucien Lelong.

15 | *Above* Advertisement for Parfums Lucien Lelong, c. 1935.

ELLE.ELLE

LE NOUVEAU PARFUM
DE
LUCIEN LELONG

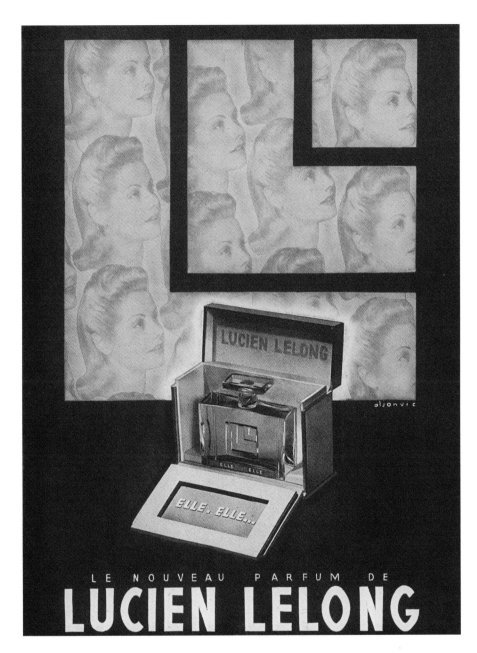

16 and 17 | Advertisements for
Lucien Lelong's perfume *Elle Elle*,
launched in 1941.

1   Lelong was describing his perfumes for the August 1928 issue of US *Vogue*. Colette, who had become friends with Lelong,
    also raved about his perfumes in *Femina*, October 1928: 'One of them, *Tout Lelong B*, is perfect for the great outdoors and
    sporting activities: it is green, woody and vivacious. *Tout Lelong A* is as dark as a beautiful night, and redolent of luxurious,
    softly lit homes, deep wardrobes, the wisteria- and coral-coloured silk chiffons which are nowadays known as 'lingerie',
    lawn cloth drapes and clutch bags… Lastly, *Tout Lelong C*, the most floral and youthful [of the three], seems to have been
    created especially to sweeten the steps of the lithe, doe-eyed darlings whose fleshless figures give them an adolescent allure:
    the Beauties of 1927.'

PORTRAIT OF A MARRIAGE

Natalie, *N,* was the young woman Lelong married in August 1927.[1] Natalie Paley was a Romanov princess and the granddaughter of Tsar Alexander II. Her father and brother had been murdered by the Bolsheviks, but she and her sister managed to escape to Finland and then France, where they were joined by their mother, Princess Paley.

Like many Russian exiles of that era, Natalie had to work to support her family. After a brief spell at a small couture house founded by fellow Russian Yteb, she started modelling for Lelong.

Lelong knew the Paley family well. Each year he took part in the princess's charity events in aid of Russian refugees. In an October 1925 issue of *L'Art et la Mode,* André de Fouquières described one of these soirées: 'We must thank M. Lucien Lelong, an artist with impeccable taste, for the after-dinner show, in which he presented a range of delightful evening gowns which were absolute perfection.'

The next year their names were linked on two more occasions. The first was in Paris, at the 'Dîner des 300', a gala dinner organized by the princess in Lelong's own mansion, for which the couturier provided a sea of flowers and lavish catering. The press reported that the 'luxury couturier of Avenue Matignon, a fine artist' had just been awarded the Légion d'Honneur medal.[2] The second was in Biarritz, where Lelong had opened a boutique in Rue Gardères. *L'Art et la Mode* reported that 'Princess Paley was the heart and soul [of the occasion]. That evening, in the magnificent setting of the Royal Pavilion, we were shown M. Lucien Lelong's stunning collection, which was superbly staged.'[3]

The wedding ceremony took place on 10 August 1927 in Paris, in the Russian Orthodox cathedral of Saint-Alexandre Nevski. The bride wore a dress of white panne gathered in at the waist and a silver lace bonnet with a tulle veil secured by bands of pearls.

18 | Portrait of Natalie Paley. Les Arts Décoratifs, Musée de la Mode et du Textile, Paris.

Had Natalie married beneath herself? After all, her sister Irène had wed a Russian prince, while in those days most couturiers were still regarded as suppliers. But Lucien Lelong was different. Born to parents who belonged to the 'grande bourgeoisie', along with Chanel he was one of the first couturiers to be received into the highest echelons of society.[4]

The Lelongs set off to New York for their honeymoon. When their steam liner, the *Île-de-France*, docked, they were met by a barrage of press photographers: in the shots, Natalie looks like a shy young girl, with her rosy cheeks and half-smile.

Natalie's perfume, N, would also be worn by her best friend Baba de Faucigny-Lucinge, another legendary society figure of the time. Perhaps, like others, she fell for the fragrance's inimitable character, which Lucien François described in 1945: 'Cool, sharp perfumes are rarely successful. This one is as bitter as tonic with its astringent notes of wood, tea, ylang-ylang and damp leaves, yet its aristocratic coolness is what makes it the most haughty, attractive and taboo fragrance that I know.'[5]

...

As the decade drew to a close, the fashion press found it increasingly difficult to distinguish from collection to collection and from season to season. Fashion was dragging its (dainty) heels. Women all looked the same and the couturiers were not coming up with fresh ideas. France began to wonder where fashion was headed, and in 1927 the director of the Premet couture house declared: 'If fashion stays the way it is, it will become a public menace. Clothes nowadays don't vary enough from one collection to the next. In 1914, last season's designs looked positively antiquated...'[6]

Two years later the Wall Street Crash sent shockwaves around the globe. Not just a season but an entire decade of fashion suddenly looked antiquated.

19 | Lucien Lelong in his office.

1   Lelong's second marriage took place only one month after his divorce from Anne-Marie Audoy, the mother of his
    daughter Nicole, was finalized.
2   *L'Art et la Mode,* 28 August 1926.
3   *Ibid.*, 9 October 1926.
4   'The Lelongs were in our circle of friends. Together with Chanel, Lucien Lelong, who was from an upper middle-class
    background, was the first to be "accepted"', Jean-Louis de Faucigny-Lucinge, *Un Gentilhomme cosmopolite* (A Cosmopolitan
    Gentleman), Éditions Perrin, Paris, 1990, p. 83.
5   Lucien François, *Paris et la beauté féminine*, Société d'éditions modernes parisienne, Paris, 1945, p. 53.
6   Interview with M. Winter, director of Premet, in *Les Cahiers de la république des lettres, des sciences et des arts*, Paris, summer 1927,
    p. 85.

A Return to Harmony

The fashion watershed of 1929 will forever be associated with Jean Patou, whose autumn/winter collection signalled the death knell of the garçonne. He sent his models out in tailored dresses with waist-lines back up at the waist and hemlines down to mid-calf. Women in the audience started pulling at their skirts to cover their knees. Backstage, the buzz went round: 'They already feel out of fashion!'

In reality Patou didn't kill the garçonne; he merely dealt the final blow. The old silhouette had been on the wane for at least two years, with couturiers such as Molyneux and Louiseboulanger working hard to produce an updated new look. Lucien Lelong had started dropping his hemlines in 1927; by 1928, his waists were more defined and his evening dresses had grown shorter at the front and longer at the back, or had extra panels at the sides which gave them added length.

Waistlines rose further in 1930, blouses were tucked back into skirts, and hemlines dropped to 34cm (13 in.) from the floor for day wear, 25cm (10 in.) for tea time, and down to the ankle for dinner. Evening dresses skimmed the floor. In May, *Vogue* published three key silhouettes: 'morning', 'sport' and 'afternoon'. The third silhouette, designed by Lucien Lelong, was described as 'a soft suit, the look of the season. The jacket is tightly nipped-in at the waist and flares gently outwards to form a very short bustle at the back. The yoked skirt gradually widens out from the hips to the hemline; although it is moderately full, it falls almost vertically.'

In October, *Le Jardin des Modes* featured a photograph of 'a look typical of Lelong's collection': a long evening dress in 'transparent satin-finish tulle fabric printed with small white flowers over a black lining with a silver metallic pattern, [...] gathered at the waist with front drapes and back tail sweeping round to the front in two panels joined together by fan-shaped ruffles.' Fortunately the dress, with its beautifully elegant lines, was much simpler than the caption.

'The garçonne is finished, long live femininity.' The caricaturists found plenty

20 | *Opposite* Natalie Paley in a three-quarter-length coat by Lucien Lelong, 1934. Photograph by Studio Dorvyne. Musée Galliera, Paris.

21 | *Above* 'Afternoon' silhouette from an outfit by Lucien Lelong. French *Vogue*, May 1930.

22a and 22b | Evening dress
in salmon-coloured silk crêpe
lengthened at the front by a
central panel; same-coloured
lining in taffeta and silk
muslin; embroidered with
pink, white, silver and clear
pearl beading, crystals and
gold lamé thread, 1928.
Musée Galliera, Paris.

to inspire them in this development, while the fashion press were largely welcoming. *Art, Goût, Beauté* enthused that 'women were women again' thanks to 'the return of the long dress', and that 'the "go everywhere" dress has had its day, let's leave uniforms to the schoolgirls.' Some couturiers doggedly stuck to the old silhouette, such as Jenny, for example, who insisted that longer-length skirts made women look older. But in 1930, Vogue was categorical: cardigans were out, fitted jackets were in; goodbye beads and baubles, hello discreet jewelry, draping, boleros, and sophisticated hairstyles.

. . .

The 1930s were Lelong's finest decade. When the Musée Galliera in Paris held its 1987 fashion retrospective 'Paris-Couture Années Trente' (Paris Couture in the Thirties), Lelong was chosen for the front cover of the exhibition catalogue: the photograph of Natalie Paley in a breathtaking black velvet coat with enormous sleeves in silver fox fur by Lelong seems to express the quintessence of the decade.

In 1931 fashion began to settle down again. Shoulders were wide, waists tight, skirts straight. 'The spotlight has turned to the area from the shoulder to the elbow', *Vogue* declared, likening the silhouette to a mushroom. Lelong's ravishing coats and suits were both elegant and understated, with high-cut waists that made legs go on for ever.

Evening wear was a different story. Here Lelong allowed his imagination to run wild, experimenting with innovative fabrics such as Rosalba and Phosphora crêpe in 1933, and rayon the following year. He promoted these innovative textiles so enthusiastically in the press that the pages read like advertorials.

While day wear became more austere and structured (sometimes with military precision), evening wear was increasingly escapist, romantic, and insubstantial, as if to distance itself from the reality of a world quietly marching towards war. This period has often been compared to the years preceding the French Revolution, when

the frivolous aristocracy retreated into a bubble of giddy ignorance, blind to what was happening around them. Lelong was no exception. As the 1930s went on, his designs attained an elegance that was ever more rarefied and detached from reality, like a beautiful orchid sustained by nothing but air.

Natalie herself was turning into this rarest of flowers. After her marriage to Lelong she seemed to grow taller, so slender was she in body and face. Her emaciated cheeks, ash blond hair, wistful eyes and sad mouth conjured an air of mystery that appealed to the era's greatest photographers: Cecil Beaton, George Hoyningen-Huene and Horst. Her face and body drove men mad: in his *Journal Inutile* (Useless Journal), writer and poet Paul Morand evoked 'her fixed gaze and her long body, slender, young, supple and narrow' – in other words, the body of a boy.

According to her biographer Jean-Noël Liaut, 'Natalie exuded an extreme femininity which flirted with androgyny, a femininity which was at its best in severe clothes [...]. She eschewed everything traditionally associated with femininity: showy furs, printed fabrics, pastel colours, embroidery and other fripperies, to create an ever more pared-down look.'[1]

Androgyny, like sports wear, has a timeless quality. Images of Katharine Hepburn and Greta Garbo in their 1930s slacks look as modern now as they did then; and Yves Saint Laurent's female tuxedo, 'Le Smoking', revived by Hedi Slimane, will never age. But androgyny is not just about borrowing from men's wardrobes: it also entails a certain body type, and a physical and moral stance that is as far from masculinity as it is from cloying femininity.

For Lelong, elegance would always be linked to this type of woman – not only his wife with her boyish body, but also the modern-day miracles that were Marlene Dietrich and Baba de Faucigny-Lucinge, both friends of Natalie. He dressed all three (Marlene only partly, Natalie and Baba from head to toe). Whenever they were photographed for *Vogue*, they always wore Lelong.

Previous pages

23 | Natalie Paley in a hat by Reboux. Photograph by George Hoyningen-Huene. French *Vogue*, 1931.

24 | Natalie Paley in a dress by Lucien Lelong and a hat by Maria Guy. Photograph by George Hoyningen-Huene. French *Vogue*, 1931.

25 | *Opposite* Detail of salmon-coloured silk crêpe evening dress (see page 38), 1928. Embroiderers would soon start going out of business. Musée Galliera, Paris.

26 | Natalie Paley and Horst in a still from an amateur film directed by George Hoyningen-Huene, 1932.

27 | *Opposite* Photographs from Baba de Faucigny-Lucinge's personal album. In the centre, Lucien Lelong is pictured with Coco Chanel.

Baba would visit Lelong's salon every Thursday for clothes fittings. Her daughter, Ysabel de Ravenel, recalled their interminable afternoons at Avenue Matignon: 'And afterwards we would have to go to Reboux to try on hats!'

Natalie would usually arrive at the salon in the late morning, and either try on clothes or advise on the latest creations (as 'consultant' to the in-house designers). She would pass two or three hours at Avenue Matignon, often over lunch time, which she would either take or skip. She ate little and went out a lot, never missing a single ball, premiere or private view; she would spend a couple of months in the summer on the Côte d'Azur or in Venice, and a month in the winter in the mountains with her friends Christian Bérard, Jean-Michel Frank, Édouard and Denise Bourdet, Marie-Laure and Charles de Noailles, Jean-Louis and Baba de Faucigny-Lucinge. They all appear in Baba's photo albums, in images captioned Saint-Moritz, Venice, Juan-les-Pins...

Among the Babas, Bébés, Mimis and Johnnys, Natalie is the only one to escape a pet name. Sometimes she is Natalie, sometimes Natasha, and, less often, Mme Lelong. Her husband also makes an appearance, in tank top or shirt and tie, sometimes with skis on his shoulders or wearing immaculate white mechanic's overalls. Two shots stand out for their rarity: Natalie laughing out loud, and Lucien and Natalie on pedalos, for once together.

1   Jean-Noël Liaut, *Une Princesse déchirée* (A Fashionable Princess), Filipacchi, Paris, 1996, p. 97.

NATALIE

NATHALIE. .LUCIEN.

NATASHA

...IEN. .LILIA. .BABA. .CHARLIE. .NATHALIE.

BABA NATACHA SERGELIFAR HOYTIE WEIB

CoCo CHANEL. .LUCIEN.

LUXURY PRÊT-À-PORTER: THE FIRST STEPS

The effects of the global economic crisis hit hard from 1932. Some couture houses closed, others restructured or merged. As US clients became scarce, there was a sharp fall in takings. French fashion was in the doldrums, and to keep his own company afloat Lucien Lelong dreamed up a revolutionary concept: luxury prêt-à-porter. In 1934, he launched France's first ever luxury prêt-à-porter collection.

The invitation card announced: 'Lucien Lelong has created the Edition collection for you, featuring eighty designs made entirely in our Avenue Matignon studios using brand name fabrics. Prices range from 750 fr. to 1,450 fr.'. The pieces were half the price of an haute couture dress. Other Parisian couturiers were nonplussed, with Schiaparelli the first to voice her disapproval. America, meanwhile, was enthusiastic, and US *Vogue* dedicated a whole page to the event, including an interview with Lelong: 'Lelong branches out!'

28 | *Opposite* Woollen outfits by Lucien Lelong designed for travel or the mountains. Illustration by André-Edouard Marty. *Femina*, June 1932.

29 | *Below* Invitation card to the launch of Lucien Lelong's 'Edition' collection, 1934. Illustration by André Dignimont.

LUCIEN LELONG

LUCIEN LELONG

LUCIEN LELONG

L ucien Lelong a fait pour la plage une série de
petites robes à transformations dont on verra
ici les différents aspects. A gauche, par exemple,
on voit une jupe en jersey vert foncé portée sur
un maillot de bain en djersa crème. Sur ce costume se place la petite veste, reproduite à côté,
en tricot rayé vert, rouge et blanc. La figurine
couchée montre le costume de dos combiné pour
le bain de soleil. Au milieu, costume en toile
blanche posé sur un maillot rouge vif dont le dos
est formé seulement de bretelles entrecroisées ; la
cravate est en toile blanche rayée multicolore.
En haut, robe en jersey vert laitue avec petite
veste de tricot rayé blanc, rouge, vert et mar-
ron. Quatre bretelles entrecroisées sont main-
tenues dans le dos par des boutons de nacre.
(Modèles déposés P.A.I.S. Reproduction interdite)

CHANEL

LUCIEN LELONG

LUCIEN LELONG

Toutes les robes de plage ont un dos très décolleté, simplement retenu par des bretelles boutonnées. Voici par exemple, en bas, à gauche, ensemble de plage en sinellic bleu roi et blanc garni de boutons bleus. La jupe est croisée devant; la blouse et la veste sont blanches. Ceinture de piqué blanc. Au milieu, robe de sinellic blanc dont on voit le devant et le dos fait de bretelles entrecroisées et boutonnées à la taille; le petit boléro en tricot rayé rouge, blanc et vert est brodé de rouge. (Modèles déposés P. A. I. S. Reproduction interdite.) En haut, à droite, ensemble de shantung imprimé rouge et blanc, composé d'une robe combinée pour le bain de soleil et d'un boléro à manches longues en même tissu. Portée avec le boléro et le petit chapeau à bords plats, cette robe de plage reprend l'allure d'une robe de ville.

Asked whether he is about to start mass-producing dresses, Lelong responds: 'Not at all... The term 'Robes d'Édition' means that my dresses will be made in limited editions... I shall constantly renew the models...as soon as a model has been sold too much, it will be withdrawn from sale and replaced by another.'

'How do you manage this obvious de-luxe quality with such low prices?'

Lelong: 'By agreement and collaboration with the manufacturers, who are studying with me methods of dyeing and weaving that achieve great quality for minimum cost.'

'Are your Robes d'Édition quite separate from your great collection?'

Lelong: 'Entirely. They are in no sense adaptations of models shown a few months before. Only their sense of beauty and their workmanship are the same.'

The article goes into more detail: the clothes come in five sizes; alterations cost 50 fr.; two fittings will double the price. Garments are stored on a different floor, but as soon as a woman has chosen the size, design and colour, the staff will phone the stockroom and the garment will be sent down in the lift.[1]

...

Lelong was counting on women to rush into the salon and check out the exciting new line, but despite a cinema advertising campaign and the incentive of a free beauty consultation with the editor of *Votre Beauté*, he couldn't conjure the clients, and the success he was hoping for failed to materialize. His big idea, that 'women should be able to buy clothes at prices which reflect the state of the economy', was a stroke of genius, but the world wasn't ready: it would take another thirty years for luxury prêt-à-porter to take off, in the 1960s.

It is no surprise that Lelong, ever the innovator, should have pioneered prêt-à-porter. His frequent trips to the United States had given him ample opportunity to study how fashion could be mass-produced and sold at affordable prices without compromising quality. Most importantly, he recognized that fashion was slowly but surely becoming more democratic, and that it was futile to try and stop it. There was

Previous pages

30 | Copy of an article published in *Femina*, July 1932, featuring a series of beach dresses by Lucien Lelong.

31 | *Opposite* Evening ensembles by Lucien Lelong: *left* green crêpe de Chine dress and ermine fur jacket; *right* white Roman crêpe dress and short jacket with mink trim.

a whole market of women out there who could not afford haute couture, and Lelong tried various other ways of reaching them. Three years later, he offered readers of *Votre Beauté* a pattern for a printed dress; and after the Second World War, he offered fashion advice to readers of *Elle* magazine, via his head seamstress. In 1948, his highly accessible 'morning collection' was singled out by *Women's Wear Daily*.

1   US *Vogue*, 15 December 1934.

COUTURE-SCULPTURE I

The sculptural elegance of neoclassical draping dominated 1930s fashion. In 1931 *Vogue* ran a photoshoot by Hoyningen-Huene inspired by the Parthenon marbles: the ethereal model, Sonia, looked like she might float away, and Vionnet's dresses were worthy of a Greek goddess. The passion for Grecian styling reached its apogee in 1935 when *Vogue* published another seminal shoot, this time by Horst, featuring a series of sumptuous white draped dresses photographed against a star-studded backdrop adorned with classical architectural elements.

At Lucien Lelong the mood extended to his salons, which were redecorated in pure white by interior designer Jean-Michel Frank to give a dreamy, surreal feel.

32 | *Opposite* 'Two dresses by Lucien Lelong in matt crêpe with beautiful draping effects and heavy pleats. Jewelry by Mauboussin'. Photograph by Horst. French *Vogue*, April 1935.

33 | *This page, left* Draped dress by Lucien Lelong in white Faribole crêpe by Ducharne. Jewelry by Cartier; console by Jean-Michel Frank. Photograph by Horst, from 'starry night' shoot published in French *Vogue*, October 1935.

34 | *This page, right* Evening dress in Capucine crêpe with long draped panels at the left shoulder and hip. Diamond brooch by Mauboussin. French *Vogue*, May 1936.

35 | *Right* Staircase decorated with drapes, part of the decor by Jean-Michel Frank for Lucien Lelong's new salons. Photograph by François Kollar, 1937.

36 | *Below* Moulded plaster drapery with concealed lighting by Alberto Giacometti for Lelong's perfume salon. Photograph by François Kollar, 1937.

37 | *Opposite* Dress by Lucien Lelong modelled by Margot Taylor; jewelry by Boucheron. Photograph by Horst. French *Vogue*, 1937.

38 and 39 | Advertisements for Parfums Lucien Lelong, c. 1935.

40 | *Below* Evening dress in black silk crêpe, c. 1930–35, Musée Galliera, Paris.

41 | *Opposite* Evening dress by Lucien Lelong, 1930s.

Long, white plaster drapery ran from floor to ceiling. A 1937 issue of *Marie Claire* described the salon: 'There is a colonnaded entrance. The interior walls feature drapery moulded in white plaster which looks as soft as fabric... The airy, octagonal-shaped perfume salon on the ground floor is decorated in the same unusual way, with white plaster drapery and concealed lighting designed by Alberto Giacometti which suffuses the space with clear, bright light. Giacometti also created the sculptural niche at the centre of the room, a breathtaking fountain of light which displays the precious perfume bottles to perfection.'[1]

The most precious of these bottles, designed for *Indiscret*, evoked the fluid lines of the decor. *Indiscret* had been launched in 1935 just after the perfume salon was completed. The bottle's glass drapes recalled the soft pleats of a Lelong evening dress (and in fact a few years later Lelong was to design an evening dress inspired by this bottle).

The bottle also conjured up another image: that of a silk handkerchief 'indiscreetly' dropped by a lady at a soirée and picked up by a man who instantly recognizes the owner by the scent – an olfactory fairytale whose ending was left to the imagination.

Or perhaps Lucien Lelong dropped his own handkerchief to help the bottle designer visualize the effect he was looking for...

Dress or handkerchief – ultimately it is unimportant. What matters are the soft, flowing pleats that affirm the supremacy of the drape during that period, be it large-scale, small-scale, in Rosalba crêpe, silk, plaster or glass.

1   *Marie Claire*, 10 September 1937.

A Fashion Icon

In 1931, during a trip to Venice, Natalie had an affair with Russian-born dancer and choreographer Serge Lifar. The following year the French poet, painter and film maker Jean Cocteau fell under her spell. Cocteau had just achieved success with his debut film *Le Sang d'un Poète* (The Blood of a Poet). Both artists were irresistibly drawn to Natalie's pure, innocent beauty.

The Romanov princess and fashion icon held a special place in Cocteau's personal mythology. Their love affair, conducted in a swirl of opium smoke, took an unexpected turn when Cocteau began dreaming of having a wife and family. He became convinced that Natalie had conceived his child and had terminated the pregnancy during a trip to Switzerland. Plunged into despair, Cocteau asked to meet with Lelong, and tried to persuade him to leave Natalie so that she would be free to marry him. Lelong was irritated and disbelieving. 'He's a peculiar gentleman', he would later say of his 'rival'.[1]

After a long holiday – possibly a period of convalescence – Natalie finally returned home to her husband in Saint-Cloud. The reunion was short-lived. Soon afterwards, she moved into her own apartment in the Paris district of Les Invalides. She went on to launch a film career, first in France and then in the United States. Natalie and Lelong parted on good terms, and she remained an ambassador for the couture house until they divorced in 1937.[2]

42 | Natalie Paley in a design by Lucien Lelong. Photograph by Studio Dorvyne, 1934. Musée Galliera, Paris.

1   There are multiple accounts of this episode. See, in particular, Jean-Noël Liaut, *Une Princesse déchirée, op. cit.*; Claude Arnaud, *Jean Cocteau*, Gallimard, 'Biographies', 2003, and Paul Morand, *Journal inutile*, Gallimard, Vol. I, 2001, pp. 561–71.

2   In 1937 Natalie left France for America, where she married the theatre producer John Chapman Wilson and worked with the famous couturier Mainbocher. After her husband's death in 1961 she became increasingly reclusive. She died on 27 December 1981.

THE CRISIS YEARS

In 1935 the luxury French ocean liner *Normandie* set off on her maiden voyage. Colette and Lelong were both on board: Colette made radio broadcasts of her impressions during the trip, while Lelong and several other Parisian couturiers presented their new collections. 'Pretty models, new lines, opulent fabrics and luxurious furs all contributed to the atmosphere of these supremely stylish shows. The audience was packed with appreciative Americans who had come to admire the impressive *savoir faire* of the French fashion industry.'[1]

These collections marked the come-back of volume, and with it the triumphant return of heavier, stiffer fabrics such as taffeta, surah and faille. These appeared in a variety of guises: 'crinkled, quilted, high-sheen, shot through with cellophane for a metallic effect, softly pleated, or in tiers of ruffles as light as radium', read *Vogue*. The fabrics were ideal for full, sweeping evening dresses that rustled noisily (the 'singing' of a taffeta was a mark of its quality), but were also used for simpler day wear. Textile firm Bianchini announced the replacement of crêpe de Chine with a dress-weight taffeta that was equally soft and light.

The March edition of *Le Jardin des Modes* pronounced Lucien Lelong's spring collection to be very feminine, graceful, 'optimistic' and bursting with new ideas. 'Volume, evident in the day wear, really comes into its own in the evening, with a profusion of ruffles and hemstitching... Suits have tailored jackets cut shorter at the front. Slimline coats are worn over full dresses with voluminous sleeves and intricate necklines.' The article was illustrated with a dress in iridescent taffeta featuring a draped bodice and ample bustle at the back.

That year Lelong produced one of his most stunning evening dresses: a pale pink satin gown with large brocaded sun motifs and wide pleats at the back which created a sleek silhouette and gently fanned out at the slightest movement. The bodice was tightly fitted at the waist but ended in a flourish of exuberant ruffles at the shoulders.

43 | Long evening cloak by Lucien Lelong in dark plum taffeta with dark plum velvet lining and trim (*left*); and black matt crêpe dress with long bustle at the back in cellophane-embroidered tulle (*right*). Photograph by Georges Saad. *Excelsior Modes,* winter 1936.

The year 1935 also signalled the end of an era for French high society and the haute couture industry. The following year saw the rise of the Popular Front in France. As factory workers went on strike, employees of couture houses followed suit, fighting against payment by piecework and demanding higher wages, a forty-hour week and two weeks' paid holiday. They won their case, reaching a settlement on 8 June 1936, just in time for preparations for the August fashion shows. The couturiers breathed a collective sigh of relief.

The Chambre Syndicale de la Couture (the governing body and guild of the French haute couture industry) was forced to revise all its statutes to accommodate the new working practices. It was a huge undertaking. In June 1937 the chairman, M. Gerber, resigned, asking to be replaced by a 'new man'. Lucien Lelong seemed the perfect candidate. Not only was he a shrewd businessman who knew the fashion industry inside out, but as one of the few French couturiers who regularly travelled to America, he had added insight into the way Parisian couture was perceived on the world stage. Although he did not officially apply for the job (as he was always quick to point out), Lelong was unanimously elected as the new chairman.

The same year, the French government asked him to produce another report on the state of the fashion industry on both sides of the Atlantic. While the United States was booming, France was in freefall: in 1935 the French haute couture trade exported only a tenth of what it had in 1925. The Great Depression and global economic crisis had led the US government to levy protectionist taxes on imported goods, and Parisian haute couture was being so highly taxed (at over 90%)[2] that American clients found the cost prohibitive. Instead of finished garments, US fashion industry buyers were therefore purchasing textiles and patterns (which were tax-exempt) direct from the French fashion houses. America was thus able to mass-produce cheap copies of original French designs, with minimal return to the French couturiers.

Not only was French couture selling poorly in America, French women had begun to lust after the American fashions they saw at the cinema. The readers of

44 | Evening dress with moss green handkerchief-style bodice extending to the ankles, and orange skirt. Illustration by Christian Bérard. British *Vogue*, April 1936.

45 | Afternoon outfit, white velvet jacket and brown velvet skirt.

46 | Lilac silk crêpe evening dress, 1932. Musée Galliera, Paris.

Vogue still held society women up as their role models, but the rest of the nation dreamed of looking like Hollywood film stars. Curiously, however, while the French press acknowledged cinema's influence on the beauty industry, it stubbornly refused to recognize its impact on fashion. For years the French fashion magazines continued to perpetuate the myth that Americans lacked style, and that Paris had the monopoly on class and elegance. So it was highly significant that *Marie Claire*'s second ever issue in 1937 featured a double-page spread on the influence of the big screen on fashion.

It was difficult to tell any more who was copying whom. Did French haute couture create the wide-shouldered look of the 1930s? Many gave credit to Marcel Rochas, whose *Bali* dress (with shoulders shaped like the roof of a pagoda) was inspired by his visit to the Paris International Colonial Exposition of 1931; though Elsa Schiaparelli

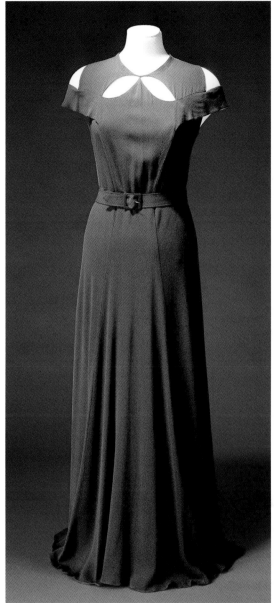

47 | Evening dress in green
crêpe and gold lamé, c. 1935.
Musée Galliera, Paris.

48 | Dress by Lucien Lelong
with fur sleeves. Illustration
by Pierre Mourgue. US *Vogue*,
December 1933.

also laid claim to having invented the silhouette. Others looked to Hollywood, and
Adrian, designer to the stars: his dress with huge organdie frilled shoulders, worn
by Joan Crawford in the film *Letty Lynton*, was copied a thousand times over. Film stars
were fashion icons; it was becoming impossible to deny.

When an American journalist asked Lucien Lelong if the French fashion industry was taking its lead from Hollywood, his reply was characteristically diplomatic:
'We all take our inspiration from the same sources. Couturiers can't live without the
cinema and the cinema can't live without us. Our fashion instincts are confirmed or
denied by them, and vice versa.'

Although Lelong would qualify his statement two years later in French *Vogue* by
suggesting that Paris still led the way ('Hollywood dresses films, Paris dresses women'),

49 and 50 | Lucien Lelong, dubbed the 'French ambassador of style to Hollywood', with Tilly Losch (*left*) and Loretta Young (*right*). French *Vogue*, January 1938.

51 | *Opposite* Mac Arthur, Lucien Lelong, Carole Lombard and Mitchell Leisen. French *Vogue*, January 1938.

he was well aware that cinema presented female role models who seemed more alive and alluring than the stiff models used by couturiers.

Couture and cinema joined forces in a 1938 film called *Artists and Models Abroad*, which featured outfits by celebrated Hollywood costume designers Travis Banton and Edith Head, alongside dresses by a roll-call of Paris couturiers: Paquin, Worth, Patou, Schiaparelli, Maggy Rouff, Lanvin, Alix, and Lelong.

1 *Vogue*, August 1935.

2 Marylène Delbourg-Delphis, *Le Chic et le Look*, Hachette, Paris, 1981, p. 171: 'To protect its own product, the American government decided to impose a customs duty tariff on imported clothing, exempting textiles and patterns, which agents were allowed to buy direct from the French fashion houses... In an effort to avoid losing their clientele, they made a deal that was commercial suicide.'

PORTRAIT OF THE ARTIST:
A DIGRESSION

L ucien Lelong turned forty-eight in 1937. The 'young, ebullient coutu-rier'[1] described by Colette in her memoirs had not changed much physi-cally. The moustache may have gone, but he was as razor sharp as ever. 'He talks plainly, moves deftly, and has a keen eye for detail', observed *Marie Claire,* which defined him as 'the most American of the [French] couturiers, and the most Parisian of those who are in love with the American dream and way of life... Which doesn't exclude him from being an artist.'[2]

It was not as an artist, however, but as an astute businessman that Lelong was first and foremost perceived. Maybe it was because he had studied at the Hautes Études Commerciales, Paris's premier business school, but some only saw Lelong as a marketing genius rather than a creative talent. They were completely wrong, of course: although Lelong, like his contemporary Patou and many other couturiers before and since, did not actually design his clothes, he alone provided the spark, the inspiration, the driving force. When one journalist asked him where his ideas came from, he answered with the classic couturier's response: his ideas reflected the spirit of the times. 'When I saw the first mass-produced vehicle designed by one of our famous car manufacturers a few years ago, the thing that struck me most was that it had mass appeal. So I immediately produced a coat which also had mass appeal.'[3]

Lelong would decide on the theme for each of his collections, brief his team of designers, and follow every stage of the creative process, from the choice of fabric all the way to the finished garments.[4] The model Praline, who started her career at Lelong, gives us an idea of his level of involvement. During one show in which she was the lead model, she recalled that Lelong was even more 'hands on' than the army of designers fussing around her backstage to make their final adjustments: '...the boss was always there, having been responsible for ten of the twenty dresses I was modelling.'[5] Lelong was also happy to attend the fittings of some of his clients, as French actress Michèle Morgan remembered: 'He would mark the alterations to be

52 | 'This crêpe satin dress is masterfully constructed with a series of pin tucks which provide both decoration and structure. The dress is finished with an enormous ruffle in frothy purple tulle.' Photograph by Horst. French *Vogue,* December 1934.

made, suggest a few changes, in short he would do everything couturiers normally do.'[6]

Marie Claire's 10 September 1937 issue revealed some of Lelong's passions and personal details: he was a heavy smoker (Filtra brand cigarettes), enjoyed sports (particularly sailing yachts) and collected porcelain (white and Chinese). For a period he had been interested in psychoanalysis, before taking up sculpture. The article ended by noting: 'Distinguishing feature: women adore him.'

And Lelong adored them back. In an interview with *Votre Beauté* about 'The ideal woman' (1934), he confessed to loving all types of women: tall, short, brunette or blonde. 'I particularly admire women with good proportions: a petite head, long neck and limbs, delicate wrists and ankles... I don't find pale complexions or

53 | Hélène Bigotte in a casual outfit by Lucien Lelong, 1930s.

gaunt faces attractive. At first sight I am more attracted to blondes, at least to those whose skin complements their eyes. Nothing shocks me more than a radiant blonde with dark, mascara-laden lashes... A blonde with silky, long, dark gold lashes is the epitome of femininity.' He hated platinum blond hair ('I find it tiresome and unforgiving with clothes'), and disapproved of gold- or silver-tinted powders, and nail polish. For him, the key to successful make-up was keeping it natural.

Lelong's models were all different, all 'ideal' in their own way. Among the most gorgeous were Sophie, the future Mme Bleustein-Blanchet, Lise Lalune, who became the director of his salons, and Hélène Bigotte, who was his favourite model from the late 1920s onwards. Lelong's affection for her is clear from postcards he sent her in 1941, when she was being treated in an Haute-Savoie sanatorium. 'Darling Hélène', as he called her, appeared to be part of the family. He would pass her titbits about his home life and give her news on his daughter and on how the couture business was going.[7]

54 | Black silk velvet dress tied at the shoulders with small gilt metal chain straps. French *Vogue*, October 1934.

55 | 'Lucien Lelong lights up his black moire velvet sheath dress with a ruffled "Medici" collar. Jewelry by Mauboussin.' Photograph by George Hoyningen-Huene. French *Vogue*, October 1934.

After Natalie ceased modelling for Lelong, a string of other Russian beauties took her place, including Mona, Tania, Galina, Genya and Ludmilla, nicknamed Lud, who appeared in a famous shot wearing a sunray pleated dress by Lelong adorned with a gold chain which wrapped around the shoulders, neck and waist. The dress itself was repeatedly photographed and sketched, and sometimes confused with a similar design by Madeleine Vionnet which appeared in the famous Man Ray photograph of a woman sitting in Oscar Dominguez's surrealist 'Wheelbarrow' armchair. Lelong's sensual dress, in bright pink with pleats entwined by the gold chain, was even more modern. He christened it *Pensive* (see page 74).

56 | *Opposite* Solarized photograph of Natalie Paley in a dress by Lucien Lelong. Photograph by Man Ray, *c.* 1935.

57 | *Above* Woman wearing a dress by Madeleine Vionnet in Oscar Dominguez's satin-lined 'Wheelbarrow'. Photograph by Man Ray.

1   Colette, *Le Voyage égoïste* (Journey for Myself: Selfish Memoirs), 'Bibliothèque de la Pléiade', Vol. II, p. 1163.

2   *Marie Claire*, 23 September 1938.

3   *Marie Claire*, 10 September 1937.

4   Lelong's knowledge of textiles was legendary. As Cecil Beaton explained in *The Glass of Fashion,* it was with Lelong that Dior 'learned the importance of what he today considers to be the essential thing in dressmaking: the eccentricities and behaviour of different dressmaking fabrics.' (*op. cit.* p. 252).

5   Praline, *Mannequin de Paris* (Parisian Model), Le Seuil, Paris, 1951, p. 60.

6   Interview with Michèle Morgan, January 2004.

7   After the closure of Lelong's couture house, Hélène Bigotte was appointed style consultant for children's fashion and women's lingerie at French chain store Monoprix, where she worked until 1970.

COUTURE-SCULPTURE II

Towards the end of the 1930s Lucien Lelong developed a passion for sculpture. In order to work in peace, he would escape in the evenings to his artist's studio in the Parisian district of Montparnasse, where he spent hours modelling, cutting and perfecting his sculptures. One of them won a prize at the Paris Salon of 1938, but apart from a female bust and a few photographic portraits of Lelong as a sculptor, little else remains of his work.

In a 1937 interview, he highlighted the close relationship between couture and sculpture. For Lelong, the implicit harmony of sculpture provided a welcome counterpoint to the increasingly tense political situation: 'It seems to me that this art form – which consists of realities, beautiful, concrete realities – can bring a calming sense of balance to our chaotic world…'

Interviewer: 'So should we see what we might call a sculptural quality in modern fashion?'

'That's right… Couturiers instinctively work with volumes to free the forms within them, just like architects and sculptors; and like them, we strive for perfection through a process of progressive refinement. Let's take my *Olympienne* black silk jersey evening dress: the bare shoulders and pure, simple lines give a sense of unity, and the drapery at the hips expresses the strength and finish of a block of stone cut with scissors.'

The same philosophy lay behind Lelong's *Pensive* and *Mouette* dresses. The latter, a design from 1939, looked all the more sculptural when modelled by a statuesque young woman who resembled a caryatid. For Lelong, this blonde giant was the ideal incarnation of fashion and beauty: it was almost as if she and the dress she was wearing had been hewn from the same material.

58 | *Opposite Pensive* evening dress in bright pink sunray-pleated raw silk, 1930–39. Musée Galliera, Paris.

59 | *Below* Portrait of Lucien Lelong as a sculptor.

In the world of fashion, couture and sculpture often go together: Balenciaga's dresses recalled abstract sculpture, Charles James invented the first 'fluid sculptures' (in the words of Dalí), Alix's (sewn) drapes seemed designed for antique statues, and Lelong's drapes and pleats, like Vionnet's, shimmered and slid over women's bodies, transforming them into living sculptures.

Previous pages

60 | *Bella* evening dress in blue silk muslin worn with blue-dyed rooster feather capelet.

61 | Six evening outfits by Lucien Lelong worn by Hélène Bigotte, his favourite model in the 1930s.

62 | *Opposite left* Afternoon dress in crêpe de Chine, 1930s.

63 | *Opposite right* Evening ensemble, 1930s.

THE COMING OF WAR

In September 1938 the Munich Agreement was signed. Lucien Lelong fully understood the gravity of the situation, but he was galvanized, preaching in an interview with *Votre Beauté* that 'Designers must not be impeded by the crisis. It is their duty to be committed to their cause. The more elegant French women appear, the more our country will show that it is not afraid to face the future.'

As the threat of war loomed ever larger, couture sought refuge in a nostalgic elegance. Huge gigot sleeves, full skirts and Second Empire crinolines all made a come-back. Couturiers gave full expression to the neo-romanticism that had been in the air for the last few years. Lelong themed his summer 1939 collection around 'the sea and the waves' and created evening dresses enveloped in wide ruffles which began at the shoulder and spiralled all the way down the dress to the bottom of the hem. The fabrics' textures and prints evoked foamy waves, and tulle was covered with seashells over a white satin lining.

Paradoxically, fashion took off on a pure flight of fantasy at the most critical moment. In late summer 1939, *Vogue* ran the headline: 'The key to the problem is the corset.' When war was declared on 3 September, the magazine had already hit the newsstands.

Men in uniforms crowded the train platforms, some civilians fled Paris, and those who remained carried gas masks with them around the city. The couture houses closed down, some of them completely (Vionnet), others partially (Chanel only kept her perfume boutique open). Mainbocher and Schiaparelli left Paris for America. Lelong was called up, then exempted ten days later.

From the very outset, he had three main goals.

The first was to save Parisian haute couture at all costs. In spite of its frivolous image, it was a heavyweight contributor to the national economy. 'Couture is an industry whose importance goes far beyond its physical end product', he insisted.[1]

64 | *La Mer*, evening dress printed with green, blue and white pattern, 1930–39. Musée Galliera, Paris.

Saving couture meant saving the jobs of hundreds of thousands of skilled workers employed in the fashion industry. Lelong's second goal was to keep them working, continue to foster their talent and protect their famous *savoir faire*.

His final goal was to ensure that French haute couture maintained its high profile abroad, or the industry risked collapse by the end of the war.

In January 1940 Lelong's determination paid off. He successfully persuaded American buyers to return to France after their no-show at the mid-season collections. There were no limits to what he was prepared to do to achieve this. He personally invited 150 New York buyers, arranged for their ship to dock in Italy, and laid on a special train to whisk them to Paris. There they were given a glamorous gala reception at the Interallié club, hosted by the French ministry for trade and industry.[2]

On 25 May the Chambre Syndicale called a meeting to discuss emergency measures: they compiled lists of employees to be exempted from mobilization and those willing to join the armed forces, and nominated a civil defence officer for each couture house. There was also the question of where the Parisian couture houses should relocate to. They chose the southwest, where some couturiers had already established new bases. Molyneux and Patou even offered to allow other houses to operate in their premises.[3]

On 15 June, the Germans entered Paris. Two days later, Marshal Pétain asked Germany and Italy for terms of surrender, and on 18 June General de Gaulle made his historic appeal from London. On 22 June Pétain signed the armistice, and France was cut in two.

Lelong was stuck in Biarritz at the time. In a letter of 17 July sent to Émilie Dupas, who was running the couture house in his absence, this normally resolute man sounded uncharacteristically hesitant: 'Since the armistice was signed I have been trying my very hardest to get back to Paris by any means possible [...]. Please use the utmost caution when visitors come calling, be they employees or suppliers. Who knows what the future has in store.'[4]

65 | *Above left* Statuette by
J. Sapey-Triomphe in a copy
of a dress by Lucien Lelong;
in the background, a miniature
version of Renoir's *Les Roses
au rideau bleu* (Roses in Front
of a Blue Curtain), Palais
de France, San Francisco.
'Plaisir de France' exhibition,
July 1939.

66 | *Above right* Bas-relief by
Mme Max Vibert for the
French pavilion at the 1939
New York World's Fair, in
a dress designed by Lucien
Lelong, 1939. 'Plaisir de
France' exhibition, July 1939.

67 | *Left* Advertisement for
Parfums Lucien Lelong, 1939.

Events would unfold rapidly. On Saturday 20 July five Nazi officers arrived at 102, Rue du Faubourg-Saint-Honoré, the headquarters of the Chambre Syndicale de la Couture, and were shown around the premises by the secretary, Daniel Gorin. They claimed to have been sent on a fact-finding mission to gather information on the current state of French haute couture, but their real purpose was to size up the offices. Eight days later, on a Sunday, they broke into the building and requisitioned the archives, which included the complete set of files on American buyers.

Having made his way back to Paris, Lucien Lelong was visited by German officers at the end of July. They outlined the Nazis' master plan for the French haute couture industry: it was to be integrated into a German organization based either in Berlin or Vienna; the French ateliers would provide the skilled workforce; a training college would be founded in Berlin so that French professionals could teach couture to young German women; and eventually, French couturiers and their houses would be transferred to Berlin or Vienna, where they would, of course, be given excellent jobs.

Lelong refused point blank: 'You can make us do anything by force, but French couture will not move, either wholly or in part. It will stay in Paris, or cease to exist.' He was asked to go to Berlin to put forward his case.

With the full support of the Chambre Syndicale and a mandate from the French Minister for Industry, Lelong travelled to Berlin in November 1940, accompanied by Daniel Gorin. He asserted the right of every country to produce its own fashion, and reaffirmed that the couturiers along with their hundreds of designers and thousands of seamstresses, factory workers and other employees would not be able to create anything if taken out of their home environment. It was down to the German fashion industry, which was undergoing a revolution, to prove that it could exist independently from Paris. On the question of the training college, he remained vague.[5]

His mission was successful: not only did the Germans agree to allow haute couture to remain in Paris, they also returned the archives of the Chambre Syndicale.

Lelong's role as guardian of the fashion industry was subsequently formalized. From October 1940, each sector was placed under the management of an organizing committee. The Textiles committee was subdivided into ten sections: Cotton, Wool, Dyeing, Clothing, etc. Because of its importance, Clothing was further divided into seven separate groups: Couture, Furs, etc. Lucien Lelong was made managing director of Group 1: couture.

He was thus ideally placed to help the industry procure what it was most desperate for: fabric. The distribution of woollen fabrics in particular was severely restricted, with the lion's share (over three-quarters) going to the Nazis, a further 17% to the Vichy government, and the remaining 3% to the rest of France.[6] In his endeavours to secure a better deal, Lelong pointed out that 'haute couture uses a minimal amount of raw materials for a maximum workforce, and it would require only a tiny levy of 0.5% on textile stocks to ensure that the industry could keep going at a reduced rate'.[7] The argument worked. A number of couture houses were eventually granted an exemption, and obtained a fixed quota pegged at 60% of the quantity of woollens they had been using in 1938. Lelong also helped devise a special incentive card scheme for haute couture clients, the 'Couture Création' card.

However, the German authorities balked at exempting all the couture houses, and entered into protracted negotiations to determine how many should be eligible. Figures were bandied around until in November 1941 they first agreed on seventy-one houses, which was subsequently reduced to fifty-four in September 1943.[8] The number of designs per collection was also regulated, and upper quotas were imposed on certain materials. The Nazis were intransigent throughout the wrangling, but despite its compromised position, the French couture industry refused to let itself either be integrated, or disintegrate. To the Germans, this defiance was inexcusably arrogant.

1   After the war, Lelong would sum up his arguments in the *Revue de Paris:* 'Our country does not have the means to export wheat or steel, particularly at the moment. But we can export ideas and style... Before the war, it was estimated that for every haute couture dress we sold abroad, we could import ten tonnes of coal, for every litre of perfume, two tonnes of oil, and for every bottle of champagne, three kilos of copper.'

2   See Colin McDowell, *Forties Fashion*, Bloomsbury Publishing, London, 1997, p. 138.

3   Archives of the Chambre Syndicale de la Couture.

4   Letter from Biarritz dated 17 July 1940, addressed to Mlle Émilie Dupas in Paris. Lelong continues: 'Once I am back in Paris I will need to get in touch with the acting authorities to take whatever decision necessary... I hope that my attempts to return to Paris will soon be successful, and I would be grateful if you and M. Cabé could see to it that the house is more or less in order... If I should have to stay here for a while longer, I will try my best to send someone up to you by train in order to assist you and help make decisions.' (Musée Galliera Archives, Paris).

5   See Dominique Veillon, *La Mode sous l'Occupation* (Fashion during the Occupation), Payot, Paris, 1990, pp. 151–54.

6   See Colin McDowell, *op. cit.*, p. 138.

7   Didier Grumbach, *Histoires de la mode* (History of Fashion), Le Seuil, Paris, p. 29.

8   See Dominique Veillon, *op. cit.*, p. 161.

ELEGANCE: THE SECRET WEAPON

On the streets of France, women were also making a stand. Parisiennes responded to rationing by turning their creative fingers to anything they could lay their hands on. They made skirts out of headscarves and suits out of their husbands' cast-offs, they unravelled knitwear and reknitted it, and spread walnut oil over their legs when they couldn't find stockings; in short, they still managed to look beautiful from head to toe. And although there was less of a spring in their step – leather was requisitioned, so they had to make do with wooden soles – they customized their clunky shoes into flamboyant artworks and one-offs. Hats, meanwhile, became towering constructions of flowers, tulle, stuffed birds, wood chips and newsprint. Everything seemed done on purpose to snub the occupying forces. Carmel Benito, who worked with the great milliner Reboux, recalled how extravagant hats boosted morale. When the felt ran out, hats were made first from muslin, then straw, and finally plaited paper. They were a symbol of French creativity in protest against the strict German regulations.[1]

Times were hard but the couture houses kept on working, often for a new clientele that did little for their image: the wives of officials in the occupying regime, mistresses of collaborators or German officers, and the 'nouveau riche' black marketeers who peddled rarities such as butter, eggs and cheese at prices that rivalled gold.

In contrast to what was happening on the streets, the war stifled the creativity of the couture houses, where there was neither the means nor the desire to innovate, other than in the practical arena. The silhouette remained more or less the same – wide shoulders and short skirts – although there was a shift in 1941, when the so-called *tonneau* (barrel) and *amphore* (amphora) silhouettes made their appearance. These featured ruffles, pin tucks, complicated bodices and drapery which added width to the hips without marring a slender figure.

Lucien Lelong's autumn/winter collection of 1943 contained a whisper of novelty: dubbed 'avant-garde' by October's *L'Art et la Mode,* the key looks were rounded (rather than boxy) shoulders and voluminous skirts and coats.

Accessories were more imaginative. Lelong designed belts with buckles in the shape of spanners, scissors and lanterns. His wooden 'log' bag of 1941 was frequently copied, as were his oversized handbags cut from the same material as his clothes – often tartan, which was very fashionable.

In spite of the difficulties, Lelong's couture house continued to be one of the most successful in Paris. Lelong was a superb manager with a knack of choosing talented staff. After Jean Ebel, his chief designer in the 1930s, he hired two young assistants who would soon prove to be especially gifted: Christian (Dior) and Pierre (Balmain). Dior started on 6 October 1941, and Balmain returned[2] to the couture house on 1 December of the same year.[3] They got on well with each other and both became friends with Janine Sagny-Marsay, one of the post-war period's top models. She was later to acquire the nickname 'Praline' and would work at Pierre Balmain's own couture house.

French haute couture had been saved, for the time being at least; but Paris still had to find a way of maintaining its presence abroad. It was a challenge: the borders were closed and exports banned.

In March 1942 Lelong organized a fashion show for some twenty couturiers in Lyon, which lay in the free zone. The evening took the form of a gala benefit in aid of France's Secours National relief agency, and featured a dance performance starring Serge Lifar. There was a dual agenda, however: the underlying aim of the event was to inform buyers and couturiers about the free zone.

Needing at least two hundred passes for the industry professionals he had invited, Lelong decided to attend a lunch

68 | *Opposite* Seersucker silk striped print evening dress, *c.* 1937.
Musée Galliera, Paris.

69a and 69b | *Above* Double-breasted redingote tailored coat in
grey ratine fabric with fitted waist, longer-length turn-up sleeves
and collar. Leather-lined belt in same fabric with square buckle.
Flap pockets with grey silk lining with repeat woven inscription
'Lucien Lelong, 16 Avenue Matignon', 1947. Les Arts Décoratifs,
Musée de la Mode et du Textile, Paris.

at the Ritz hosted by the French Round Table association, which was very pro-German. Seated next to a Nazi officer, he turned the conversation around to his problem … and walked away having secured the passes.

In the event, Lelong invited over 350 professionals from neutral countries (Spain, Portugal, Turkey, Switzerland and the countries of northern Africa). They all departed with armfuls of fabrics, patterns, and new ideas.

The Germans were enraged at having been tricked, and retaliated by banning fashion shows outside European capitals.[4] They also outlawed any form of marketing or publicity for haute couture, and heavily monitored the fashion press. The Germans had tried systematically to crush couture, by drowning it in foreign competition, depriving it of raw materials, preventing it from advertising and denying it access to foreign markets. One last option remained: to mutilate it by conscripting a part of its labour force.

The figures discussed were arbitrary: between 10% and 80%. Lelong eventually managed to negotiate 10%, and the final levy was as low as 5% of the workforce.[5]

As Praline later put it, 'Lelong did a good job behind the scenes during the Occupation.' Lucien Lelong had kept haute couture alive during the war. His intelligence, diplomacy and authority made him the perfect 'Minister of Couture', and the entire profession was grateful to him.

1   Colin McDowell, *op. cit.*, p. 141.

2   Before the war, Balmain had worked first at Molyneux before joining Lelong. They were forced apart at the start of the war, until Lelong recontacted him by phone in 1941 as he was travelling through Chamonix.

3   Christian Dior had worked at Piguet before the war. At Lelong, Christian Dior and Pierre Balmain succeeded Nadine Robinson, 'the French woman who knew how to cut cloth better than anyone else'. They joined Lelong's couture house within a few weeks of each other, as Lucien Lelong told Hélène Bigotte in a letter of 1 October 1941: 'Balmain will return on 1 December, Dior arrives on Monday' (private collection).

4   Along with Vienna and Italy: see Dominique Veillon, *op. cit.*, p. 166.

5   The negotiations dragged on for the length of the Occupation. For more details, see Dominique Veillon, *op. cit.*, pp. 151–85.

70 | White crêpe wedding dress, 1939. Musée Galliera, Paris.

LIBERATION, EXONERATION

Amid this symphony of praise, there was a false note. On 22 September 1944 an article appeared in the newspaper *Ce Soir*,[1] which, without naming names, accused Lucien Lelong and Daniel Gorin of having been dictators of fashion, of having been collaborators even. 'What lies in store for the man who has been the dictator of couture since 1940, the chairman of Paris's Chambre Syndicale de la Couture and managing director of the clothes organizing committee...who once dreamed of transferring Parisian couturiers to Berlin, or at least of having them show their collections there instead of here? What is to become of this powerful puppet master who held the fate of all of the French couture houses in his hands and who decided it by rather unusual methods [...]?', asked the journalist Georgette Lavigne.

In response to these false allegations, the Chambre Syndicale issued a statement which, while it did not claim the innocence of the entire industry ('It would be dangerous to assert that none of the couturiers had been collaborators', commented Raymond Barbas, head of Patou), did pay tribute to the hard work of Lucien Lelong and Daniel Gorin.

The couturiers also faced the incomprehension of the Allies when they liberated Paris in the autumn of 1944. British and American women had respected the austere dictates imposed on them by their governments, and had dressed in dowdy, uniform-like clothes that were in keeping with the war effort. Even the British Queen had subjected herself to the restrictions. But when the Allies arrived in the French capital, they were met with an astonishing spectacle: thousands of Parisiennes parading around in sexy, coquettish, frivolous outfits, looking as if the war had never happened.

The foreign press condemned the autumn 1944 collections as 'excessive', almost to the point of indecency. Lelong tried to explain himself to US and British *Vogue* in a cable dispatch. Yes, he could understand why the Allies were shocked, but French couture and French women had also suffered, and these collections reflected the euphoria of imminent victory rather than the deprivations of the war years.

71 | Portrait of Lucien Lelong, 1940s.

The hint of contradiction in his comments betrayed an evident unease. It was not easy to convey to the Allies the reality of life during the Occupation, and even less to convince them that when your stomach is empty, elegance can be an act of courage, style an expression of defiance.[2]

Despite his lunch at the Round Table, for which he was investigated by the Court of Justice, Lelong did not have real cause for concern. He was acquitted in 1945. The judge ruled that he had cooperated minimally with the Nazis in order to safeguard both his country's cultural heritage and the workers employed in his industry.

1   The French daily *Ce Soir* was published from 2 March 1937 to 2 March 1953, with a brief intermission from the end of August 1939 to August 1944.

2   Lelong would return to this point in his article 'Défense de la mode' (In defence of fashion) published in the *Revue de Paris* (*op. cit.*): 'Some soldiers in their khakis couldn't believe their eyes and declared, "They can't have suffered as much as they told us." But the ones who looked a little closer noticed that the rouge was hiding pale cheeks, and that the ruffled bodices were covering up threadbare fabric. They admired the efforts [the French] had made to remain stylish in the face of adversity, and saw it as a mark of courage and dignity.'

72 | Outfit (*left*) featuring
new draping design by Lucien
Lelong. Woollens by Anfrie.
*L'Officiel de la Couture et de la Mode
de Paris*, October 1946.

THE 'THÉÂTRE DE LA MODE'

Foreign clients and buyers had not been able to travel freely to Paris during the Occupation. Now that the war was over, Paris would travel to them, in the shape of the 'Théâtre de la Mode', a miniature theatre of fashion. The idea was simple: to showcase French fashion flair in an international 'theatre' tour featuring dolls in couture clothes. The entrance fee for the Théâtre de la Mode would be donated to the French Entr'aide charity.

Although the idea of fashion dolls seemed novel, there were precedents. Similar dolls had been made during the 18th century to model the fashions of the day, and more recently, couturiers had dressed dolls just before the war. When King George VI visited Paris in 1938, the young Princesses Elizabeth and Margaret Rose were presented with a whole collection on behalf of the children of France. The dolls came with a wardrobe of three hundred miniature outfits designed by Paris's top couturiers.[1]

There was also a pre-war precedent for the concept. In 1938, puppet master Jacques Chesnais decided to take his 'troupe' of ninety marionettes abroad and stage a mini fashion show of the latest Parisian designs. He asked Maggy Rouf, Schiaparelli, Lanvin and Lucien Lelong to create outfits for some of the puppets (which he had made himself). Lelong had produced two very different dresses: the first in dark tulle embroidered with midnight blue and contrasting pale sequins, the second in pale pink satin studded with crystal teardrops, with a dark fitted bodice.[2]

Unfortunately this model-marionette project was a flop: war was declared just as the tour began, and public and media attention was understandably focused elsewhere. Chesnais staged one show in Amsterdam during the Phoney War, but it all ended there.

The Théâtre de la Mode of 1945, on the other hand, was a runaway success which brought together some of the top creative talents of the day. The theatre sets were designed by Christian Bérard, lighting by Boris Kochno, and decor by Cocteau, Touchagues and Wakhevitch among others. Eliane Bonabel made the wire-framed figurines, which were dressed in beautifully finished outfits by Paris's leading couturiers.

73 | Roger Schall, 'Théâtre de la Mode' dolls on stage set designed by Christian Bérard. One of the dolls wears a miniature version of Lucien Lelong's *Faïence* dress, 1945.

Following pages
74 and 75 | Puppet dolls dressed by Lucien Lelong for Jacques Chesnais's marionette theatre, 1938.

76 | *Opposite* Jacques Chesnais's marionette theatre, 1938.

77a | *Above* Cover of programme for the 'Théâtre de la Mode' with illustration by Christian Bérard, 1945.

77b | *Above right* Inside spread of programme with (*left*) advertisement for Parfums Lucien Lelong and (*right*) list of credits for the thirty-six fashion designers, twenty hair stylists, as well as shoe designers, jewellers and accessory-makers who took part in the 'Théâtre de la Mode' project.

The accessories also showcased France's finest: Van Cleef provided the lilliputian jewelry and Paris's best milliners and shoe designers created the hats and dainty foot wear. Even the hairstyles were the work of a top professional, Alexandre.

The dolls represented the height of French fashion in 1945, which they would successfully export abroad. Although the war was not quite over, the return of exuberant colours and luxurious fabrics heralded a new-found sense of freedom. Waists were emphasized, sometimes tightly nipped in by girdles and corsets, and skirts (both narrow and wide) were longer.

Lelong's designs seemed to anticipate the New Look, particularly the short, full-skirted turquoise polka dot dress, the ballerina dress with a tight-fitted pink bodice and voluminous black skirt, and the long evening dress in ivory tulle embroidered with sequins over a grey-blue lining. Could it even be that these three pieces had been designed for Lelong by Christian Dior himself…?

The exhibition was launched at the Musée des Arts Décoratifs in Paris before setting off for London, Leeds (the UK's textile capital), Barcelona and Stockholm. The whirlwind schedule took its toll on the outfits, and the dolls had to be retouched and redressed between exhibitions. When the Théâtre finally reached America, it took New York and San Francisco by storm. The Chambre Syndicale de la Couture was delighted: the exhibition had fulfilled its dual purpose of raising money for Entr'aide (more than a million francs) and showing the world that Parisian fashion was alive and well and more dazzling than ever.

But behind the smiles of satisfaction there was anxiety. The United States had been forced to fend for itself in fashion for the last four years, having been cut off from Paris for the duration of the war. The French feared that instead of becoming frustrated, the Americans had relished the opportunity of cutting the apron strings once and for all. From the outset some journalists had been jubilant. 'American women, who for years had taken their lead from Paris in matters of fashion, were no longer looking in this direction. The artistic creativity that once blossomed in Rue de la Paix was suddenly dead.'[3]

While the Théâtre de la Mode had brilliantly proven otherwise, the fact remained that the war had changed the status of Parisian fashion abroad. The Chambre Syndicale sent Lucien Lelong back to the US to investigate, this time with Raymond Barbas, who had headed up Patou since the death of its founder. The Chambre hoped that their report would provide the key to reforging links between the two countries. Lelong and Barbas presented their findings on 28 June 1945.

Lelong concluded that they shouldn't rush into things: 'The USA expects us to produce perfection, but we're not in a position to do that.' France was devastated, its communication lines destroyed, and raw materials were even more scarce than they had been during the war. 'We would be better off coaxing Americans over to Paris, and discussing an attractive marketing strategy with the Ministry for Tourism.'[4]

This was to be one of Lelong's final missions as chairman of the Chambre Syndicale. On 5 November 1945, he tendered his resignation. His decision, he emphasized, was final. He was duly appointed honorary chairman for life.

1   See Colin McDowell, *op. cit.*, p. 40. The three hundred outfits were designed by top Parisian couturiers including Lanvin, Patou, Piguet, Vionnet and Worth, with hats by Agnès, Reboux and Suzy, furs by Weil and jewelry by Cartier.

2   The marionettes were photographed by Geiger at the start of the war. In 1941 Jacques Chesnais sent each of the couturiers a photo album of the 'collection', from which the pictures published here were taken (collection of Marion Chesnais).

3   Dominique Veillon, *op. cit.*, p. 155.

4   Archives of the Chambre Syndicale de la Couture.

THE END OF THE AFFAIR

After the First World War, Lelong had been ready to conquer the world. After the Second World War, things were very different. For five years he had worked tirelessly to save the couture industry, all the while trying to ensure that his own business remained afloat. He was burned out; worse still, his staff were beginning to desert him.

Pierre Balmain was the first to go, in 1944. Balmain felt that his creativity was being stifled, and the saga of his *Petit Profit* dress convinced him that Lelong didn't understand or appreciate his work. The dress, a simple design in black crêpe, was copied hundreds of times before Lelong reluctantly accepted it. This was the final straw: Balmain left to set up his own couture house, taking Juliette with him. She would become his head seamstress. They were joined soon afterwards by Praline, Lelong's one-time top model.

Christian Dior followed in 1946, along with Raymonde Zunacker, Lelong's studio director, who became Dior's second in command.

They were replaced by Hubert de Givenchy, who worked on the collections with two other designers, Serge Kogan and Serge Guérin. Givenchy got on well with Kogan, less so with Guérin. Most of all, he hated having to present his work before the 'tribunal', as he called it, consisting of Lucien and Nicole Lelong and their director, Baroness d'Avilliers. In his biography he described the experience as 'very unpleasant'.[1]

There appears to have been little love lost between Lucien Lelong and Hubert de Givenchy. When asked by a journalist in the 1950s to list his designers, Lelong replied curtly, 'Christian Dior for four years, Pierre Balmain for seven years, and Hubert de Givenchy for a minute or so.'[2]

By 1946 there was none of the happy vitality that had characterized the couture house between the wars. The young Bettina, who was just beginning her modelling career, remembered the atmosphere on entering Avenue Matignon: the place seemed

78 | Evening dress showing the new silhouette: shorter at the front, long at the back. The close-fitting velvet bodice contrasts elegantly with the tulle skirt. *L'Officiel de la Couture et de la Mode de Paris*, October 1946.

79a and 79b | *Opposite* Suit in
white, beige and brown tweed
and viscose rayon twill mix
fabric (details). Fitted jacket with
four pockets, two at the breast.
Single Corozo button fastening
at the waist. Straight four-
panelled skirt with zip fastening,
1943–44. Les Arts Décoratifs,
Musée de la Mode et du
Textile, Paris.

80 | *Above* Nicole Lelong
(standing at centre) and team
choosing fabrics.

81 | *Right* Christian Dior
and Sanda Goudeket.

austere and gloomy, with a cathedral-like solemnity. Nevertheless, to the outside world Lelong continued to project its image as a leading couture house, indeed the best in Paris. Jacqueline Delubac credited the couturier with an infallible 'genius for choosing'. 'He never lets a mistake slip past him. Being dressed by him means feeling safe'.[3] Michèle Morgan also had fond memories of Lelong: 'It was a great couture house, one of the finest. I met Lucien Lelong once or twice, when he attended my fittings. He was refined and polite, a gentleman. His clothes had a wonderful elegance about them, a classic elegance that you simply don't see nowadays'.[4]

When Michèle Morgan left for America after finishing her film *La Symphonie Pastorale* (Pastoral Symphony), *Elle* magazine dedicated a full page to her, in which she is pictured wearing a dress by Lelong. 'An enchanting, delicate dress in white and blue, which Lelong has named *Faïence*', read the caption, which went on to mention that the actress had also picked out a navy blue coat dress and a black suit.[5]

. . .

Lelong's first post-war collections were generally well received by the fashion press, even if there was little new for them to get excited about. Curiously, his winter 1946 collection reminded them of the line he produced after the First World War, in 1920. The winter 1946 issue of *L'Art et la Mode* observed: 'Every one of Lelong's dresses and coats resembles something our mothers would have worn twenty years ago. Hobble skirts, 1920-style coats pulled in at the waist, necklines that resemble fish platters, lashings of fur on hats and cuffs and tidal waves of woollen fabric: Lelong's women look like the surrealist 1920 ballet *Le Boeuf sur le toit* (The Ox on the Roof)...'.

On 12 February 1947 Lucien Lelong attended the launch of the New Look, which instantly confirmed its creator as one of the most important couturiers of the century. *Elle* magazine ran a double page spread on the event featuring a historic photo of Lelong at Christian Dior's show: the master and pupil. Lelong is pictured gazing intently at *Green*, a green twill dress with small white polka dots. The caption observes:

'Lucien Lelong was there, as [Dior's] old boss, a friendly neighbour, and master'.[6]

The two couturiers would always hold each other in the highest regard. Lelong regularly attended Christian Dior's shows, and Dior would look back fondly on his years at Lelong. 'I had a wonderful job with none of the pressures of a managerial position or the constraints of a representative role. In short, it was a very peaceful existence', he recalled in his autobiography.[7]

In February 1948 Lelong showed designs inspired by the New Look, featuring rounded shoulders, wasp waists and wide skirts falling to just above the calf. The collection was televised – a groundbreaking development – and also covered by the Keystone photo agency.[8] A set of photographs shows Lelong and legendary photojournalist Robert Capa surrounded by cameramen. In other shots, Lelong can be seen laughing and clinking glasses with his daughter, future wife, models and staff.

But this would prove to be a farewell toast: beset by health problems, Lelong finally decided to close his couture house in summer 1948. *Elle* magazine paid homage to him in its 10 August 1948 issue: 'Lucien Lelong is quietly shutting his doors and tip-toeing out. Following his second collapse, his doctor told him that if he carried on, his heart would give up. Lucien Lelong decided he would rather give up couture.'

De Molyneux, deux variations
sur les longs manteaux de velours

Bérard

Une combinaison heureuse de Lucien Lelong
Jaquette de velours et robe de taffetas.

Lucien Lelong
Moire lamée blanche, velours vert

Bérard

Lucien Lelong
Taffetas rouge
et satin
blanc peint

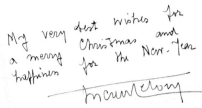

Previous pages

84 | Velvet jacket and taffeta dress by Lucien Lelong (*right*). Illustration by Christian Bérard. French *Vogue*, October 1936.

85 | Dress design by Lucien Lelong in white lamé moire and green velvet. Illustration by Christian Bérard. French *Vogue*, October 1938.

86 | Dress design by Lucien Lelong in red taffeta and white printed satin. Illustration by Christian Bérard. French *Vogue*, April–May 1940.

87 | *Opposite* Evening coat by Lucien Lelong. Illustration by Christian Bérard. French *Vogue*, April 1938.

88a and 88b | *Above* Greetings cards written by Lucien Lelong. Illustrations by Pierre Pagès (above) and Runacher (below).

1   Givenchy added: 'They would choose the sketches they liked and we could then start cutting the cloth. This was my one consolation because the clothes that came out of those ateliers were finished to an astonishingly high quality, in the best tradition of pre-war haute couture', quoted by Jean-Noël Liaut in *Hubert de Givenchy*, Grasset, Paris, 2000, p. 46.

2   Anny Latour, *Les Magiciens de la mode* (The Magicians of Fashion), René Julliard, Paris, 1961.

3   Quoted by Lucien François, *op. cit.*, p. 21.

4   Interview with Michèle Morgan, January 2004.

5   *Elle*, 26 March 1946: ' Michèle Morgan will be leaving for America with a magnificent wardrobe of outfits which will publicize French haute couture over there. She first called at Lelong where she ordered a navy blue coat dress *(Papillote)* and a black suit *(Stéphane)*.' The *Faïence* dress she wore in the photograph had appeared in miniature version in the 'Théâtre de la Mode'.

6   *Elle*, 4 March 1947.

7   Christian Dior, *Christian Dior et moi* (Christian Dior and Me), Bibliothèque Amiot-Dumont, Paris, 1956, p. 14. He went on to write: 'I am so grateful to Lelong for understanding that once my mind was made up, there was no turning back! We parted company on friendly terms, and with great sadness' (*op. cit.*, p. 20).

8   *Elle* magazine reported: 'At Lelong there was another eye on the clothes: that of the television camera, which filmed his collection along with those of a few other couturiers in order to show them on American TV.'

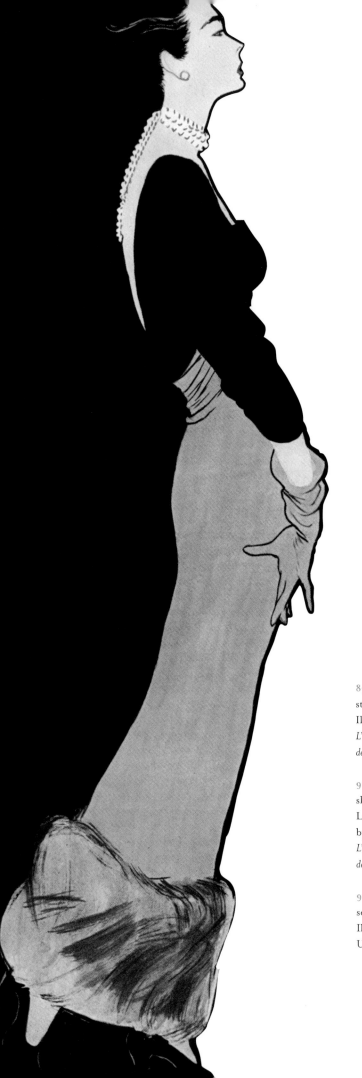

89 | *Opposite* Draped dress in striped moire fabric by Staron. Illustration by René Gruau. *L'Officiel de la Couture et de la Mode de Paris*, October 1946.

90 | *Left* Yellow woollen sheath skirt with marmot fur trim by Lucien Lelong, black bodice by Coudurier-Fructus-Descher. *L'Officiel de la Couture et de la Mode de Paris*, October 1947.

91 | *Right* Black velvet sheath dress set off by a pink satin bolero. Illustration by René Bouché, US *Vogue*, November 1945.

92 | Advertisements for
Parfums Lucien Lelong:
Orgueil, Elle Elle and *N*, 1940s.
Illustrations by Jean
Picard Le Doux.

LUCIEN LELONG, PERFUMER

Despite being exhausted by his wartime efforts, worn down by managerial issues and financial problems, and dogged by illness, Lelong was keen to hold on to his perfume business. He opened a gorgeous boutique at 6, Place Vendôme, which was to make a fleeting appearance in the film *Gentlemen Prefer Blondes*, in the scene where Marilyn Monroe and Jane Russell go on a whirlwind shopping spree taking in Balenciaga, Dior, Schiaparelli, and Parfums Lucien Lelong. In summer 1948, *Parfumerie de France* reassured its readers: 'We can confirm that Parfums Lucien Lelong, which is a completely separate company [from the couture house], will carry on as before. Discerning perfumers will no doubt be delighted.'

The following year Lelong launched *Cachet Bleu* at a soirée thrown by the famous interior designer and society hostess Elsie de Wolfe, aka Lady Mendl. Six hundred guests were invited to admire the new perfume, which was displayed like one of the crown jewels in a cylindrical red box placed on a vintage piece of furniture. The launch was covered by various magazines including *Beauty Fashion*, which marked Lelong's renaissance by declaring him to be 'back in splendid health'.[1]

In the course of his career the couturier created some thirty perfumes. As well as being the quintessential accessory to feminine elegance, perfumes were, for Lelong, the most effective way of diversifying. From the very start he had set up a branch of his perfume company in Chicago, and he often created new products specifically with the US market in mind. As with his couture house, Lelong wasn't content simply to look after the business side of things. His flair for sculpture enabled him to design the perfume bottles himself, some of which are now highly collectable. Yet apart from *Indiscret*, his perfumes have now largely been forgotten. Who remembers *Mélodie, Bois Vert, Murmure, Mon Image, Jabot, Sirocco, Orgueil* or *Elle Elle*?

Elle Elle cleverly played on the 'LL' of Lelong's double initials, and was exploited graphically as effectively as Chanel did with her 'CC', or Jean Patou with his 'JP'. The two right-angled 'L's nestled within each other inside a square. The logo adorned everything from perfume bottles to labels, boxes and chic cosmetics cases.

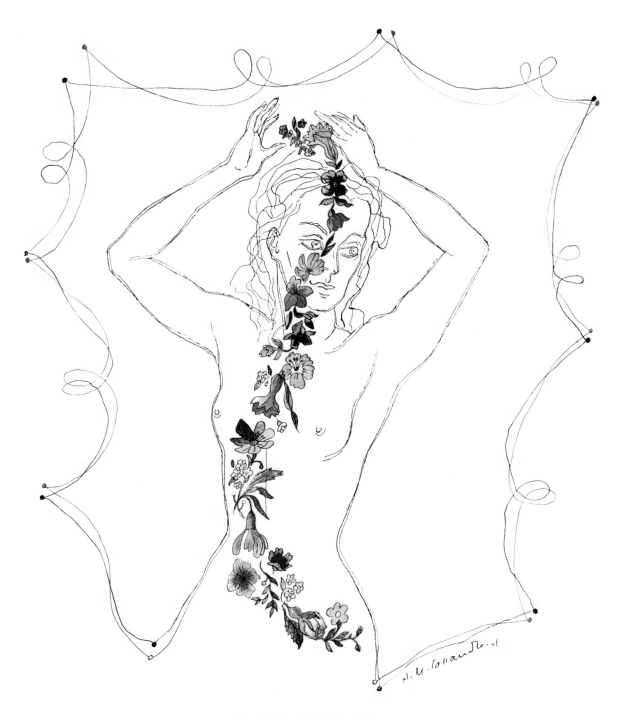

PARFUMS

LUCIEN LELONG

PARIS

PARFUMS

LUCIEN LELONG

PARIS

PARFUMS
LUCIEN LELONG

PARIS

"N". Indiscret. Passionnément. Elle-Elle

PARFUMS
LUCIEN LELONG

PARIS

Most of the bottles were inspired by two distinct worlds: couture and architecture. The best-known 'couture' bottle was created for *Indiscret,* featuring drapes which mimicked those of an evening dress. Other bottle designs were equally noteworthy, however: *Jabot*'s knot, *Cachet*'s embroidered pattern, and the jewel-like *Plumes* bottles which doubled as brooches or earrings.[2]

The very first 'architectural' bottle was designed by Lalique in the late 1920s, for the fragrances *J* and *N*. The black lacquered design evoked the Chrysler Building at night, and was presented in a chrome and black lacquered box decorated with the same sparkling garlands. Similarly, *Penthouse* recalled a skyscraper's penthouse suite, while the tower-like designs of *Balalaïka* and *Sirocco* were reminiscent of ziggurats. The mirrored casket of *Mon Image* echoed the sleek, minimalist interiors of 1930s Art Deco, and *Orage* (renamed *Opening Night* for the American market) came in the form of a crystal pyramid.

From 1937, Lucien Lelong scents were regularly advertised in women's magazines. Lelong worked with the best illustrators of the time – Cassandre, Lila de Nobili, Picart Le Doux and (latterly) Gruau – to create a romantic universe peopled by harlequins, ballet dancers and flower-festooned women, who exuded all the elegance of haute couture. Lelong would later commission photographers (Blumenfeld, for example) and even artists: a shelved project by Mondrian later exchanged hands in the auction houses.

The French fashion press reported on Lelong's latest editions. *Vogue*'s Easter 1950 issue mentioned 'a new travel-sized bottle in a robust container shaped like a weekend bag'. In 1956 Lelong introduced another innovative idea: a flat bottle which was 'light, easy to carry' and could be 'slipped into a travel holdall'.

Lelong would eventually start producing lighter eau de toilette fragrances such as *Cologne of the Hour* and *Eau Extra Sec for Men*, which reflected the changing mood of the times. These modern scents could not have been more different from the heady, warm and lingering perfumes of his earlier career: perhaps Lelong had grown to prefer the delicate smell of the roses he was cultivating in his garden in this final chapter of his life.

1   *Beauty Fashion*, October 1949.
2   Lelong's bottles were not always designed with a specific perfume in mind, just as one perfume sometimes inspired a number of different bottle designs. *N*, for example, had a bottle created by Lalique, and another much rarer one with rounded contours. Lelong also regularly issued 'présentations', limited edition bottles made for a particular occasion, such as Christmas, or to give an imaginative new lift to his established perfume lines. These one-off bottles were often produced for the American market, such as *Ting a Ling* which was decorated with real bells, *Castel* and *Plumes*.

Previous pages
93 and 94 | Advertisements
for Parfums Lucien Lelong,
c. 1945. Illustrations by
A.M. Cassandre.

Following pages
95 and 96 | Advertisements
for Parfums Lucien Lelong,
c. 1945. Illustrations by
René Gruau.

PARFUMS LUCIEN LELONG

PARFUMS LUCIEN LELONG

A Fine Garden Near Biarritz

Lelong moved away from Paris in the early 1950s. In 1954 he married for a third time, to the spirited Sanda Dancovici (later Goudeket). The couple settled in Anglet, near Biarritz, where Lelong spent two years and a fortune restoring the estate of Courbois. The fine 18th-century building housed the China porcelain he had been collecting since the 1930s: the figurines and an extremely rare Chinese bowl were displayed in the drawing room, in four glass cabinets lined with red fabric which beautifully set off the gleaming white objects.

Beside the house, a square outbuilding was converted into a wine cellar, and the old tennis court was transformed into a rose garden designed by Lelong himself, in which he grew hundreds of different species. The Lelongs led a calm life: they put away their sports racquets, sold their boat and emptied the swimming pool decorated with mosaics. They did, however, play golf. It was on the golf course that they met the Duke of Windsor, no doubt dressed in red and green, or raspberry-coloured plus-fours. Their social life revolved around lunches and formal dinners at Courbois. Christine, the Lelongs' daughter, remembered the cars that would flood into the courtyard: 'The chauffeurs would wait in their Rolls-Royces, Cadillacs and Bentleys.' Among the guests was the Marquis Guy d'Arcangues, who organized evening events for the Biarritz casino – Wednesday night dinners for young people, theatrical productions, and dance performances whose rehearsals took place in his own home. 'Lucien Lelong loved to come along,' he recalled. 'He enjoyed watching all the young people dancing. He was a cheerful man with a glint in his eyes, and in spite of the age gap we had a lot in common, and could relate to each other, man to man.'

The Lelongs were invited to everything, including the costume ball thrown by the Marquis de Cuevas at Chiberta on 1 September 1953. It was a magical evening straight out of *Swan Lake*. Lucien Lelong dressed up in Chinese garb, and even borrowed a Pekinese lapdog for the occasion. In his long, elaborate cloak, he looked like a little old man, weak and stooped.

97 | *Opposite above* Lucien Lelong and Sanda Goudeket.

98 | *Opposite left* Sanda Goudeket in the garden of the Courbois estate.

99 | *Opposite below* Sanda Goudeket at a ball in the 1950s.

During the night of 11 May 1958, Lelong suffered a heart attack and died, six months after Christian Dior. *Sud-Ouest* published a long obituary to him.[1] He was buried two days later. Maurice Goudeket, the widower of Colette, came to the funeral; a few months later, he married Sanda, Lelong's widow.

1   See *Sud-Ouest,* 14 May 1958.

100 | *Above* Greetings card sent by Lucien Lelong. Illustration by Lila de Nobili.

101 | *Opposite* Black woollen crêpe afternoon dress with three-quarter sleeves and sweetheart neckline with drape effect and sunray pleated skirt (detail), 1947–50. Les Arts Décoratifs, Musée de la Mode et du Textile, Paris.

LUCIEN LELONG, A TIMELESS GENIUS

We might well question how Lucien Lelong, one of the most influential couturiers of the 1920s and 1930s, came to spend so long in relative obscurity. He was not the only one: Piguet, Mainbocher and Molyneux (among others) suffered the same fate. The reason lies in the way that fashion history is constructed, with its focus on particular key dates, especially the 'revolutionary' years of 1905, 1925, 1947 and 1966[1] – the triumphant years of Poiret, Chanel, Dior and Courrèges.

But a feature of revolutions is that they fade away.[2] Defining the spirit of their time, they are firmly of their time, and inevitably are tainted by its flaws as well as its achievements. The elegance of the 1930s, on the other hand, epitomized by Lelong, seems to transcend time. Cinema may play a part in this: the glorious fashions of Hollywood's Golden Age retain a firm hold in the collective consciousness. But above all, the essence of Lelong's designs, their timeless elegance, is in the detail – the pared-down styling, the simplicity of the lines, the very way they define the silhouette. In this, Lelong belongs to a lineage of designers running from Madeleine Vionnet to Mme Grès via Jean Patou.

There are many books about the history of fashion; but no-one has yet written the history of elegance – which, unlike fashion, is timeless. This book on Lucien Lelong would be a key chapter.

102 | David Seidner, the 'Théâtre de la Mode', *Faïence* design by Lucien Lelong, 1990. Evening gown in ivory tulle embroidered with white paillettes and grey-blue floral motifs appliquéd to grey-blue satin fabric.

Following page
103 | A 1940s advertisement for Parfums Lucien Lelong. Illustration by René Gruau.

---

1   These are the dates singled out by Françoise Vincent-Ricard in *Clefs pour la mode* (Keys to Fashion), Seghers, Paris, 1987. Apart from 1947 and the launch of the New Look, the dates of the other events can be shifted by months or years (Poiret actually arrived on the scene a little later, Chanel a little earlier), but the chronology is useful overall.

2   With the obvious exception of Chanel, who managed to be revolutionary and timeless at once. The recent come-back of a Courrèges design, for example, was no doubt much more circumstantial.

PARFUMS LUCIEN LELONG

CHRONOLOGY OF A LIFE

1889

11 October Lucien Lelong is born in Paris to Valentine Éléonore Marie Lambelet and Arthur Camille Joseph Lelong, who run a small couture house in Rue Vignon named A. E. Lelong. Nine years later they move to 18, Place de la Madeleine.

1909

Lelong carries out his military service in the 4th Hussar Regiment.

1911–13

Lelong attends the École des Hautes Études Commerciales business school in Paris.

1914

2 August France mobilizes its troops. Lelong is forced to cancel the presentation of his first collection.
4 August War is declared and Lelong joins the 2nd Cuirassier Regiment.

1915

22 January Lelong is appointed Reserve Second Lieutenant and deployed in the French military attachment to the British army.

1917

24 May Lelong is wounded by shrapnel.

1919

After a long period of convalescence, Lelong rejoins the family business.

1920

The couture house is renamed Lelong et Fried (Fried is Lelong's associate). A year later it is definitively renamed Lucien Lelong. Nicole is born to Lelong and his wife Anne-Marie Audoy, whom he married immediately after the war.

1924

Lelong leaves Place de la Madeleine and moves to 16, Rue Matignon in Paris's new fashion district, near the Champs-Élysées roundabout. The same year, he registers his future perfume company.

1925

June Lelong takes part in Paris's Exposition Internationale des Arts Décoratifs et Industriels Modernes (International Exposition of Modern Industrial and Decorative Arts), presenting his designs in the 'Elegance' pavilion on Siegel display mannequins. His collection, in which he debuts the 'kinétique' silhouette, attracts a great deal of attention. Lelong makes his first trip to the United States.

10 October Lelong attends a charity benefit evening in Biarritz organized by Princess Paley in aid of Russian refugees.

1926

Lelong launches his first three perfumes, *A*, *B* and *C*, collectively named 'Tout Lelong'.
May Lelong is awarded France's highest decoration, the Légion d'Honneur medal.
5 June The 'Diner des 300' gala dinner organized by Princess Paley is held in Lelong's mansion.

1927

July Lelong and Anne-Marie Audoy divorce.
9 August Lelong marries Princess Natalie Paley. The same year, he launches the perfume *N*, named for his young wife, and *J* (for 'Jasmine').

1928

Lelong opens an American branch of his perfume company in Chicago.

1929

The Wall Street Crash: America imposes protectionist taxes in response to deepening economic crisis. Parisian haute couture becomes prohibitively expensive to American clients. Patou's collection signals the end of the boyish 'garçonne' silhouette.

1934

Lelong's show salons are redecorated with white plaster moulded drapery designed by Jean-Michel Frank and lighting by Alberto Giacometti. Lelong presents 'Edition', the French fashion industry's first prêt-à-porter collection.

1935

Indiscret is launched, Lelong's best-known perfume. He takes part in the Exposition Universelle in Brussels.

1936

Couture factories and workshops go on strike.

1937

24 June Lelong is elected chairman of the Chambre Syndicale de la Couture (the governing body and guild of the French haute couture industry). He makes a six-week trip to the United States.

1938

Lelong dresses a puppet doll for Jacques Chesnais, who plans to take his 'troupe' of marionettes on an international tour.

1939

Lelong shows his collections in Europe and the United States.
3 September War is declared. Temporary closure of French couture houses.

1940

14 June The Germans enter Paris. Many couture houses relocate to southwest France.
October Lelong is appointed managing director of the Couture group.
November Lelong travels to Berlin and persuades the Nazis to allow the French haute couture industry to remain in Paris.

1942

Lelong encourages the press to report on the continuing survival of the French haute couture industry. He organizes a fashion show for clients from neutral countries, without prior approval from the Germans.

1945

27 March The 'Théâtre de la Mode' is launched.
May Lelong travels to New York with Raymond Barbas in an attempt to re-establish links between the US and French fashion industries.
5 November Lelong steps down from the Chambre Syndicale.

1946

The perfume *Orgueil* is launched.

1947

Lelong attends the launch of Christian Dior's first collection: the 'New Look' is born, and Dior becomes an overnight success. Lelong's daughter Nicole drops out of medical school to work with her father.

1948

4 February Lelong's latest collection is filmed for television.
Summer Continuing health problems lead Lelong to close his couture house, while keeping his perfume business open.

1949

Cachet Bleu is launched and the Parfums Lucien Lelong boutique opens in Paris's Place Vendôme.

1954

Lelong is married for a third time, to Sanda Dancovici. The couple move to Anglet, near Biarritz.

1958

11 May Lelong dies of a heart attack.

 PARFUMS LUCIEN LELONG

SELECT BIBLIOGRAPHY

Claude Arnaud, *Jean Cocteau*, Paris, Éditions Gallimard, 2003

Christine Bard, *Les Garçonnes*, Paris, Éditions Flammarion, 1998

François Baudot, *A Century of Fashion*, London, Thames & Hudson, 1999

Cecil Beaton, *The Glass of Fashion*, London, Weidenfeld & Nicolson, 1954

Sarah Berry, *Screen Style*, Minneapolis, London, University of Minnesota Press, 2000

Célia Bertin, *Paris à la Mode: A Voyage of Discovery*, London, Victor Gollancz, 1956

Anne Bony, *Les Années 10*, Paris, Éditions du Regard, 1991

Anne Bony, *Les Années 20*, Paris, Éditions du Regard, 1989

Anne Bony, *Les Années 30*, Paris, Éditions du Regard, 1987

Anne Bony, *Les Années 40*, Paris, Éditions du Regard, 1985

Colette, *Les Vrilles de la vigne* and *Le Voyage égoïste*, Paris, Éditions Gallimard, Bibliothèque de la Pléiade, vols I and II

Michel Collomb, *La Littérature Art déco*, Éditions Klincksieck, Méridiens, 1987

Lucie Delarue-Mardrus, *Embellissez-vous*, Paris, Éditions de France, 1926

Marylène Delbourg-Delphis, *Le Chic et le Look*, Paris, Éditions Hachette, 1981

Yvonne Deslandres, *Le Costume, image de l'homme*, Paris, Institut Français de la Mode, 1976; Éditions du Regard, 2002

Yvonne Deslandres, Florence Müller, *Histoire de la mode au XXᵉ siècle*, Paris, Somogy, 1986

Christian Dior, *Dior by Dior*, London, Weidenfeld & Nicolson, 1957

William E. Ewing, *The Photographic Art of Hoyningen-Huene*, London, Thames & Hudson, 1986

Jean-Louis de Faucigny-Lucinge, *Un gentilhomme cosmopolite*, Paris, Éditions Perrin, 1990

Pierre Faveton, *Les Années 20*, Paris, Éditions Temps Actuels, 1982

Rose Fortassier, *Les Écrivains français et la mode*, Paris, Éditions des Presses Universitaires de France, 1988

Lucien François, *Comment un nom devient une griffe*, Paris, Éditions Gallimard, 1961

Guillaume Garnier, *Paris-Couture Années trente*, Paris, Musée de la Mode et du Costume, Palais Galliera, Éditions Paris-Musées et Société de l'Histoire du Costume, 1987

Madeleine Ginsburg, *Les Années folles de la mode*, Paris, Éditions Celiv, 1990

Didier Grumbach, *Histoires de la mode*, Paris, Éditions du Seuil, 1993

Anny Latour, *Kings of Fashion*, London, Weidenfeld & Nicolson, 1958

Jean-Noël Liaut, *Une princesse déchirée*, Paris, Éditions Filipacchi, 1996. New edition published as *Natalie Paley, princesse en exil*, Paris, Éditions Bartillat, 2005

Jean-Noël Liaut, *Hubert de Givenchy*, Paris, Éditions Grasset, 2000

Michelle Maurois, *Déchirez cette lettre*, Paris, Éditions Flammarion, 1990

Christie Mayer Lefkowith, *The Art of Perfume*, London, Thames & Hudson, 1994

Colin McDowell, *Forties Fashion*, London, Bloomsbury, 1997

Paul Morand, *Journal inutile*, Paris, Éditions Gallimard, 2001

Princesse Paley, *Souvenirs de Russie 1916–1919*, Éditions de la Couronne, 1989

Praline, *Mannequin de Paris*, Paris, Éditions du Seuil, 1951

Maggy Rouff, *La Philosophie de l'élégance*, Paris, Éditions Littéraires de France, 1942

Gérard-Julien Salvy, *Balmain*, Paris, Éditions du Regard, 1995

Suzanne Train, editor, *Le Théâtre de la mode*, Paris, Éditions du May, 1990

Nancy J. Troy, *Couture Culture*, Cambridge, Massachusetts, The MIT Press, 2002

Alexandre Vassiliev, *Beauty in Exile*, New York, London, Harry N. Abrams, 2000

Dominique Veillon, *Fashion under the Occupation*, Oxford, Berg, 2002

CATALOGUES, SYMPOSIA, ARCHIVES

'Cocteau et la mode', *Cahiers Jean Cocteau No. 3*, Paris, Éditions Passage du Marais, 2004

Le Vêtement, colloquium held at the Centre Culturel International, Cerisy-La-Salle, July 1998, directed by Frédéric Monneyron, Paris, Éditions L'Harmattan, 2001

Exhibition pamphlet *Le Théâtre de la Mode*, with foreword by Lucien Lelong, Paris, 1945

Lucien Lelong in Paris: archives of the Musée Galliera and the Musée des Arts Décoratifs

Lucien Lelong in New York: archives of the Metropolitan Museum of Art

District archives of Paris; archives of the Chambre Syndicale de la Couture; archives of the Musée Galliera; archives of the Bibliothèque Historique de la Ville de Paris

Magazines, Newspapers, Journals

Art, Goût, Beauté, L'Art et la Mode, Femina, Le Jardin des Modes, Vogue, L'Officiel, Elle, Beauty Fashion... (collections of the Bibliothèque Forney, the Musée Galliera, the Musée des Arts Décoratifs and the Bibliothèque François-Mitterrand)

Vogue USA, Harper's Bazaar (collections of the Metropolitan Museum of New York)

Les Créateurs de la Mode, Paris, Éditions du Figaro, C. Eggimann, 1910

Sud-Ouest, Bibliothèque Municipale, Bayonne

Les Cahiers de la république des lettres, des sciences et des arts, special edition dedicated to fashion, Paris, *Les Beaux-Arts*, 1927

Revue des Deux Mondes, 'La Mode, courants et contre-courants', August 2001

Paris et la beauté féminine, by Lucien François, Paris, Société d'Éditions Modernes Parisienne, 1945

Correspondence

Letters from Natalie Paley to Jean Cocteau, Fonds Cocteau, Bibliothèque Historique de la Ville de Paris

Letters from Lucien Lelong to Hélène Bigotte, private collection

Letter from Lucien Lelong to Émilie Dupas, archive of the Musée Galliera

Letter from Lucien Lelong to Jacques Chesnais, private collection

ACKNOWLEDGMENTS

Thanks to Jean Chalon, who first had the idea for this book and who introduced me to Sanda Goudeket. And of course to Sanda herself, who gave me access to documents relating to her life with Lucien Lelong, to whom she was married before she became the wife of Maurice Goudeket.

I am grateful to the following people: Christine Pellistrandi, daughter of Sanda and Lucien Lelong, who shared with me details of her parent's life in their house near Biarritz; Ysabel de Ravenel and her daughter Ariel, who permitted me to consult their family albums and to reproduce several images; Jacques Polge, who generously allowed me access to his collection of autographs and documents relating to Lucien Lelong, some of which are reproduced here; Anne Melin, who shared with me letters from Lucien Lelong to Hélène Bigotte, as well as a number of photographs of Bigotte that appear in this book; Clarence Duchêne, who helped me to recreate (and illustrate) the career of Lucien Lelong the perfumer, thanks to his rich archive of perfume advertising.

My thanks also to Guy d'Arcangues, Maïmé Arnodin, Françoise Auguet, Mariella Berthéas, Claudine Boulouque, Jacqueline Bromberger, Robert Capia, Carven, Jean-Louis Coulombel, Alexandre de la Cerda, Marion Chesnais, Anne Etot, Amy Feldman, Christophe Girard, Jacqueline de Guitaut, Thomas Gunther, Peter Lamborghini, Marie-Françoise Leclère, Jean-Noël Liaut, Frédéric Mitterrand, Nine Moati, Michèle Morgan, Jean de Mouy, Dominique Paulvé, Marie-Christine Perreau-Saussine, Lynn Povich, Alexis de Rédé, Olivier Saillard, Marie-Ethel Siméonides and Alexandre Vassiliev.

I owe special thanks to Catherine Join-Dieterle and the team at the Musée de la Mode and the Costume-Palais Galliera: Dominique Revellino, Annie Barbera, Sylvie Roy, Sophie Grossiord, Sylvie Lecallier, Françoise Vittu and Fabienne Falluel, whose expertise and kindness were a constant support; Pamela Golbin at the Musée des Arts Décoratifs and Didier Grumbach at the Chambre Syndicale de la Couture for the assistance they gave me in opening up their archives; and lastly Valérie Guillaume, who helped me get started with my research. In the US, I offer thanks to Stéphane Houy-Towner at the Costume Institute of the Metropolitan Museum of New York, whose substantial files allowed me to assess the importance of Lucien Lelong in the United States.

And thank you, finally, to Paule Verchère, who, with his extensive and subtle knowledge of the 1930s, was my friend and companion throughout the writing of this book.

PHOTO CREDITS AND SOURCES OF ILLUSTRATIONS

WHEN

TRADITION

AND

AVANT GARDE

UNITE THE EFFECT
IS SENSUAL,
SENSATIONAL.

THE KISS, THE VOW. *HERE AND NOW*

The past made present, the future, perfect,

IN THESE NOT SO SUBTLE NUPTIALS FOR
THE BRIDE THAT DESIRES TO SHINE.
UNBRIDLED BY CONVENTION,
SHE IS UN-BRIDALED IN INTENTION.
AN INDEPENDENT SPIRIT
TO HAVE AND TO HOLD.
MYRIAD, MULTIPLE, MYSTERIOUS,

Crystal

REFLECTS, REFRACTS,
ATTRACTS THE EYE.
AND ILLUMINATES EVERY

'I do'.

WHEN

TRADITION
AND
AVANT-GARDE
UNITE

THE EFFECT
IS SENSUAL,

THE KISS, THE VOW.

The past made present, the future, perfect,

IN THESE NOT SO SUBTLE NUPTIALS FOR
THE BRIDE THAT DESIRES TO SHINE.
UNBRIDLED BY CONVENTION,
SHE IS UN-BRIDALED IN INTENTION.
AN INDEPENDENT SPIRIT
TO HAVE AND TO HOLD.
MYRIAD, MULTIPLE, MYSTERIOUS,

Crystal

REFLECTS, REFRACTS,
ATTRACTS THE EYE,
AND ILLUMINATES EVERY

I do.

CRYSTALLIZED™
SWAROVSKI ELEMENTS
THE ELEMENTS BRAND OF SWAROVSKI

CONCEPT + IMAGE

CREATIVE DIRECTOR Stephen Todd
FASHION EDITOR Sophia Neophitou
DESIGN EDITOR Caroline Roux
ART DIRECTOR Marcus Piper
EDITOR Marion Hume
ETIQUETTE CONSULTANT Marion von Adlerstein
PRODUCTION Bruno Semeraro, Emilie Erbin, Christey Johansson
ART ASSISTANT Vanessa Titzé
RETOUCHING Faith Denham

COVER
Dress and coat John Galliano
Photography Sofia Sanchez & Mauro Mongiello
Styling Marina Burini
Model Querelle at City Models

PRINTED BY
Graphicom
Viale dell'Industria 67
36100 Vicenza
Italy

Published by Swarovski AG, Droeschistrasse 15, 9495 Triesen, Principality of Liechtenstein.

ISBN: 978-3-033-01401-5

ON COVER: VEIL SOPHIE HALLETTE GLOVES DENISE FRANCELLE

UNBRIDALED

THE MARRIAGE OF
TRADITION AND
AVANT GARDE

MODERN MARRIAGE

Tradition & the Individual Spirit

TEXT JOHN ARMSTRONG

It's only a minor exaggeration to say that the modern idea of marriage began in 1994. That was the year of *Four Weddings and a Funeral* – the most commercially successful British film to date. What it did was to put modern romance back into harmony with the grand tradition of weddings as wonderful social theatre. It combined realism about how we love and live with a happy sense of the fun and fineness of marriage. The film teases, but is genuinely affectionate about ritual and ceremony. Hugh Grant might curse delightfully as he tries to button his waistcoat; but he doesn't throw it aside. And the film is movingly frank about the longing to be married. All these charming people are direct: they want to find love and they want to get married. After a brief hibernation, marriage was back as one of the great and natural goals of life.

Modern marriage is the meeting point of tradition and the individual spirit. The impulse today is to be generous to tradition. We like the sense of continuity. We like the idea that there's a meaning to marriage that's bigger than us. We are charmed by the idea that there's an inherited wisdom in this social institution.

Looking at *The Village Wedding* painted by Sir Samuel Luke Fildes in 1883, we can feel both close and distant to the image. We are touched by the mixture of seriousness – on the faces of the couple – and the general festivity; there is a beguiling sense of place: the whole village is there. But, there's also a sense of dis-tance. We don't live like that; we don't look like that anymore.

Modern marriage is guided by the longing to be sensitive to, and expressive of, the self: our own particular vision, the shape of an individual life. We're not passive in the face of the past. History is now. If we're marrying a tradition, it's also true that the tradition is marrying us. Of course, there are many traditions: love, weddings and marriage are reinvented in the light of each civilization. We are cosmopolitans to the extent that we are insiders in more than one civilization, to the extent that we are involved in the conversation of more than one culture. Modern marriage is increasingly cosmopolitan: able to absorb and hold multiple cultural meanings.

CLASSIC AND ROMANTIC VISIONS OF LOVE

We are the inheritors of two distinct ideals of marriage – in fact two distinct ideals of love, which can be summed up under the great banners of culture: Classic and Romantic.

The classic conception sees marriage as a contract: a purposeful and pragmatic alliance between two parties. This was connected to the practice of giving a dowry and of negotiations between families. Marriage, in this view of life, is a profoundly public act; it needs an audience. An extreme version of this vision of marriage is illustrated in a magisterial painting, now in the Louvre, painted by Rubens. The picture is a fantasized record – painted some twenty-five years after the actual event – of the

The Kiss
Gustav Klimt, 1907-1908
Belvedere, Vienna

marriage of Marie de Medici to Henri IV of France. Their union would produce the future King Louis XIII. Here, marriage is all about dynasties, politics, power, land and money. We may blanch at the pure realpolitik of the Medici marriage; but something similar, if much less grand, is actually quite important. This is just the most dramatic version of something much more pervasive and ordinary. Marriage was – and generally still is – to do with survival and security: with coping well in the material world.

At this less dramatic level, there is a corresponding vision of love: a vision of what is loveable. Good humour, reliability, industry, self-control and persistence are characteristics that – on this view of life – make a person attractive. We catch sight of this pragmatism in the Japanese custom of guests giving a cash gift to the couple whose wedding they attend. This frankness about economics – which is also kindness – has a larger significance. It's a reminder – at a moment when we might need to be reminded – that a marriage is, amongst other things, a practical alliance. The specific material help is a touch of realism.

The Romantic conception of love focuses on the uniqueness of each person; what we love is their individual essence, their soul – to speak in the Romantic manner. When we fall in love, on this view, we meet someone who can touch the hidden and secret parts of our personality, who can know us through and through, and is delighted by what they find. The most Romantic statement in the history of art is a single line from Verdi's opera *La Traviata* (first performed in Venice in 1853). Violetta, the central character, sings 'love me Alfredo. Love me as much as I love you'. It's the core of the Romantic conception: that the intensity and depth of love is returned, is met, is shared.

And so there is almost always doubt: the essential Romantic fear is that one is not loved enough, not longed for as truly and deeply as one longs for the beloved other. In comparison with this longing, everything else seems of lesser worth. In Klimt's 1908 painting, *The Kiss*, we see the moment of fulfilment: from within that picture all doubt is banished. The twining of hands, the enveloping golden mantle speak of complete closeness; and the flattened, decorative background – the absence of anything else going on – is brilliantly perceptive. The lovers are in a world of their own; a world in which

nothing matters besides this moment; there are no distractions, no rival demands. The Romantic view of marriage is an expression of such love; marriage is a spiritual state – it need hardly be announced to the world.

The vitality of modern marriage arises from the creative tension between these two ideals: each is important; each speaks appealingly and seriously to us. Yet they are potentially at odds with one another. Each marriage is an individual response to the question: how can they be united?

A wedding is one privileged moment where tradition meets the individual spirit. Like any fine work of art, a wedding grows out of history; it makes sense within a long line of ritual and procedure that comes from others. But we are contributing to this; the tradition needs us; it wouldn't be a tradition, it wouldn't have life, if it were not taken up and used in the service of the individual.

THE MARRIAGE OF STYLES

One reason why Jane Austen has such enduring appeal – and such strong appeal in today's world – is that she puts her finger on something we know is important but find hard to talk about directly. Few writers have been more in love with love; she has created enduring stories of the search for a soul mate, the search for that special someone without whom we cannot be whole. And yet she never loses sight of the fact that life is not pure romance. We are complex creatures with many different kinds of need. We have to live in the world we have. So Jane Austen pays loving and serious attention to the mechanics of happiness: where do people live, how will they dine, what will their social life be like? Marriage – in the eyes of Jane Austen – isn't only the union of two souls, it's the union of two lives. So she's pointing at one of the critical issues of modern life. Marriage isn't just the sacred force of love: it's an expression of our full humanity – its linen cupboards, and nice cutlery, its Wellington boots and elegant hotel bedrooms. These longings don't spoil love: they are ways of finding love together, of expressing ineffable longings in particular physical things.

In a way, we have all to become our own Jane Austens. We have to become the authors of our own vision of love; we are the artists of modern marriage. It's as if we're always starting from the Klimt Kiss – that mesmerising image

of complete mutual absorption in all its purity and intensity, that world of love – and having to add in the background. The maturity of modern marriage is founded on an awareness of tomorrow; on a sense that the background counts too. It's no betrayal of Klimt's picture and what it stands for to recall that people have careers, and friends and enjoy travelling and kicking back and watching television. We have classic needs as well as romantic needs. What we need to do – the art we need to cultivate – is that of joining the two pictures together; we have to discover ways of filling in the realistic background without disturbing the couple.

Home is the outward expression of marriage; our home expresses who we are, and it's the place where the two inescapable sides of life – emotional and material – most naturally come together. The style of our home is really the story we are telling ourselves about how we make sense of what Jane Austen was so concerned about. She was so brilliantly aware that lovers also live in the world; and that a marriage is a philosophical epic about how something as special and fugitive as the feeling of love comes to be made solid in two complex lives.

THE PHILOSOPHY OF TEARS

When people cry at weddings, it's often because there's a sense that something deeply impressive is taking place. They're not tears of sorrow; they're much harder to explain. It's as if we're humbled and delighted by the feeling that this is the truth of life: this is the real thing and it's here and now. As if life were being summed up and presented to us in one single awesome moment. We can feel this even if we just happen to be passing at a crucial moment when a newly wedded couple are jumping into a limousine.

This is really a way of recognizing that there is a solemnity about marriage and about a wedding. Solemn has nothing to do with glum or tedious. It's the sense that something momentous is happening. There is perhaps no finer expression of this 'solemnity' than Poussin's 1647 picture of marriage in the National Gallery of Scotland in Edinburgh. A wedding is an iconic moment, a special moment in life, because it sums up and emphasizes in a single moment the meaning of life as a whole. The birth of a child is like this too. The confusing complexity of existence, the bustle and business of everyday life recede – for a moment. We are confronted with

Couple with a Standing Screen
Kitagawa Utamaro, Jihei, 1797
Japanese, Edo period
William S. and John T. Spaulding Collection
Museum of Fine Arts, Boston

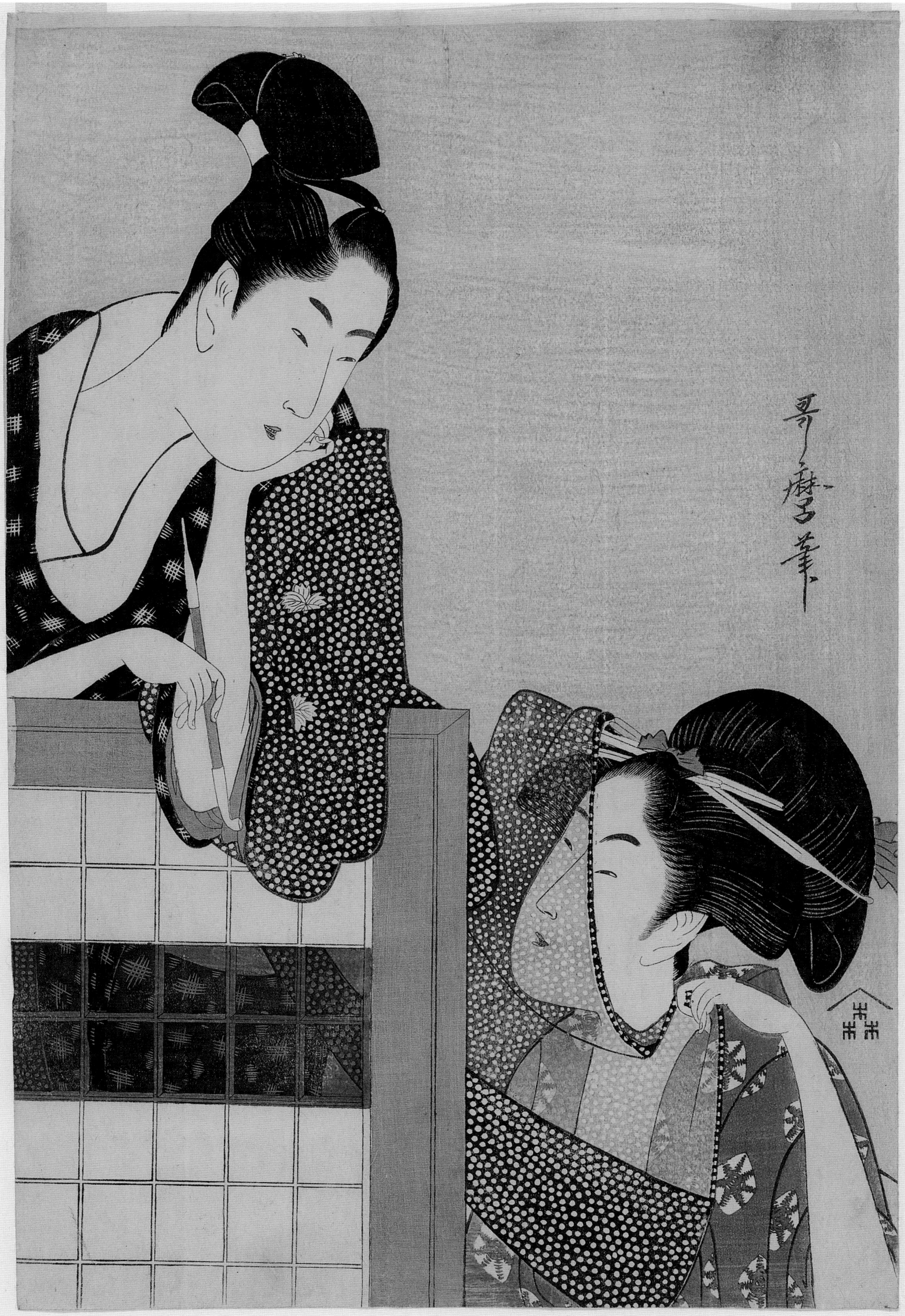
哥麿筆

TOP LEFT *The Sacrament of Marriage*
Nicolas Poussin, 1647-1648
Duke of Sutherland Collection
on loan to the National Gallery of Scotland

TOP RIGHT *Le Mariage par Procuration de Marie de Medici
et d'Henri IV,* Peter Paul Rubens, c. 1623-25
akg-images, London, UK

BOTTOM *The Village Wedding,* Sir Samuel Luke Fildes, 1883
The Sir Andrew Lloyd Webber Art Foundation

the elemental ideas: hope, love, trust, commitment. We know a million and one other things; we know all there is to know about the less lovely truths about people. But at this moment they are held at bay and we are confronted with a pure vision of human dignity.

If we look closely, it's in fact quite a modest scene. The couple are crowned with simple garlands of flowers; there's a feeling of stillness and concentration. The architecture, though elegant, is plain and undecorated. It's as if Poussin doesn't want anything to distract our thoughts from what is happening. Poussin always wanted us to see the universal in the particular. This isn't meant to be simply a representation of one particular wedding; it aims to show us something that is true of all marriages.

Like many of his pictures, there is a contrast between the straightforwardness, the simplicity of the characters in the picture and the very real grandeur of the work of art within which they are placed. The careful geometry of the windows and the columns give this picture a monumental rhythm. We – the spectators looking in from our world – can see something they do not: the huge weight and significance of what is going on. This is the solemnity of marriage. And when we catch sight of it, for a moment, we are humbled, moved and exhilarated.

THE FEAST

The history of the word 'feast' is curious in that it blends two apparently separate notions. One (perhaps more familiar) sense is primarily that of a sumptuous meal: a banquet, often with a large number of guests. But its older sense – which lingers on – is that of a festival, a public holiday: it marks an occasion. And our idea of a wedding is really a feast in both these senses.

Few works of art convey the imaginative resonance of a wedding feast more powerfully than a huge, lavish work by Paolo Veronese. Painted probably in 1562, *The Wedding Feast at Cana* takes its origin in a specifically religious story. But the picture has a clear secular voice as well. It speaks of our natural delight in abundance, but it is tempered with style; people wear splendid clothes and hold themselves in fine attitudes; here there is courtesy and wit and intrigue and flirtation. This is a picture unashamed of our love of beauty.

This masterpiece is so very civilized because it understands the alliance between beauty and solemnity. We need beauty because it expresses what we long for; it gives material – outward – show and form to our inner longings. This alliance is central to our humanity. Beauty has a dual significance. It looks, from one side, onto our physical nature: it gives us the touch of silk, the luxury of fine lines, the natural, powerful appeal of gilding and brightness; beauty knows that we are physical creatures, excited and charmed by elegance. But beauty looks, at the same time, towards our ideals, towards our deeper and more delicate moments of reflection. That is why we can love, and not merely like, beauty. It is as if beauty knows our surface and our depths; and wonderfully unites them. The promise of beauty is that we can be complete. And that is why beauty is an essential in life. Material beauty is the natural expression of spiritual longing; it is the natural sign of love. Beauty looks the way love feels.

THE GROWTH OF LOVE

When things grow, they change in appearance – although if we follow the process of development we can see the continuity. Our hopes for love are rooted in this vision of growth.

In Mozart's astonishingly beautiful opera *Cosi Fan Tutte,* first performed in Vienna at the end of January 1790, the theme of painful growth is explored. The opera's title is a bit irritating: 'they [women] are all like that' sounds, when we first think about it, a mean-spirited note of world-weary disillusion. The work carries a subtitle: the school for lovers. And indeed it really does teach a startlingly serious lesson. The opera follows a battle between a cynical philosopher and two young men who are deeply in love with two women who return their love with equal ardour. The cynic holds that love is never true, and by artifice puts love to the test. The men depart, as if heading off to war, only to return five minutes later in elaborate disguise. They then proceed to win the affection of their own sweethearts. And so it seems as if the hard-hearted philosopher is justified.

But, in the end, love triumphs. All is forgiven and the lovers return, a little wiser, to where they were in the beginning: each pair happy in themselves. Following the dictates of unity of time, the whole action is compressed into a single day – but the logic, if allowed a longer span, is perfectly serious. The lesson at stake – the lesson which needs to be absorbed for the reconciliation and return of love – is that one's beloved is not perfect. The young men in *Cosi Fan Tutte* started out with that very normal fantasy.

But it's not the love of perfect people for one another that counts in life. We need to be able to do something more relevant and important: the real love of imperfect people. It's one thing to love someone who has no faults. It's more human and more relevant to love someone who has their blemishes and weaknesses. Mozart keeps faith with our hopes. Hope and loyalty are all the more precious, all the more valuable, when we are clear-eyed about ourselves. The deepest stream of the history of love is the development of – and profound admiration for – love in the face of imperfection.

And we come to realize that Cosi isn't really about women in particular; it is about the human condition in general. It is we who are 'all like that': all imperfect.

HAPPINESS

The natural goal of marriage is the mutual happiness of two people – of two lives. And the happiness of a life is a complex thing. It's not like the happiness of a particular moment: unalloyed, pure delight and wellbeing that we experience from time to time. A life cannot be purged of sorrows and distress. A happy life is one that includes suffering; but in which suffering is bearable, partially overcome and compensated for. The same necessarily holds for married life. The happiness of marriage cannot lie in the magical banishment of difficulty.

There's a wonderful short story by Tolstoy, called *Family Happiness*, which introduces the powerful ideas of a second happiness and a second love. What this really suggests is that as love grows over time it sheds its original skin. It becomes a more developed and deeper version of itself. But the shedding process is real and can be painful. For Tolstoy's characters, Masha and Sergey, it is traumatic. The shedding of the first bloom of love is experienced as a painful loss. As that happens, they cannot see it for what it is: a necessary stage in the development of their relationship. Tolstoy is trying to tell us something at once simple and difficult, the combination that marks the essence of wisdom. To marry is to join together. But the large meaning of marriage is not just the union of two people; it involves the union of different aspects of human nature: emotional and worldly, flesh and spirit. It requires the union of our ideals and our pragmatism. It is solemn and festive. It is a tradition and it is our future.

PHOTOGRAPHY PAUL WETHERELL
STYLING LUCY EWING

Dress Vivienne Westwood Gold Label

Dress and Headpiece LOLITA LEMPICKA

13

*"I believe
that I should make the
past and present cohabit
in all my styles,*

*SO I ALWAYS LEAVE
AN OLD TOUCH
IN MY DRESSES*

*in order to show
the beautiful image
of old traditions."*

– Zuhair Murad

DRESS COLLETTE DINNIGAN

DRESS 3.1 PHILLIP LIM

"*Crystals help create a fantasy,*

evoke a dream,
TO REALIZE what every woman
dreams of as a child."

– Phillip Lim

"Where I come from – Lebanon – weddings are like competitions: everyone tries to do the biggest and most GLAMOROUS. So each time you go to a wedding, you think it's the best, but then you go to another even bigger and better one. It's like this all the time. But of course, the best wedding is the one of a friend or a member of my family, where there's WARMTH and feelings from the heart."

— Elie Saab

Dress (left) ELIE SAAB
(right) ARMANI PRIVÉ

DRESS ZUHAIR MURAD

DRESS REEM ACRA

23

*"Crystals are really
the ultimate in beauty and finesse.*

A BRIDE LIKES TO BE SEEN AS DAZZLING, LIGHT AND PRECIOUS,

*and this really sums up
what Swarovski is all about."*

– Antonio Berardi

HEADPIECE MARIOS SCHWAB

Dress ALBERTA FERRETTI

"A crystal's brightness
*IS A DREAM
IN ITSELF.*"

– Alberta Ferretti

"THE MOST IMPORTANT THING FOR A WOMAN

IS TO HAVE WONDERFUL COMPORTMENT

– carrying herself properly and paying attention to every detail."

– Vivienne Westwood

Dress VIVIENNE WESTWOOD
GOLD LABEL

DRESS ROMONA KEVEZA

Hair Jimo Salako at JedRoot agency
Makeup Shinobu using Chanel
Models Indre and Egle at FM, Bara at Union Models
For more details see page 207

31

SHOES GIUSEPPE ZANOTTI

Photographer Gavin Bond
Art direction Bradley Garlock for Garlock-DeGuiceis
www.garlockdeguiceis.com

Florist Floral Arts, using peonies and orchids.
Floral Arts, Venice Beach, CA

TEXT MARION VON ADLERSTEIN

THE CITY OF ANGELS *is a heavenly place to tie the knot. Between paparazzi flashes and mega-watt glamour, the modern bride truly shines. Action!*

Photography Metz & Racine
Styling Kanako B. Koga

Headpiece ERICKSON BEAMON

Gloves (white & peppermint) Christopher Kane
(lace & mesh) Dany Mizrachi
Bustier Rossella Tarabini for Anna Molinari

TABLEWARE BODO SPERLEIN

ZUHAIR MURAD

ESCADA SWA

Stephen Jones
MILLINERY

the naked b

Swarovski by Juha Acknown

"CRYSTALS are great to help set off and add a magical sparkle to the dress.

CRYSTALS are perfect to frost the shoulders, add gloss and shimmer to a décolleté and bring an extra finesse to the most magical dress a girl will wear.

CRYSTALS are all the colour and glamour you need on a white wedding dress."

– JOHN GALLIANO

Photography Sofia Sanchez & Mauro Mongiello
Styling Hector Castro

Coat John Galliano
Hat Stephen Jones for John Galliano

DRESS VIKTOR & ROLF

DRESS AND CARDIGAN 6267

43

"*A wedding dress is really* *THE ULTIMATE IN FANTASY.* LIKE HAUTE COUTURE, *IT SHOULD FIT THE WEARER LIKE A GLOVE,* MAKING HER DREAMS COME TRUE.

But it also needs to be modern and forward-thinking."

— ANTONIO BERARDI

Dress DANIEL SWAROVSKI
Hat STEPHEN JONES FOR JOHN GALLIANO

45

Dress Julien Macdonald
Necklace (on head) Daniel Swarovski

"The veil and the head dress are the ultimate finishing touch for a bride. Normally, all is okay, but when they put the veil on they know they're getting married

THE BEWILDERED, SHOCKED AND ECSTATIC REACTION ALWAYS ENDS IN A BURST OF TEARS."

— STEPHEN JONES

TIARA AND VEIL STEPHEN JONES

Hair Romina at Airport Agency
Makeup Alex Box at D&V Management
Model Daul Kim at Storm
For more details see page 207

Photographer Vikram Bawa
Producer and floral designer Sheetal Mafatlal,
using rose petals and white mogra

Among the rich adornments that characterize a HINDU *wedding are masses of fragrant flowers. Rather than carry a bouquet, the bride wears a garland given to her by the groom in exchange for one she bestows on him. Red, the colour of floral offerings made to female deities, often predominates, as it does in the opulent piece on the opposite page. Fashioned from ROSE PETALS AND A LOCAL FLOWER CALLED MOGRA, this garland, threaded through with Swarovski crystals, is draped on an altar in front of the Gateway of India in Mumbai with other important elements in the marriage ceremony (vivaha). When the groom arrives – sometimes dramatically on a white horse – he is showered with rose petals. Swags of blooms cascade from the canopy – called a mandapa – under which the most important parts of the ceremony take place. As for her wedding dress, a Hindu bride is resplendent in an elaborate and vibrantly-coloured silk sari or a garment typical of the region of her heritage – perhaps a lehenga woven with pure gold or silver thread. To fit the festive mood, she adds a sultan's hoard of jewellery.*

TEXT MARION VON ADLERSTEIN

SHOULDERPIECE LEMARIÉ

54

CHOCOLATE BOX **GODIVA**

TEXT MARION VON ADLERSTEIN

Photographer Peter Hunt
Styling Andreas Skoularikos

Florist Wild at Heart, using English roses.
www.wildatheart.com

Carrying A POSY such as this one of roses in cream, white and blush-pink, a traditional ENGLISH bride wears something old, something new, something borrowed and something blue. On her way to the village church, tradition has it that she should look for a good luck sign, but as chimney sweeps are rare in England these days, sunshine should suffice... After the ceremony, the newly weds are showered WITH ROSE PETALS, RICE OR CONFETTI. The peal of wedding bells, which we now find lyrical and joyous, has its origins in the wish to ward off evil spirits.

"CEREMONIES AND RITUALS
OFTEN REVOLVE AROUND AN OBJECT,
AN ALTAR OF SORTS.
*THE EPERGNE, OR TABLE CENTREPIECE,
IS ONE SUCH OBJECT.*

*Although it has been largely ignored
by contemporary design, we felt that it was
worth exploring in the context of
modern marriage – an epergne gives an
instant feeling of grand celebration and luxe.*"

– Patrik Fredrikson & Ian Stallard

Epergne Fredrikson Stallard

PHOTO METZ & RACINE STYLING KANAKO B. KOGA

Garland Joris Laarman/Demakersvan

PHOTOGRAPHY ROBERT WYATT
STYLING LUCY EWING

DRESS RICHARD SORGER

Dress and Hat with Veil **Marios Schwab**
Shoes **Gina**

DRESS ZANDRA RHODES

"One of the most distinct elements in a traditional Middle-Eastern dress is the use of detailed embroidery and beadwork. My design utilizes these two elements, but I give them my own personal touch. I use non-conventional methods in pattern and work-execution and I use basic dress structures with Western influence and just the right amount of deconstruction. The use of Swarovski crystals is also a must in my book, as it gives my designs an extra ZING. I like to think of my designs as unique, eclectic and very glamorous."

— FURNE ONE

Dress, Mask, Rings Amato by
Furne One

DRESS ROKSANDA ILINCIC
HAT NOEL STEWART FOR
ROKSANDA ILINCIC

DRESS VERA WANG
TIARA HAUTE BRIDE

"A wedding gown is about self-expression,

ABOUT CREATING SOMETHING
THAT'S TRUE TO A WOMAN'S STYLE.

The bride should choose
a gown that reflects
who she is before all else."

— Vera Wang

Neckpiece MANIK MERCIAN
Skirt VIVIENNE WESTWOOD (VINTAGE)

"A wedding dress is a challenge in the sense that it is attached to so many traditions, and to a certain extent, rules. I LOVE the constraints of a wedding dress, all the pomp and ideas of what it should look like."

– Erdem Moralioglu

Dress Erdem

Hair Nicolas James at Premier
Makeup Kelly Cornwall at Premier using Chanel
Model Melissa at Select Model Management
For more details see page 207

Magnum Ornament Crystallized™ Design Team for Moët & Chandon

Knife CHRISTOFLE
Bag BRACHER EMDEN
Bird FLEUX

(LEFT) DRESS ALBERTO RODRIGUEZ
(ABOVE) NECKLACE TARUN TAHILIANI

Burka Haider Ackermann
Sandals Stuart Weitzman
Veil (on little girl) Suneet Varma

PHOTO THIERRY PEREZ STYLING CHRISTOPHE MARTINEZ

Bustier Chantal Thomass
Plates Manufacture de Monaco
Glass Domes Fleux

Screen (Detail) Linda Florence
Table Lamps Tomoko Azumi

(OPPOSITE) DRESS RAMI AL ALI
EARRINGS ROBERTA CHIARELLA
(ABOVE) DRESS BARNEY CHENG

91

Photography and Video Francesco Carrozzini
Styling Sophia Neophitou

Dress Emilio Pucci
Suit, Shirt, Bow tie Richard James

Dress, Sunglasses KAREN WALKER
Bouquet PHILIPPE FERRANDIS
Suit, T-shirt RICHARD JAMES

Fur Coat FENDI STUDIO, *Shoes* AZZARO

DRESS ANNE BARGE
DRESS (ON HANGER) SOHAD ACOURI
(*BROOCH* DANIEL SWAROVSKI)

Green Dress Awatif Al-Hai, *White Dress* Sohad Acouri
(*Brooch* Daniel Swarovski), *Handpainted Dress* Zaki Bin Aboud

Hooded Dress Martin Grant, *Sandals* Gina
Suit, Shirt, Bow tie Richard James

"*The challenge is to not fall into the classic 'princess' tradition, without freaking out the grandmother and the mother of the bride.*"

— MARTIN GRANT

Dress S<small>INHA</small>-S<small>TANIC</small>, *Sandals* G<small>INA</small>
Suit, Shirt, Bow tie R<small>ICHARD</small> J<small>AMES</small>

Dress Azzaro, *Sandals* Gina
Skirt (worn as dress) Anna Molinari for Miss Blumarine
Barrettes Roberta Chiarella

DRESS NINA DONIS
SUIT RICHARD JAMES

Hair Franco Gobbi at Art Department
Makeup Mariel Barrera at Joe Management
Models Aiste, Lexie, Eric, Zaya, Anastasia, Eddie, Joele
For more details see page 207

ALTARED VISION

One bride's memory of an unforgettable day

TEXT NATASHA FRASER-CAVASSONI

You could say my 1997 wedding was fairly straightforward. Held in Paris, it was a Catholic church ceremony followed by an afternoon reception for 350 and then a debauched *après*-dinner disco. The slight difference was that *Hello!* covered the entire event. The magazine's curiosity was piqued because one of our eight witnesses was the actor Rupert Everett. He had just made *My Best Friend's Wedding* – the smash-hit film of that summer and was so famous even the priests were snapping him at the altar.

But popping flashlights aside, it was a bit of a triumph. Friends admitted to falling in love with Paris again and great fun was had by all. I write 'all' because the wedding is about the guests, not just the couple getting married. Indeed, you can have the most perfect dress, flowers and food but if the casting stinks, bang goes the ambience.

Now, being an abominable control freak (even at five, I tried to change the day of my birthday party for a larger attendance) I was fabulously well-organized. I had a green coloured cloth notebook which possessed every iota of our arrangements. I strongly recommend this for every bride-to-be. Light in weight (I've seen some that resemble a telephone book) and brilliantly sectioned off by my sweetheart, it was my bible and contained every detail, including the measurements of eight bridesmaids.

As for the budget, I was given £10,000 by my mother – biographer Antonia Fraser – with the words, 'How you spend it is your choice. If you have the urge, I mean why not on a pair of shoes?' A pair of shoes for that amount in 1997! How very Marie Antoinette of her – and this was before she wrote her best-selling book which inspired Sofia Coppola's film.

Fortunately, Christian Louboutin was designing my shoes anyway. Chanel was giving me my wedding dress. Finding the church was easy. Robert Forrest, the fashion world's favourite Mr Fix It, told me about Saint Clotilde, a beautiful basilica in the seventh arrondissement which happened to be where I was living. So that was booked before anything else. But my entire family vetoed my 'Girl Guide idea' of sailing on a Bateau Mouche on the Seine afterwards. So where to have the reception? My uncle, Michael Pakenham (then Number Two at the British Embassy in Paris) came to the rescue. A member of the Cercle de l'Union Interalliée, a private club with the most divine garden, he suggested the perfect venue. One meeting with the manager, who was so jolly and full of the delights of *hors d'oeuvres* and magnums of champagne, sold us on the place. Finally, we could print and send off our invitations.

The idea of bridesmaids felt quite alien. But I was forgetting the iron will of proud grandmothers, proud mothers. At first, hints were subtle. 'The back of your dress will look so much prettier with little girls following you,' my mother began. The penny still didn't drop

FROM LONDON
Is There a $AFE AT CRILLON?

Mum is bringing tiara.
Need to try with dress — CHANEL?
Find out when? Thursday
— TRY ON FRIDAY

Borrowing pearl earrings
from Annabel Lind say —
pink pearl + diamond drop
white pearl + diamond / pearl.
Kate Betts need to return

Necklace from Granny
of pearl + diamond

Thank you letters
to be written before Honeymoon

- ✓ Yves Saint Laurent – Smoking
  ✓ & PIERRE BERGÉ

- Emanuel Ungaro – black
  beaded dress – Laura too?

- Valentino – coat with
  fur collar.   Rome?

- ✓ Azzedine Alaia – saxe
  blue dress

- ✓ Gilles Dufour – who else at
  Chanel? TBD

- ✓ Rifat Ozbek – dress for
  civil ceremony – London or

until Rebecca, my eldest sister and mother of two curly-topped daughters, boomed: 'Listen, are you having bridesmaids or not?' Having initially been against the idea, I soon had Gilles Dufour, then at Chanel, joining me in going totally over the top. Our idea being that each little girl would be dressed like a flower: bluebells, daffodils, you get the picture. The dressmaker shook her head. 'Natasha, it's your day,' she said. 'No one will look at you if you have this circus troupe behind you.' As a result, the simplest long white cotton dresses with puff sleeves were designed. The only difference being the colour of the sash around each tiny waist.

As it turned out, the pastel-coloured sashes came in handy with the flower scheme. Being financially challenged, I couldn't afford lush gardens of lilies, tulips and roses, even if Rupert kept on calling from Los Angeles and barking 'the flowers have to be important'. True, but the problem was the vast dimensions of St Clotilde. My florist, Marianne Robic, saved the day. Instead of trying to fleece me, she suggested that we have two gigantic vases of flowers on each side of the altar, while the large copper lamps hanging from the ceiling and trailing along the church's aisle would drip with satin ribbons which were the same colour as the bridesmaids' sashes. It turned out to be inexpensive and effective.

All this was organized weeks in advance, whereas my dress was left to the eleventh hour. It got to the point where I started harassing Gilles early in the morning and sobbing down the telephone. 'Relax Max,' continued to be his mantra. 'You will lose kilos before you tie the knot, *cherie*,' he would say while munching on his breakfast toast smothered in jam, 'and there's no point starting now.' Having designed many wedding dresses, such as the spectacular gowns for his nieces, Victoire de Castellane and Mathilde Agostinelli, he knew what he was up to. From nerves, my body did melt. In fact, every

time I turned up at Madame Elizabeth's atelier, she had to take in the seams.

Then came the great day. My mother and step-father Harold Pinter were staying at the Crillon Hotel and threw a buffet lunch for the bridesmaids beforehand. It was an enchanting start: all the little girls were in an utter state of excitement, driving one or two people mad with their insistence of dancing 'ring around the roses' while the mothers were hen-like, gossiping about the night before or making last-minute decisions on their wardrobe.

With great pride, Gilles and I showed my mother the hourglass-shaped dress which had been delivered in an imposing Chanel box. Pointing out how it was embroidered around the plunging cleavage, enhanced waist and hips, Gilles explained that Jane Russell had been the inspiration. My mother nodded, then started rabbiting on about her own hat! We were both amazed at such extreme Mother-of-the-Bride fever. Then Madame Elizabeth arrived and helped me slip into the dress – lightly embellished with shimmering embroidery by Lesage – and with an invisible pull-in girdle and a sprig of pale-blue ribbon sewn into it for luck.

When Harold arrived to collect me, this great man of letters was completely lost for words. But then, I did look amazing: as I should have done, with all the help I received. Terry de Gunzburg did my make-up and Carlos Cambelopoulos created my 'I dream of Jeanie' hairdo, complete with family tiara fixed on top. And off we drove in the bubble-pink Cadillac. Harold seemed mildly uncomfortable. But at least we didn't arrive in a pony and trap which was my original idea.

No doubt, it was the delight at seeing so many people, but while we walked up the aisle I started weeping. Then so did everyone else – I arrived at the altar to find many, including my intended, Jean-Pierre, reaching for their hankies. The charged atmosphere was demonstrated

when the priest announced the sign of peace and instead of handshakes, strangers exchanged kisses. (No doubt, the English thinking it was a French custom and the French thinking it was an English one.)

When leaving the church, Jean-Pierre and I were bombarded by our bridesmaids who threw rose petals and others who chose rice. We then stepped into our Cadillac Convertible. While waving to the cheering crowds, I felt *très* Evita (Madonna's film had just come out). But the perfect moment crashed when our driver suddenly insisted on being paid the rest of his fee. So instead of heading straight to the reception, I waited as Jean-Pierre got cash out of the bank!

As for the reception, the weather was truly magnificent, the roses were in full bloom, Karl Lagerfeld appeared with a rose-cut diamond brooch for yours truly (*Hello!* was thrilled) and of course there were the speeches. Harold and the entire family made touching and appropriate ones. Then along came Rupert's. It had been censored. He'd seen my three brothers beforehand who had nixed his idea of starting with the names of all my exes. Instead, he accused me of accepting all sorts of fashion bribery, being too intimate with my girlfriends and rugger-tackling my husband into marrying me. It had everyone – myself included – in stitches.

Speeches are particularly key to a wedding because they mark the occasion. However, I have sat through a few that were seriously embarrassing. (Imagine a wedding where five golden boy bankers got up to wax lyrically about the groom's achievements and barely credited the bride!) In general, I think unless you're funny by profession, the focus should be showing that you care about the couple.

At my brother Damian's wedding in Mexico City, Alex Salvidar, who introduced Damian to his museum curator wife, Paloma, had everyone transfixed. He has a rich seductive voice and he told a delicious tale of the couple's courtship as we sat surrounded by eighteenth-century colonial splendour at the Museo de la Ciudad. Paloma was wearing a Carolina Herrera silk and taffeta wedding dress with her thick hair twisted and plaited up in a chignon, while my brother looked handsome and very nineteenth century in white tie. And then there was the glamour of the South American ladies, starting with Rosa Porraz, Paloma's mother. And how they hit the dance floor when the live Colombian band started! Were these the same women who had looked so holy in the church of Santo Domingo with its marble floor and towering gold candlesticks? Mexicans are deservedly famous for knowing how to party.

The same, of course, could be said for writers. New York editor Kate Betts' wedding to award-winning journalist Chip Brown was that perfect mix of intellect and glamour: from Bob Woodward, the best selling author and star of the *Washington Post* to American *Vogue* editor-in-chief Anna Wintour, as well as generations of an East Coast American wasp world. Vows were exchanged at the Old Whaler's Church in Sag Harbour (scribe territory since Melville and Steinbeck) although Kate, who is Miss Punctual, was hideously late owing, according to Christian Louboutin, to her veil having been sewn inside out and needing to be fixed. Still, the bride arrived looking sensational in a bias-cut Galliano dress with a now-perfect veil above her famous strawberry-blond mane of hair. It all felt very F. Scott Fitzgeraldish, as we headed off to the twenty acres of prime beachfront that is the Fireplace Estate in the Springs, East Hampton, where not only the grand vista impressed, but also the attention to detail – from the pots of daisies which lined our path to the Chateau Plagnac served with dinner. Fun gossip was to be had later, as a certain stylist was observed chasing Bob Woodward around a marquee decorated with hydrangeas and tuberose and reminding him that they had shared a Jacuzzi in the 1970s.

There appeared to be no dramas at the nuptials of fashion stylist Franciane Moreau and theatrical designer Riki Bouscasse, for the simple reason that we were always on the move. Held on the sunny island of Porquerolles near Toulon, there wasn't a moment when we weren't jumping on a boat, squeezing into a bus or back at sea. Franciane, who is now part of the Marc Jacobs team at Vuitton, had planned it that way, reckoning that if their wedding were

mobile, people were less likely to be bored and that with so much travelling, guests who didn't know each other would be forced to communicate. It worked. The wedding ceremony was at a tiny church in Giens, where Franciane's mother, known for her voice, sang. Riki was tieless and decked out in a Smalto ivory suit, and Franciane wore a Lesage-embroidered cardigan over her Gilles Dufour corseted dress which was made of *broderie anglaise*. Back at the Mas du Langoustier where the dinner was held, the atmosphere resembled a 1960s Brigitte Bardot film, as the likes of Claudia Schiffer, Linda Evangelista, hairstylist Odile Gilbert and others tossed off their shoes to dance.

Although equally lovely in atmosphere, Francesca Malgara's wedding to Nino Tronchetti Provera was more sedate, perhaps because it was the blending of two dynasties. Giulio Malgara, Francesca's father, is an entrepreneur in the food world as well as the founder of Auditel which measures Italian television audiences. Nino's uncle is Marco Tronchetti Provera, the telecommunications billionaire. Guests included Silvio Berlusconi, while Luca Marzotto, the fashion textile heir, was best man. Still, although there were camera crews in the village nearby – the buzz on the power event was considerable – no media circus was allowed into Ca'Paruta, their sixteenth-century home, notable for being from the school of Palladio Villa Veneta.

Francesca wore a simple silk dress designed by Tom Ford (her sister Cristina was and remains a PR principessa at Gucci) and because the ceremony was in the family chapel downstairs, she must be the only bride known to arrive two minutes before the priest. Naturally, the lunch for 300 held *al fresco* was delicious. Saffron risotto was followed by *chianina*, a melt-in-the-mouth beef from Tuscany, and then *1000 foglie*, the traditional Italian wedding cake, made last-minute and consisting of layers and layers of strawberries. However, it was the charm of the newly weds who stopped and thanked everyone individually for coming that made the most lasting impression.

Acclaimed art consultant Abigail Asher's marriage to banker Douglas Schoninger combined an international flavour with overwhelming warmth. It was my second Jewish wedding and held in London's Victoria & Albert – a favourite museum since childhood. The ceremony with the Rabbi took place in the Raphael Cartoon room. Afterwards, Abigail – whose

clients include Tom Cruise – had to walk around her husband seven times. Happily, her fears that her husband might get wrapped, mummy-like in acres of silk tulle proved unfounded.

The dinner was given in the museum's entrance where the main central ticket office was covered beyond recognition with voluminous draped silk and an enormous vase filled with pale pink and white cascading flowers. As for the placement of the tables of eight, so much trouble had been taken that each of us felt we were attending our own dinner party. I was seated next to Christie's wunderkind auctioneer Tobias Meyer and *Tatler*'s Geordie Greg. As for the marvellous food, it had taken the bride's family twenty tastings to agree what should be served, but by Abigail's own admission, they are all 'serious foodies'.

Over the years I have attended countless weddings in locations around the world – ranging from a grand Habsburg family affair in Salzburg to a Bel Air extravaganza where all the bridesmaids were the bride's personal shoppers. And now my two little girls have finally made it as bridesmaids. When my youngest brother, Orlando, announced his engagement to Clementine Hambro, who grabbed the public's attention as Princess Di's youngest bridesmaid more than 25 years ago, I was over the moon. But I have to confess that part of the excitement was imagining my twin daughters with flowers in their hair and white satin ballet slippers on their footsies. Was I a stage momma about it? You betcha! And Clemmie was an incredible sport, managing to cope with 16 bridesmaids in her wedding entourage. Admittedly, I am biased, but it was adorable seeing the long train of hot sticky hands behind her. As for the actual ceremony – held at the protestant church of St Margaret's where her great grandparents Winston and Clementine Churchill and my maternal grandparents Frank and Elizabeth Longford all exchanged vows – it was utterly perfect; from the music, to the display of white lilies on the altar, to the speeches later, during the reception at Claridge's.

Of course, a successful wedding seems to be all about the details – the pearly smile of the bride, a linen tablecloth fluttering in the wind or the party drunk trying to stand straight. Yet it's hard not to think that, whether traditional or not, what is paramount is that the best intentions come from the heart. Weddings are so glorious because love is in the house.

Time? PARKING —

FRIDAY

Café de l'Époque lunch

° seating with Jean-Pierre ♡?

Melon for those who
don't eat foie gras?

✳ Melon for kids? _Yes_

chips for kids
WINE — how much
Check about piece
montée — who is collecting it.
How TALL is CAKE?
Ask Kathryn Ireland
to decorate tables — Need
bag, cell — Find out where stays

small chairs — high chairs?
Tumblers not stemmed glasses
C# / Pt juice; Apple juice (No Coke
Kids on Terrace

(LEFT) DRESS BEN DE LISI
(MIDDLE) VEIL ERIK HALLEY
(OPPOSITE) NECKLACE SWAROVSKI

Throughout history, two of CHINA's most enduring floral emblems have been the PEONY AND THE PLUM BLOSSOM. Because of their positive connotations, they are often depicted in elaborate embroideries on wedding dresses as an alternative to the customary dragon-and-phoenix design. So, it follows that when a Chinese bride decides to carry a bouquet in the Western style, these are among the first flowers she might consider. In this bouquet, shot at the corner of the north gate to the Forbidden City in Beijing, peonies harmonize with phalaenopsis orchids, dahlias, wonder-flowers and Swarovski crystals.

TEXT MARION VON ADLERSTEIN

Photographer Shannon Frady
Producer Ray Lee

Florist Ikebana, using Chinese peonies, phalaenopsis orchids, dahlias and wonder-flowers

NINA DONIS FOR SWAROVSKI 2007

Other cities may strive to be the most romantic in the world but few can rival VIENNA, *the city on the Danube on which history has bestowed a magnificent legacy – a way of life that epitomizes grace and culture. A wedding in the capital of Austria takes place against a backdrop of architectural and decorative splendour that spans seven centuries, from Gothic through Renaissance, Baroque, Rococo and Biedermeier to Modernism and beyond. All the senses are indulged: the patisseries for your wedding cake are the best in Europe. Then of course, there's the majestic Vienna Waltz. Though if your taste is not for Strauss, many other great masters of music were based here, including Haydn, Mozart, Schubert and Mahler.*

Photographer Emilie Erbin

Florist Sädtler GesmbH & Co KG
using hydrangea, orchids and baby's breath
www.saedtler.at

Sleeping Mask Pascal Saint André
for Kopenhagen Fur
Ring Box Kris Van Assche
Plates Deyafa Gallery
Apples Hervé Gambs

126

INVITATION CARD BOX *(Top Left)*
CREATIVE INTELLIGENCE
Note Paper and Invitations (Top Right)
CRANE & CO
Pen CARAN D'ACHE
Invitation Card Boxes and Invitations
(Bottom) REDBLISS

THE FAMILIES OF *Amy*
REQUEST THE HONOUR OF
SATURDAY, THE FIRST OF DE
ST. COLUMBA'S CHAPEL, 55 W

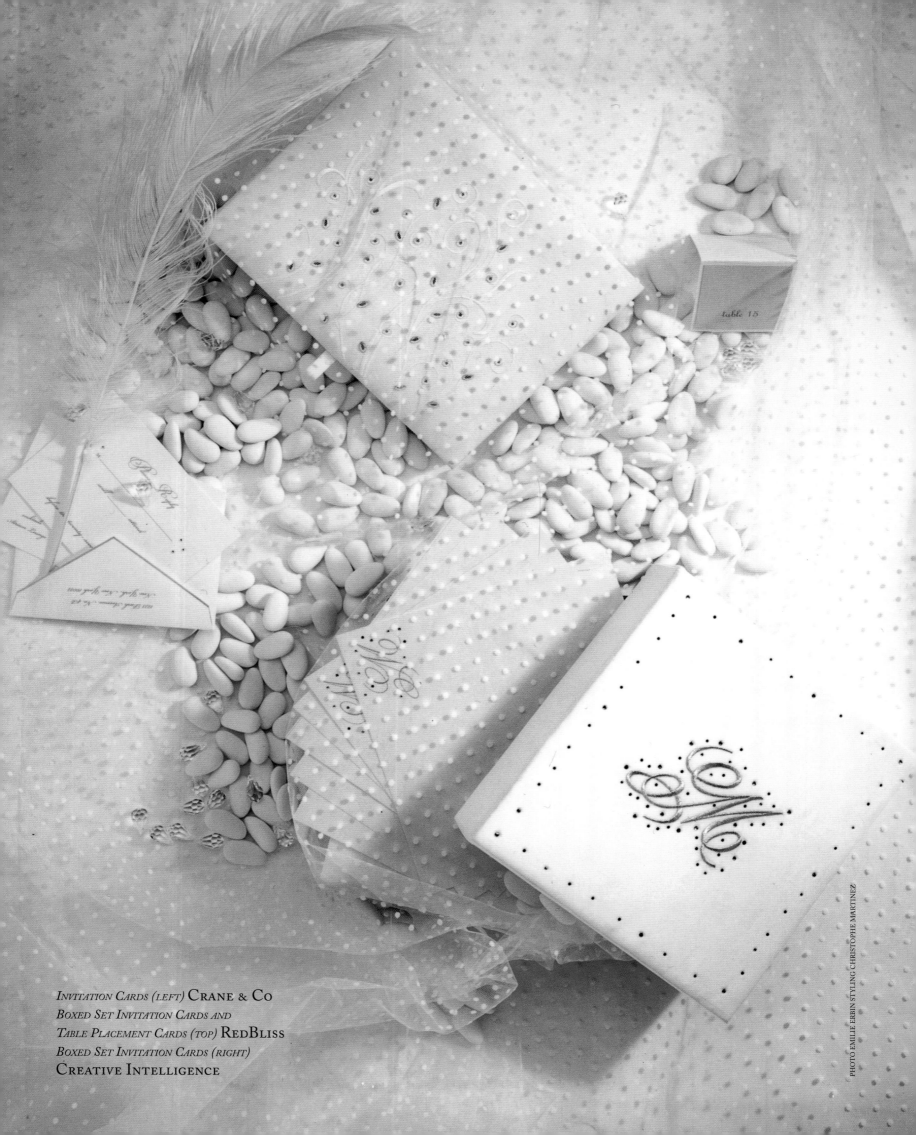

INVITATION CARDS *(LEFT)* CRANE & CO
BOXED SET INVITATION CARDS AND
TABLE PLACEMENT CARDS (TOP) REDBLISS
BOXED SET INVITATION CARDS (RIGHT)
CREATIVE INTELLIGENCE

Shoes LEIBER
Announcement Cards MARIANNE GUÉLY
Cake Set TOPPERS WITH GLITZ

PHOTO METZ & RACINE STYLING KANAKO B. KOGA

PHOTO THIERRY PÉREZ STYLING CHRISTOPHE MARTINEZ

(LEFT) DRESS RICHARD SORGER
(IN TREE) DRESS LOLITA LEMPICKA
TIARA BIJOU NEUMANN & WENZEL
(RIGHT) DRESS DANY MIZRACHI
TIARA HAUTE BRIDE

TEXT MARION VON ADLERSTEIN

However elaborate the festivities surrounding an ARAB wedding, the ceremony itself is short and simple. The bride and groom remain in separate rooms while someone schooled in Islamic law visits each to determine that their choice has been freely made and that they wish to be married. Each signs the marriage contract in front of witnesses before they are brought together as husband and wife. There are no bridesmaids, but young girls carry BASKETS OF ROSE PETALS to scatter before the bride. It is not traditional for a Muslim bride to carry flowers but those with experience of Western practices often do.

In the months before her wedding, the bride is pampered with beauty treatments. She also goes on a shopping spree. At a henna party, a few nights before the marriage, her arms, hands, feet and legs are patterned with elaborate designs. Her body anointed, her hair perfumed, her limbs hennaed, her eyes rimmed with kohl, and clad in sumptuous silks, with rings on all her fingers, the Arab bride is ready for her bridegroom.

Photographers Darrin James and Ayaad Damouni
Damouni James Photography
www.djphotography.net

Florist Lala Lenon at Worood Florist, using red, white and
pink roses, spray roses, sanini, pink wild chrysanthemum,
orchids, hyacinth and baby's breath.
www.worood.com

*"A WEDDING RESONATES AS
THE ULTIMATE SPECIAL OCCASION,
not just for the bride and groom. It carries everyone to the
summit of sentimentality – whether you are bearing
the ring or designing the dress."*

– Giorgio Armani

MINK JACKET AND DRESS ARMANI PRIVÉ
SHOES RENÉ CAOVILLA

*"IT IS IMPORTANT
TO ADAPT*

TRADITIONAL IDEAS,

*translating them
into modern,
more relevant styles
for this new age."*

– Akira Isogawa

Photography Martina Hoogland Ivanow
Styling Dan May

Dress Akira Isogawa

Baptismal Gown Dries Van Noten

Kimono Scena D'uno

Kimono CHISO

KIMONO YUMI KATSURA

"I believe the fusion of 'tradition' and 'modernity' is essential.
I always seek a way to express the artistry of Japanese
traditional techniques by blending with European
traditional beauty in order to create designs accepted
by any bride all over the world today."

Linking East and West in one dynamic city,
ISTANBUL *is a democracy that manages to be multicultural, multi-faith and secular, all at the same time. A burgeoning population of talented, energetic and worldly young people, with high disposable incomes and a fascination with fashion, is shaping this ancient metropolis into a prototype for cities of the future.*

So, the contemporary bride in Istanbul has the freedom to dip into a limitless store of the world's wedding traditions, pull out what she fancies, then put it together with her own modern style. A white wedding gown by a top international designer might now combine with the foreign custom of a bridal bouquet, such as PARROT TULIPS, RANUNCULUS AND HYPERICUM with a trail of Swarovski crystals, photographed here against the backdrop of the mighty Bosphorus at Ortakoy, one of the city's hippest neighbourhoods. In today's Istanbul, anything goes, as long as it's on the fashion world's radar.

Photographer Koray Birand
www.koraybirand.com
Producer Defne Kocabiyikoglu

Florist Selvi Kayin Guverin for
Hana Ihsan Aksoy Sokak
www.hanacicek.com

TEXT MARION VON ADLERSTEIN

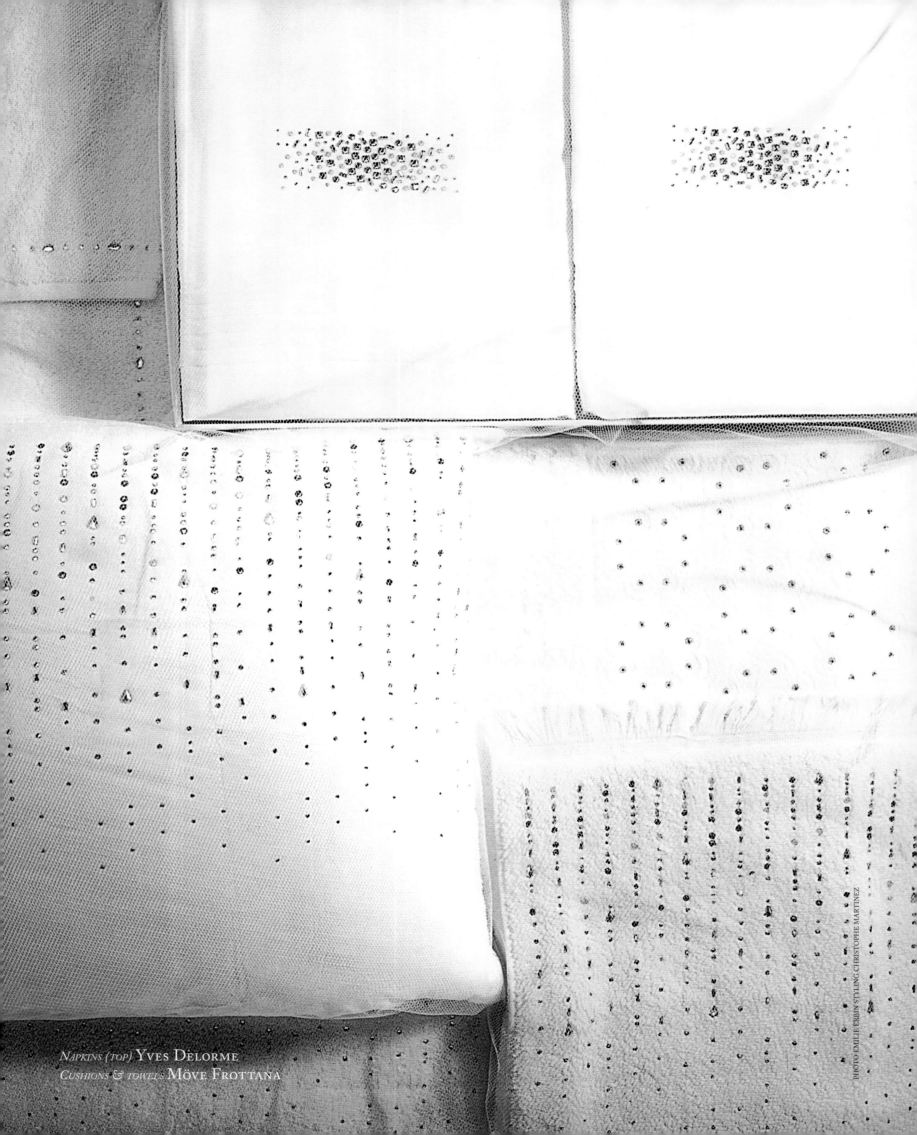

Napkins (top) YVES DÉLORME
Cushions & towels MÖVE FROTTANA

Skirt, Top & Veil SUNEET VARMA

Headpiece Alberto Rodriguez
Hairpieces Barney Cheng
Tiaras Bijou Neumann & Wenzel
Nightgown Only Hearts
Bird Fleux

photo metz & racine styling kanako b. koga

BUSTIER ROSSELLA TARABINI FOR ANNA MOLINARI
FLOWERS DOUBLE PENSÉE

In TEL AVIV, *this opulent, variegated bouquet blends Swarovski crystals with* HYDRANGEA AND THREE KINDS OF ROSES *woven into a trail of* BOUGAINVILLEA. *It also contains a pomegranate, one of seven species of crops with which Israel has been blessed. In Jewish tradition, the service is performed under a canopy (chuppah) representing the home the newly weds will make together. As a reminder of the fragility of happiness, the groom shatters a glass with his foot. The most exuberant dance is the Hora, when bride and groom, seated in chairs, are lifted into the air and bounced about in time to music.*

Photographer Ariel van Straten

Florist Kathi Tommen for Chris Weys Flowers Design & Decoration, using bougainvillea, pomegranate and hydrangea with "Lady Jane", "Cool Water" and "Black Magic" roses
www.chris-weys.com

TEXT MARION VON ADLERSTEIN

Jewelled Biscuit Box
IRINA VOLKONSKII
FOR LADURÉE

Honeymoon Travel Set
LIBERTY OF LONDON

Photographer Claudio Sardone
With thanks to Daniela Natale & Paola Cernigliaro

Florist Cento Rose e un Tulipano
www.centoroseuntulipano.it

TEXT MARION VON ADLERSTEIN

The style of MILANESE *women is legendary, so the finery a bride wears to her wedding in Italy's fashion capital is as elegant as it is individual. The Roman Catholic Church regards marriage as a divinely-blessed contract between baptised adults and the ceremony usually takes place within a Nuptial Mass. Before they undertake such a deep commitment, the engaged couple are required to see their priest regularly to prepare them for what lies ahead.*

Dog Collar Manfred of Sweden

Dress John Galliano

Bouquet Philippe Ferrandis

Photography Serge Leblon
Styling Jamie Surman

Dress Silvia Tcherassi

"HOW DO I APPROACH DESIGNING A WEDDING DRESS?

With twenty questions and a lot of diplomacy!"

— MARTIN GRANT

Dress Wacoal Dia

Dress Celestina Agostino

DRESS AZZARO

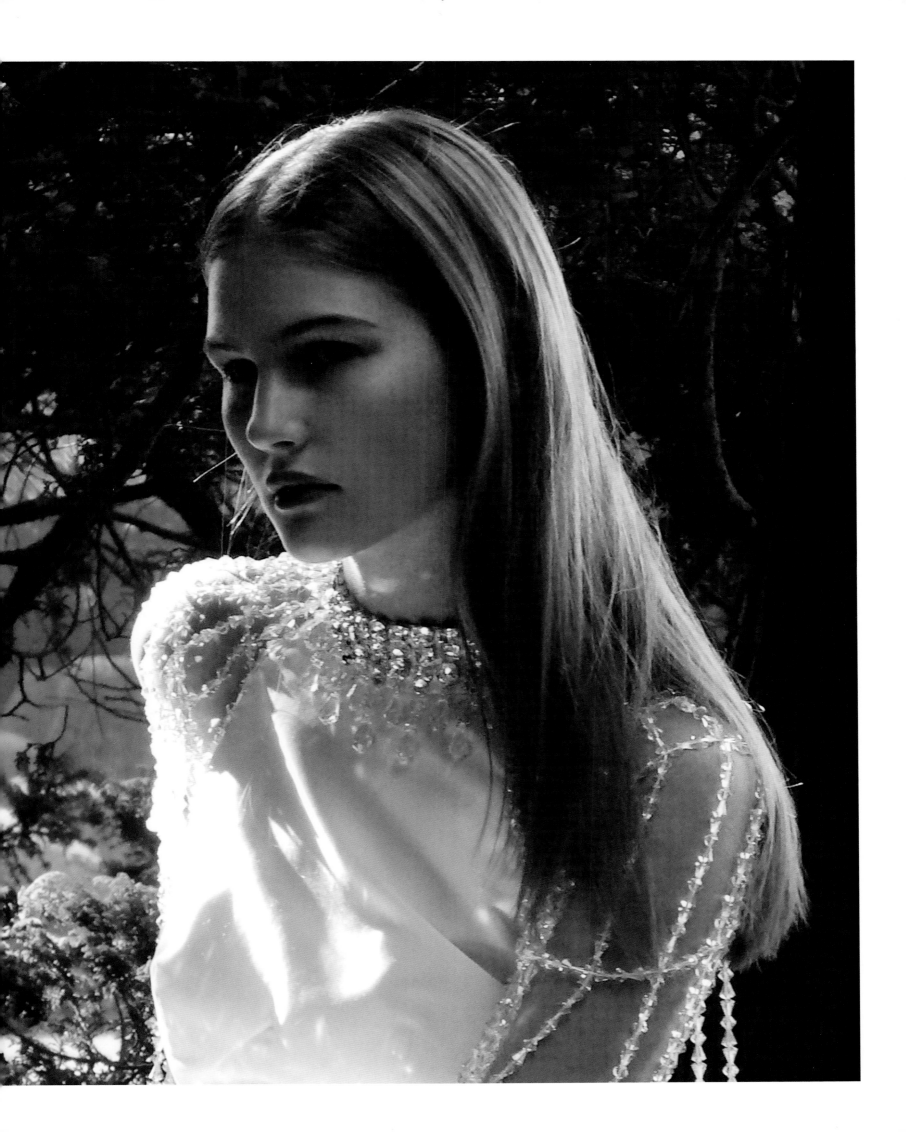

Dress ESCADA

Hair Chi Wong at Untitled
Makeup Florrie White at D&V Management
Model Bobby Wiens at Elite Paris

"Nynke and I adore the concept of sharing a lifetime: TWO SWANS THAT NEVER LEAVE EACH OTHER.

*Within our iconographic collections
the candle and candle holder symbolize Hope.
These two archetypal but oversized candle holders
(to celebrate everyday life and make us appear humble)
are joined by a thick, never to be broken, ring."*

– Job Smeets

Candlestick Sculptures Nynke Tynagel &
Job Smeets (Studio Job)

NEW YORKERS *of all denominations flock to Central Park to celebrate their nuptials in the open air. They may live in steely skyscrapers and modern lofts, but nothing gets local hearts racing like a sentimental journey around the Park in a horse-drawn carriage. Just watch out for those crazy cab drivers…*

Photographer Gavin Bond
Art direction Bradley Garlock for Garlock-DeGuiceis
www.garlockdeguiceis.com

Florist Tom Borgese, using calla lilies
tom@tomborgese.com

Photo Album, Wrapping Paper SHEPHERDS

Sofa SQUINT
Shoes JONATHAN KELSEY

TABLECLOTH PAUL RENWICK
BRACELET SWAROVSKI

In FRANCE, *the bride and groom go through two wedding ceremonies. First, a civil one at the town hall which legalizes their union. Here the newly weds are given a livret de famille, a small book in which to record milestones in their future life together. The second ceremony is a religious one and may proceed only after the civil marriage certificate is presented. And then, a party, with the traditional wedding cake, a croquembouche – a glazed pyramid of profiteroles filled with confectioner's custard – as the centre-piece.*

Photographer Emilie Erbin

Florist La Fontaine fleurie, using roses, lisianthus and ivy

TEXT MARION VON ADLERSTEIN

"The royal wedding of the Prince of Wales and the Duchess of Cornwall was the best wedding I ever attended. The excitement of seeing the royal couple walking down the aisle in something I had designed was the highlight of my career so far."

– PHILIP TREACY

Dress Monique Lhuillier

Dress Giambattista Valli

Headpiece
DANIEL SWAROVSKI

DRESS AND HEADPIECE
ALICE TEMPERLEY

DRESS CHRISTOPHER KANE

"Usually a wedding dress becomes a valuable piece of family history and a part of happy memories.

I ALWAYS KEEP THIS IN MIND AND PUT ALL MY EFFORTS INTO CREATING A REAL MASTERPIECE."

– IGOR CHAPURIN

VEIL CHAPURIN

Hair James Pecis at D&V Management
Makeup Alex Box at D&V Management
Model Rosa Curtain at ICM Models
For more details see page 207

THEY
SAID

.

i do

3.1 Phillip Lim

Phillip Lim launched his 3.1 Phillip Lim collection in New York in 2005 to almost instant critical acclaim. Originally studying Finance at California State University, he quickly switched courses, eventually finding a fashion internship then moving on to establish his own-name label. After only two years, the collection is available in 26 countries.

www.31philliplim.com

6267

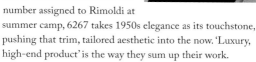

Working under the name 6267, Tommaso Aquilano and Roberto Rimondi are the newest design phenomena to come out of Milan. Named after the number assigned to Rimoldi at summer camp, 6267 takes 1950s elegance as its touchstone, pushing that trim, tailored aesthetic into the now. 'Luxury, high-end product' is the way they sum up their work.

www.castor-moda.it

Akira Isogawa

Born in Japan, Akira Isogawa emigrated to Australia in 1986 at the age of 22. Trained in fashion design at East Sydney Technical College, he launched his eponymous label in 1993. Blending key aesthetics of the East and West, his designs call upon traditional Japanese fabrics and vintage kimonos, which are resculpted into cool contemporary clothing.

www.akira.com.au

Alberta Ferretti

Alberta Ferretti is a modern romantic. Her trademark pleated, draped and swathed dresses have made her a favourite of those seeking a fresh, light approach to womenswear. Since the label's debut at Milan in 1983, it has gone from strength to strength, constantly evolving a clear vision of the modern woman's wardrobe.

www.albertaferretti.com

Alberto Rodriguez

Born in 1966, Mexican designer Alberto Rodriguez began his fashion career as an advertising creative, then as an illustrator, before deciding to launch his own-name fashion design house. His collections, he says, are an ode to the contemporary Latin female, 'a romantic woman who dreams with her eyes open'.

www.albertorodriguez.com.mx

Alice Temperley

Born in England in 1975, Alice Temperley trained in fashion design at London's Central Saint Martins College. Launching her own-name label in 2000, she became noted for her innovative approach to fabric treatments, most often having recourse to handmade techniques such as embroidery, printing and beading.

www.temperleylondon.com

Amato by Furne One

Furne One began his fashion career in the Philippines, before moving to Dubai and opening his Amato Couture fashion house in 2004. Based on traditional embroidery and beading techniques, Furne One's designs push fashion forward 'using Western influence and just the right amount of deconstruction'.

www.amatohautecouture.com

Anna Molinari

In 1995, Rossella Tarabini designed her first collection for the label named after her mother, Anna Molinari. An Arts graduate of Bologna University, Tarabini moved to London to further her studies. On returning to Italy she joined the family business, starting out as a creative on ad campaigns and fashion shows.

www.annamolinari.it

Anne Barge

As a bridal-wear specialist, Atlanta-based designer Anne Barge takes inspiration from fantasy clothing of all epochs, from the 1700s to the 1950s to today. The brand comprises three distinct lines – Black Label, Couture and La Fleur – each combining classic elegance with current style trends for the discerning bride.

www.annebarge.com

Antonio Berardi

A graduate of London's Central Saint Martins College of Art & Design, UK-based Antonio Berardi allows his Sicilian roots to cohabit with his English upbringing, resulting in designs that are at once restrained and gloriously offbeat. Elaborate and vivacious, but with an undeniably modern edge, his clothes follow a woman's form to sculptural effect.

www.antonioberardi.com

Awatif Al-Hai

Awatif Al-Hai lives and works in Kuwait, where she runs her couture fashion house, specializing in elaborately draped evening dresses and body-hugging gowns perfect for making that head-turning entrance. Her client list includes some of the most prestigious names in the Gulf States, including a new younger customer drawn to her lively daywear line.

www.awatifalhai.com

Azzaro

Since taking over the reins of Azzaro in 2003, Vanessa Seward has guaranteed a coherent future for a house renowned for its clean, modern lines. A graduate of Paris' Studio Berçot, Seward spent nine years assisting Karl Lagerfeld at Chanel before moving to Yves Saint Laurent under the tutelage of Tom Ford.

www.azzaroparis.com

Barnaby Barford

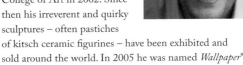

Barnaby Barford graduated with an MA in Ceramics and Glass from London's Royal College of Art in 2002. Since then his irreverent and quirky sculptures – often pastiches of kitsch ceramic figurines – have been exhibited and sold around the world. In 2005 he was named *Wallpaper* magazine's Designer of the Year.

www.barnabybarford.co.uk

Barney Cheng

Hong Kong designer Barney Cheng studied Textile Design at the Royal College of Art in London and Fashion History at the Parson's School, Paris. Armed with this experience, he returned to Hong Kong, establishing his studio there in 1993, to create custom order one-off pieces as well as ready-to-wear.

www.barneycheng.com

Ben de Lisi

New York-born designer Ben de Lisi studied sculpture at the Pratt Institute before moving to London in 1982. Launching his eponymous collection that year, he has been showing his signature glamorous gowns and sexy daywear at London Fashion Week since 1995. He offers an exclusive, one-off, made-to-measure bridal service.

www.bendelisi.com

Bijou Neumann & Wenzel

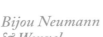

Bijou Neumann & Wenzel is a well-established Austrian company specializing in premium-quality fashion jewellery for day and evening wear. Under the design direction of 22-year-old Natalie Rausch, the label creates vibrant, fresh designs using silver, semi-precious stones and crystal.

www.newe.at

Bodo Sperlein

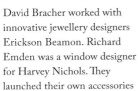

London-based product designer Bodo Sperlein specializes in home accessories such as lighting, furniture and table/giftware, as well as jewellery. In addition to developing his own collections, Sperlein also acts as a design consultant, undertaking projects for global clients as diverse as Mulberry, Dibbern, Du Pont and Lladró.

www.bodosperlein.com

Bracher Emden

David Bracher worked with innovative jewellery designers Erickson Beamon. Richard Emden was a window designer for Harvey Nichols. They launched their own accessories collection in Spring 2001, and their unashamedly brazen belts, cuffs and bags were met with immediate critical acclaim.

www.bracheremden.com

Celestina Agostino

Born in Calabria, Italy, Celestina Agostino acquired a taste for fashion from her couturière mother. She began her career in publishing, before turning to fashion, opening her first own-name boutique in 1993. Since 2002, Celestina Agostino for Le Bon Marché department store, Paris, has been supplying elegant gowns for discerning brides.

juliette.brouard@wanadoo.fr

Chantal Thomass

Chantal Thomass launched her eponymous ready-to-wear collection in 1975. Within a few years, her label had become identified as a leader in the new breed of French lingerie brands. Recreating corsetry, suspender belts and basques in refined, precious fabrics, for more than 30 years, Chantal Thomass has epitomized all that is chic in underwear.

www.chantalthomass.fr

Chapurin

The Chapurin Couture label was launched in 1992, after Igor Chapurin won a young designer contest organized by Nina Ricci, Paris. Since then the Moscovite couturier has created ready-to-wear and couture collections, achieving a savvy balance of traditional with cutting-edge. He has also designed costumes for the prestigious Bolshoi Ballet.

www.chapurin.com

Chiso

Founded over 450 years ago in Kyoto, with an extensive archive of exclusive handmade patterns, Chiso's motto is 'Create Beautiful'. Under the guidance of current CEO Souzaemon Nishimura, the house's elegant, graphic designs are the manifestation of this creed. Steeped in tradition, each Chiso kimono is startlingly modern in its allure.

www.chiso.co.jp

Christopher Kane

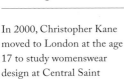

In 2000, Christopher Kane moved to London at the age of 17 to study womenswear design at Central Saint Martins College of Art & Design. His debut collection – inscribed in the body-hugging 1980s' style of Gianni Versace and Azzedine Alaïa – was shown at London Fashion Week in 2006 to almost instant critical acclaim.

studio@christopherkane.co.uk

Collette Dinnigan

Collette Dinnigan began her career as a costume designer. By 1990 she had launched her eponymous label, specializing in delicate, feminine designs in precious fabrics, evolved from the idea of underwear as outerwear. Since 1996 she has shown her collections as an official invitee of the Paris Chambre Syndicale.

www.collettedinnigan.com.au

Daniel Swarovski / Swarovski

A graduate of New York's Fashion Institute of Technology, Nathalie Colin-Roblique began her fashion career at Perry Ellis, alongside designer Marc Jacobs. In 1994 she began consulting to Swarovski on trends and design, and in 2006 she was named Creative Director of the brands Daniel Swarovski and Swarovski.

www.swarovski.com

Dany Mizrachi

Born in Tel Aviv, Dany Mizrachi began working in his family's fashion business at the age of 17 and was given the humble task of ironing the clothes. In 1991 he established his own studio and label, specializing in radically romantic bridal wear. His collections typically explore new approaches to avant garde yet sexy femininity.

www.danymizrachi.com

Demakersvan

Jeroen Verhoeven, Joep Verhoeven and Judith de Graauw were all born in 1976. All three attended the prestigious Design Academy Eindhoven, specializing in product and (in Joep's case) interior design. They graduated simultaneously in 2004, and established Demakersvan design group in 2005. For *Unbridaled* they collaborated with Joris Laarman.

www.demakersvan.com

Doshi Levien

Nina Doshi was born in Bombay and studied at the National Institute of Design in Ahmedabad. Jonathan Levien was born in Scotland, and studied furniture design at London's Royal College of Art. They met in London in 1995, married and set up the Doshi Levien design company in 2000, working with manufacturers such as Moroso.

www.doshilevien.com

Dresscamp

Born in 1974, Toshikazu Iwaya graduated from the Bunka Fashion College, Tokyo, in 1995. Beginning his career as a textile designer, he finally launched the Dresscamp fashion label in 2002, garnering immediate critical acclaim. His work has been described by the *International Herald Tribune* as 'flamboyantly decorative and naughty'.

www.dresscamp.org

Dries Van Noten

Born in Antwerp in 1958, Dries Van Noten attended the Antwerp Royal Academy. In 1985 he launched his own line and, a year later, received both international acclaim and commercial success when he presented his men's collection in London along with the 'Antwerp Six'. Van Noten's flagship store, Het Modepaleis, opened in Antwerp in 1989.

www.driesvannoten.be

Elie Saab

Born in Beirut, Elie Saab opened his first atelier in 1982 at the age of eighteen, creating garments from myriad cross-cultural influences. In 1997 Saab was invited to take part in Milan's fashion schedule. Since 2003 he has shown his haute couture collection in Paris, as an officially invited member of the Chambre Syndicale.

www.eliesaab.com

Emilio Pucci

Launched by Emilio Pucci in 1947, the Florentine fashion house quickly gained renown for its sporty lines and wild ways with print. British designer Matthew Williamson was named Creative Director in 2006. His eye for colour and pattern, and his trademark easy tailoring are pushing the house's past into the future.

www.emiliopucci.com

Erdem

Half-Turkish, half-British, Erdem Moralioglu first studied Liberal Arts in Montreal, but subsequently moved on to fashion design at Toronto's Ryerson University. Upon completing his Master's Degree at London's Royal College of Art, he worked for Diane Von Furstenberg before launching his own collection in London in 2005.

www.erdem.co.uk

Erickson Beamon

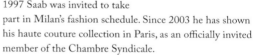

Detroit natives Karen Erickson and Vicki Beamon launched their jewellery label in New York in 1983. A spontaneous reaction to the lack of fun, funky jewellery to fit the mid-80s mood, their first collection of hand-strung crystals and beads on suede was an overnight sensation. The Erickson Beamon London flagship store opened in 1995.

www.ericksonbeamon.com

Erik Halley

Since 1994, French accessory designer Erik Halley has continually surprised with his radical jewellery designs. As well as working under his own name, Halley has also designed for prestigious houses such as Ungaro, Givenchy, Lacroix, Chanel and Mugler, bringing to each a unique concept of modern embellishment.

erikhalley@noos.fr

Escada

Founded in 1976 by Margaretha and Wolfgang Ley, Escada soared to success in the highly ornamental 1980s. Since its listing on the stock exchange in 1986, Escada has expanded into a highly recognizable global brand. Since 2006 Escada has been under the creative guidance of Italian-born designer Damiano Biella, former Design Director of Valentino.

www.escada.com

Fredrikson Stallard

Patrik Fredrikson and Ian Stallard began their creative collaboration in 1995 and have since become recognized leading exponents of radical British design. Their cutting-edge furniture and products are conceptually rigorous whilst being visually aesthetic, assuring them a place in the collections of the cognescenti.

www.fredriksonstallard.com

Gert van de Merwe

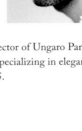

Based in Cape Town, South Africa, for twenty years designer Gert van de Merwe has provided his discerning clientele with timelessly elegant evening and bridal designs. His studio – now also available by appointment in London – specializes in exquisite fabrics and finely embellished details.

www.gertvandemerwe.com

Giambattista Valli

Born in Rome, Giambattista Valli studied at London's Central Saint Martins College of Art & Design before joining Roberto Capucci and then Fendi as senior designer. After a period spent as Art Director of Ungaro Paris, he launched his eponymous label specializing in elegant, feminine dresses in March 2005.

www.giambattistavalli.com

Giorgio Armani

From his headquarters in Milan, Giorgio Armani reigns over one of the world's most successful fashion and lifestyle design houses, with a network of over 300 exclusive retail stores in 39 countries. The epitome of understated chic, the brand comprises ready-to-wear, accessories, homewares and the exclusive Privé couture line.

www.giorgioarmani.com

Giuseppe Zanotti

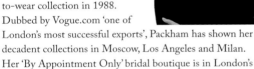

Born in the Italian shoemaking region of San Mauro Pascoli, Giuseppe Zanotti began his career as an apprentice in women's luxury footwear. Establishing his own label in 1994 with his wife Cinzia, the Zanotti label quickly became associated with rigorous design standards. 'The way the shoe is crafted is essential for its success,' says Giuseppe.

www.giuseppe-zanotti-design.com

Gunjan Gupta

A graduate of London's Central Saint Martins College of Art & Design, Gunjan Gupta founded Wrap Art & Design in New Delhi in 2006. Based on the premise that 'wrapping something attaches a new set of values to it', her work typically consists of pared-down, refined lines, embellished by a layer of precious material such as gold or silver leaf.

www.wrap.co.in

Haider Ackermann

Born in Sante Fe de Bogota, Colombia, to French parents, Haider Ackermann grew up in various cities throughout Europe and Africa. After graduating from Antwerp's Academy of Art he launched his own label in Paris in 2001. A global nomad, Ackermann's work is about contrasts – the mix of high and low, the melting pot of cultural aesthetics.

katou@michelemontagne.com

Haute Bride

Lindsie Jones studied Human Resources Management before turning her attention to jewellery design, launching the Haute Bride accessories label in 2002. Today the collection of fine bridal accessories – tiaras, chokers and brooches – is available in more than 80 bridal salons throughout the USA and Canada.

www.hautebride.com

Jenny Packham

A graduate of Saint Martins College of Art, Jenny Packham launched her signature ready-to-wear collection in 1988. Dubbed by Vogue.com 'one of London's most successful exports', Packham has shown her decadent collections in Moscow, Los Angeles and Milan. Her 'By Appointment Only' bridal boutique is in London's ritzy Belgravia area.

www.jennypackham.com

JJ Valaya

Born in Rajasthan, JJ Valaya studied at New Delhi's National Institute of Fashion Technology, graduating in 1991. He launched his own label in the same year, and opened India's largest single designer store five years later. The first 'JJ Valaya Life' international lifestyle store opened in New Delhi in 2004.

www.valaya.com

John Galliano

Born in Gibraltar, at the age of six John Galliano and his family moved to London, where in 1984 he graduated from Central Saint Martins. Since launching his label, Galliano's extravagant vision and extraordinary cutting skills have seen him named British Designer of the Year four times. Since 1997 he has designed for Christian Dior, Paris.

www.johngalliano.com

Jonathan Kelsey

Drawing inspiration from the 1920s and 1960s, Jonathan Kelsey creates unashamedly sexy shoes. After graduating from Central Saint Martins, Kelsey joined the atelier of iconic shoe designer Jimmy Choo in 1996. Five years later, he branched out on his own, working freelance for houses such as Cacharel, Gina and Giles Deacon.

www.jonathankelsey.com

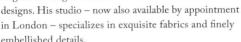

(HAIDER ACKERMANN) SOPHIE DREIJER

Joris Laarman

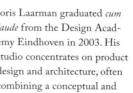

Joris Laarman graduated *cum laude* from the Design Academy Eindhoven in 2003. His studio concentrates on product design and architecture, often combining a conceptual and poetic approach with style and engineering. For his *Unbridaled* contribution he collaborated with the Demakersvan design team.

www.jorislaarman.com

Julien Macdonald

Born in Wales, Julien Macdonald studied at London's Royal College of Art. Upon graduating in 1996 he was named head knitwear designer at Chanel, and began developing his own-name line. In 2001 he became Creative Director of Givenchy, a post he held until returning to London to concentrate on his eponymous label in 2004.

julienmacdonaldstudio@btconnect.com

Karen Walker

Karen Walker is a New Zealand-born fashion designer with a reputation for original, effortless and unpretentious style. The Karen Walker clothing label is stocked in over 140 stores throughout the world in cities including New York, London, Hong Kong, Los Angeles and Sydney and in over 20 cities throughout Japan.

www.karenwalker.com

Kris Van Assche

A graduate of Antwerp's Royal Academy of Art, Kris Van Assche established his own label in 2004, at the age of 28, after working at Yves Saint Laurent Homme and Dior Homme. Van Assche's strong modern tailoring skills and inherent sense of elegance saw him named Artistic Director of Dior Homme in April 2007.

www.krisvanassche.com

Ladurée

The Parisian tea room famed for its delicious macaroon biscuits was established in 1862. Today Ladurée sells some 135 tonnes of macaroons a year in its four Parisian and two international tea rooms. Accessories and product designer Irina Volkonskii has reinterpreted the house's signature biscuit box as a wedding table centre-piece.

www.laduree.fr

La Perla

At the age of 22, Bologna-born Anna Masotti joined the family business, La Perla. Sharing her father's passion for communication, and her mother's love of fine fabrics worked into excellent product, she spent several years on research and field work. Today she is Artistic Director of the La Perla group.

www.laperla.it

Leiber

Founded in 1963 by Judith Leiber, the Leiber label was quickly recognized as a pre-eminent American luxury brand. Leiber bags alone are cultural icons. Since 2004, the label has been under the creative direction of designer Frank Zambrelli, a graduate of New York's Fashion Institute of Technology who began his career at Chanel.

www.judithleiber.com

Lemarié

Lemarié is one of the rare *plumassier* (feather ateliers) still working today. Under Artistic Director Eric Charles-Donatien, the venerable house is now part of the exclusive club of couture suppliers belonging to Chanel. Trained at the Ecole de la Chambre Syndicale de la Couture, Charles-Donatien worked for Hermès before joining Lemarié ten years ago.

e.charles-donatien@wanadoo.fr

Liberty of London

Launched in 2005 under the creative direction of Tamara Salman, Liberty of London is the stand-alone brand of 130-year-old Liberty department store. Half-Iraqi, half-British, Salman incarnates the exoticism and eclecticism on which the Liberty identity is built. Her highly decorative Arts and Crafts-inspired designs echo the store's opulent past.

www.libertyoflondon.co.uk

Linda Florence

London-based designer Linda Florence produces bespoke, hand-printed wallpaper for commercial and domestic interiors. Trained at Central Saint Martins College of Art, Florence's printing techniques incorporate a mixture of traditional and new technologies including silkscreen print, laser etching, flocking and a range of unusual surfaces.

www.lindaflorence.co.uk

Lolita Lempicka

Lolita Lempicka founded her fashion house in 1984, quickly becoming known for her romantic, elegant, feminine approach to fashion. Les Mariées de Lolita, her bridal line, was launched in 1994, specializing in fantasy robes with appellations such as 'fée' or 'siren' – looks and attitudes straight out of a fairy tale.

www.lolitalempicka.com

Manfred of Sweden

Swedish television personalities Ann and Björn Gärdsby were born in 1954. Inspired by her milliner mother, Ann began making clothes at an early age. After studying law, Björn was drawn to the world of art and music. Together they launched the Manfred of Sweden canine clothing line in 2003.

www.manfredofsweden.com

Manik Mercian

Born in 1979, Jenny Manik Mercian studied Fashion and Textiles at the University of Technology, Sydney. After working for various Australian labels, she launched her own line of hand-crafted, one-off pieces in 2005. She has since created showstoppers for Victoria's Secret, Mary J Blige and Mariah Carey.

www.manikmercian.com

Marianne Guély

Since graduating from the Olivier de Serres School of Applied Arts in Paris, Marianne Guély has become renowned for her elaborate sculptural works in paper. Often large-scale, always intricately conceived, she has created installations for luxury brands such as Cartier, Hermès, Roger Vivier, Pucci and Christofle.

www.marianne-guely.com

Marios Schwab

Twenty-eight-year-old Greek/ Austrian designer Marios Schwab studied in Berlin where he graduated with Best Student Award from Esmod. After completing an MA in Womenswear from Central Saint Martins College of Art & Design in 2003 he debuted his eponymous collection at London Fashion Week in 2006.

www.mariosschwab.com

Martin Grant

Australian-born Martin Grant launched his first ready-to-wear line at the age of 16, in 1982. A rapid success, in 1991 he moved to England to learn bespoke tailoring with Koji Tatsuno. A year later he moved to Paris, where he opened his first boutique in 1996. Sculptural silhouettes, impeccable tailoring and fine detailing are his trademarks.

www.martingrantparis.com

Miss Blumarine

In 1997, Anna Molinari and her husband Gianpaolo Tarabini established the Blumarine label. Today they are at the helm of an empire encompassing the Blumarine, Anna Molinari, Miss Blumarine and Blugirl labels. Whimsical, lyrical and feminine, Anna Molinari's designs are the epitome of modern romance.

www.blumarine.com

Monique Lhuillier

Born in the Philippines, Monique Lhuillier studied at the Fashion Institute of Design and Merchandising in Los Angeles. In 1996 she launched her first bridal collection. Five years later she developed her first evening collection. Since then, the elegant simplicity of her designs has made her Beverly Hills boutique a must-go destination.

www.moniquelhuillier.com

Nina Donis

Nina Neretina and Donis Pouppis studied at the Moscow Textile Academy, often collaborating on projects until their graduation in 1992. Since then they have come together officially under the brand name Nina Donis, a label which was included in *i-D* magazine's influential *Fashion Now: the world's 150 most important designers*.

www.ninadonis.com

Otazu

Rodrigo Otazu was born in Buenos Aires, Argentina. Inspired by the opulent designs of Emmanuel Ungaro, Rifat Ozbek and Christian Lacroix, he began making jewellery. The glamour and dramatic appeal of Otazu's designs has attracted attention from celebrities including Kelis, Lauren Hill, Aretha Franklin, Destiny's Child, and Lil' Kim.

www.rodrigootazu.com

Pascal Saint André

Pascal Saint André was born 'some time in the Sixties'. He studied design at the Ecole des Beaux Arts at Toulouse before moving to Paris to begin a career as a show designer. But he soon found his true calling in jewellery. After working with cult designer Erik Halley, Saint André accepted a position working in the atelier of Ungaro Couture.

www.myspace.com/labourette

Paul Renwick

Born and raised in Scotland, Paul Renwick studied Fashion and Textiles at Sussex University, England. After 20 years as a fashion designer for European and American houses, he launched his own company in 2006, specializing in custom textile goods. Working to order, Paul Renwick offers bespoke service on luxury table- and bedlinens.

www.paulrenwick.net

Philip Treacy

Born in small-town Ireland, Philip Treacy studied fashion at Dublin's National College of Art & Design, before moving on to London's Royal College of Art. Specializing in head-wear, his career took off when he was taken under the wing of the late, legendary fashion editor Isabella Blow. His hats are whimsical, 3-D sculptures, made to be worn.

www.philiptreacy.co.uk

Philippe Ferrandis

Frenchman Philippe Ferrandis created his accessory and jewellery design company in Paris in 1986. As well as his twice-yearly collections of finely-crafted, spectacular pieces, Ferrandis has accessorized the fashion shows of houses such as Balmain, Oscar de la Renta, Escada, Nina Ricci, Scherrer and Chanel.

www.philippeferrandis.com

Rami Al Ali

Born to a Syrian family in 1972, Rami Al Ali completed his degree in Visual Communications at the Faculty of Fine Arts at Damascus University in 1995. In 1997 he settled in Dubai, working with several prominent Arab fashion houses, before launching his own couture house in 2001.

www.ramialali.com

Reem Acra

Reem Acra studied at the Esmod School of Design (Paris) and the Fashion Institute of Technology (New York) before launching her eponymous bridal and evening-wear brand. As well as her private-order salon in Manhattan, her collections sell through some of the world's leading retailers, including Saks and Neiman Marcus.

www.reemacra.com

René Caovilla

Trained at his father Edoardo's side, René Caovilla began making hand-crafted shoes in the 1950s, forging a solid link between fashion and art. A close collaborator of couture houses such as Valentino, Christian Dior and Chanel, Caovilla specializes in dreamlike, unashamedly elaborate fairy-tale footwear.

www.renecaovilla.com

Richard James

Opening his first store on Savile Row in 1992, Richard James heralded a new era of chic male dressing. Melding the traditional sensibilities of a classical tailor with the verve of a modern retailer, Tom Cruise, Pete Doherty and Noel Gallagher were soon counted among his clientele. The first Richard James boutique opened in Tokyo in 2007.

www.richardjames.co.uk

Richard Sorger

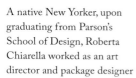

Graduating with a degree in Fashion Design from Middlesex Polytechnic in 1991, Richard Sorger worked for several years in the fashion industry before taking up teaching at the London College of Fashion. He launched his eponymous label in 2004, specializing in elaborately detailed embroideries and hand-finished details.

www.richardsorger.com

Roberta Chiarella

A native New Yorker, upon graduating from Parson's School of Design, Roberta Chiarella worked as an art director and package designer for companies such as Clinique, Ralph Lauren and Cacharel. After time spent as Vice President of Creative for Yves Saint Laurent Perfume, today her own-name jewellery collection is sold around the world.

www.robertachiarella.com

Roksanda Ilincic

After studying Architecture and Applied Arts in her native Belgrade, Roksanda Ilincic moved to London, where she completed a Masters Degree in Womenswear at Central Saint Martins College of Art & Design. She launched her own label in 2003, featuring demi-couture garments crafted from exclusive fabrics, all with a modern edge.

www.roksandailincic.com

Romona Keveza

Romona Keveza studied Fine Arts and Business before opening specialized ready-to-wear retail stores in Canada and the USA. Exclusive evening wear followed, and soon Romona Keveza became a specialist bridal designer. Today her garments are available in approaching 100 of the best bridal salons around the world.

www.romonakeveza.com

Scena D'uno

Born in 1975, multi-talented Japanese model, actress, TV celebrity and former ballerina Uno Kanda was awarded the 43rd F.E.C. 'Celebrity of the Year' prize in 1999. Two years later she launched her Scena D'uno fashion label and is now a successful designer of sumptuous bridal wear.

www.kuraudia.com

Silvia Tcherassi

Colombian designer Silvia Tcherassi began her career as an interior designer, before deciding to take up fashion. In 1987 she began making garments she sold to local stores, by 2003 she was officially invited to show her collections in Milan, and the next year in Paris. Today, Silvia Tcherassi creates ready-to-wear, couture and bridal gowns.

www.silviatcherassi.com

Sinha-Stanic

Half-Indian, half-British, Fiona Sinha was born in Scotland. Aleksander Stanic was born in Croatia. The pair studied in the same class at Central Saint Martins College of Art & Design in London. Teaming up after graduation, the Sinha-Stanic label was launched to wide critical acclaim in 2004.

www.sinhastanic.com

Sohad Acouri

Sohad Acouri graduated from the Academy Michelangelo of Fine Art, Beirut, in 1992. He had opened his own design atelier before even beginning a degree in fashion design, and launched a couture house in Jumeirah, Dubai, in 2000. His design studio focuses essentially on evening wear and bridal design.

www.sohadacouri.com

Squint

Lisa Whatmough studied Sculpture at the UK's Winchester School of Art, graduating in 1990. In 2005 she set up Squint, an interior design company specializing in the patchworking of existing objects in a riot of clashing antique fabrics. Mirrors, lamps, furniture and even teapots have all been reborn as elaborate works of craft.

www.squintlimited.com

Stephen Jones

Born in Cheshire, Stephen Jones studied at St Martins during the day and became a style icon of London by night – a regular feature at the legendary Blitz nightclub, he was always exquisitely dressed, and always crowned with a striking hat of his own idiosyncratic design. By 1980 he had opened his own millinery salon.

www.stephenjonesmillinery.com

Studio Job

Job Smeets studied 3-dimensional design at the Eindhoven Academy, where Nynke Tynagel studied graphic design. Together, they work under the banner Studio Job, producing finely-crafted pieces that often play with perceptions of function or scale. Treading a fine line between art and industrial design, their pieces reflect on the culture at large.

www.studiojob.nl

Suneet Varma

After graduating from the London School of Fashion in 1986, Suneet Varma worked at Nicole Farhi in London then Yves Saint Laurent in Paris. As well as his own couture, ready-to-wear and diffusion lines, Varma has developed fabrics and techniques for houses around the world, including Donna Karan, Caroline Herrera and Nicole Miller.

www.suneetvarma.com

Talbot & Runhof

American-born Johnny Talbot trained in Engineering at Vanderbilt University. German-born Adrian Runhof studied Business Management. The pair developed their fashion labels separately before coming together as Talbot & Runhof in 2000. Since 2005 they have shown on the official calendar of Paris Fashion Week.

www.talbotrunhof.com

Tarun Tahiliani

Starting his career with a degree in Business Management in the USA, upon returning to India Tarun Tahiliani realized the enormous potential that existed in the fine clothing sector. In 1987 he opened his first fashion boutique in India. In 1990 he founded the Tarun Tahiliani Design Studio, specializing in elaborate fashion and jewellery designs.

www.taruntahiliani.com

Tomoko Azumi

Born in Hiroshima, Japan in 1966, Tomoko Azumi studied at Kyoto University before transferring to an MA in Furniture Design at London's Royal College of Art. In 1995 Tomoko opened the AZUMI studio in London with husband Shin. She is a Research Fellow at London Metropolitan University and a tutor at the Royal College of Arts.

www.azumi.co.uk

Vera Wang

A native New Yorker, Vera Wang was a *Vogue* fashion editor for 16 years before joining Ralph Lauren as Design Director. In 1990 she opened her flagship store on Madison Avenue, specializing in fashion-forward bridal designs. In 2005 she received the Designer of the Year award from the Council of Fashion Designers of America (CFDA).

www.verawang.com

Victoria Bartlett

Victoria Bartlett graduated from the London College of Fashion before moving to New York and launching her first collection in 1989. Working for many years as an acclaimed fashion editor and stylist for magazines such as *Interview*, Italian *Vogue* and *i-D*, Bartlett launched her VPL (Visible Panty Line) collection in 2003.

www.vplnyc.com

Viktor & Rolf

Viktor Horsting and Rolf Snoeren were born in 1969. They both studied in the fashion department of the Arnhem Academy, Holland, from 1989 to 1992. They launched their haute couture collection in 1998, following up with a ready-to-wear line in March 2000. Their menswear collection was debuted in 2003.

www.viktor-rolf.com

Vivienne Westwood

Born in 1941, Vivienne Westwood began designing fashion when she met Malcolm McLaren in 1971. Her signature punk looks for the Sex Pistols marked an era. By 1984 she had moved her attention away from street style and to the salons of haute couture, splitting her brand into Gold Label high fashion and Red Label ready-to-wear.

www.viviennewestwood.com

Wacoal Dia

Atsuko Kamio has been fascinated by dress and lingerie design since her childhood in Japan. Today living between Paris and Tokyo, she oversees her Wacoal Corp label, established in 2002. Taking 'creation of new lingerie culture' as its motto, Wacoal Dia has two flagship boutiques in Tokyo, showcasing its underwear-as-outwear aesthetic.

www.wacoaldia.com

Yumi Katsura

Yumi Katsura studied at the Ecole de la Chambre Syndicale de la Couture Parisienne, opening her first bridal salon in Japan in 1964. In 1999 she became the first Asian member of the Haute Couture of the Camera Nazionale della Moda Italiana and since 2003 she has presented her collections during the Paris haute couture season.

www.yumikatsura.com

Zaki Bin Aboud

Zaki Bin Aboud studied Languages, Social Science and Business Administration before moving to fashion design. She launched her own-name clothing line in 1998 in Jeddah, Saudia Arabia. Zaki, who says her designs are 'mainly targeted at the GCC market and the United States', was named Best Saudi Designer in 2003.

info@zaki-sa.net

Zandra Rhodes

Zandra Rhodes studied printed textile design at London's Royal Academy of Art. In 1967 she established her own brand, selling her collections in New York. In 1975 she opened her own shop off London's fashionable Bond Street. She is the founder of the Fashion and Textile Museum in London, opened in 2003.

www.zandrarhodes.com

Zuhair Murad

Born in Lebanon, Zuhair Murad studied Fashion Design in Beirut before obtaining a degree in Fashion in Paris. He returned to Lebanon, opening his own atelier and boutique in 1995. In 1999 he began showing in Rome, and since 2001 has shown his twice-yearly collections during the Paris haute couture shows.

www.zuhairmurad.com

ALSO IN ATTENDANCE...

Astier de Villatte
www.astierdevillatte.com

Caran d'Ache
www.carandache.ch

Christofle
www.christofle.com

Crane & Co
www.crane.com

Creative Intelligence
www.creativeintelligence.com

Deyafa Gallery
deyafa_arabia@hotmail.com

Fendi Studio
www.fendi.com

Fleux
www.fleux.com

Gina
www.gina.com

Godiva
www.godiva.com

Kopenhagen Fur
www.kopenhagenfur.dk

Manufacture de Monaco
www.mdpm.com

Moët & Chandon
www.moet.com

Möve Frottana
www.moeve.de

Noel Stewart Millinery
www.noelstewart.com

On Aura Tout Vu
oatv@aol.com

Only Hearts
www.onlyhearts.com

RedBliss
www.redbliss.com

Stuart Weitzman
www.stuartweitzman.it

Shepherds
www.bookbinding.co.uk

Toppers with Glitz
www.topperswithglitz.com

Yves Delorme
www.yvesdelorme.com

THANKS TO THE BAND...

PAGES 10-31: Photographer's Assistant, Chris Miller. Fashion Assistant, Olly Paton. Retouching, Provision. Casting, Thomas at Pure Productions. With thanks to Sarah Eastel film locations (www.film-locations.co.uk).

PAGES 40-51: Photographer's Assistants, Antoine Cadot and Valentin Roman. Fashion Assistant, Ellie Cumming. Digital Technician, Anne-Marie Van Dogen at Dtouch. P41 Pearls, Stylist's own. P42 Pearl necklace, vintage tulle headpiece, Stylist's own. P43 Feather headpiece, Stylist's own. P44 Pearls, Stylist's own. P45 Ribbon, VV Rouleaux, Feather headpiece and pearls, Stylist's own. P48 Ribbon, VV Rouleaux. Pearls and vintage tulle, Stylist's own. P49 Feather headpiece, Stylist's own. P51 Pants, vintage tulle headpiece, Stylist's own.

PAGES 62-76: Photographer's Assistants, Jamie Smalley and Tom Jackson. Fashion Assistant, Olly Paton. Digital Operator, Simon Crane. Retouching, Michael at Loop. With thanks to: Kenwood House, London; Company of Cooks at the Brewhouse, Kenwood; Sarah Eastel film locations (www.film-locations.co.uk).

PAGES 92-109: Picture Editor, Tuomas Korpijaakko. Photographer's Assistant, Nando Ponce. Fashion Assistants, Anthony Irvine, Natalie Dembinska. Casting, Gayle Jones at Lift Productions. Thanks to Elvis, Ron Parras. PP103, 104, 109 Shoes, Stylist's own. P106 Shoes, Model's own. Production, Dan May. On-Site production and location scouting, PJ Connolly. Shot at, and special thanks to: The Little White Wedding Chapel, The Graceland Wedding Chapel, The Little Church of the West, Viva Las Vegas Wedding Chapel. Special thanks to Donna, Deva and Marek.

PAGES 131-143: Models, Stina, Leia and Juno Persson Helleday. Photographer's assistant, Oscar Richt. Special thanks to all at Adamsky.

PAGES 187-197: Photographer's Assistants, Tom Jackson, Belinda Foorde. Fashion Assistant, Tony Irvine. Digital Operator, Klaus at Little Yellow Jacket. Shot at Big Sky Studios. Thanks to Sarah at Katy Barker.

PAGES 34-35, 54-55, 58-59, 80-81, 86-87, 126, 129, 151, 153, 161, 182-183: Model, Hanna Paat at Nathalie. Photographer's Assistant, Lowe Seger. Hair, Ivan Lapeyroux at Aurelien. Makeup, Julie at Box Management. Set Designer, Nathalie Combacedes at Otos. Special thanks to: Carole Lambert; Jean François Aloisi (www.studio-aloisi.com)

PAGES 37, 82-83, 85, 88-89, 116-117, 130-131, 135, 147, 150, 160, 162-163: Models, Esther de Jong, Ilona Oswald. Hair, Christophe Martinez at Aurelien. Makeup, Audrey Gautier at Box Management. Set Designer, Maurice Meister at Techorma. Flowers, Point Vert (thanks to Katia Eichinger). Special thanks to: Thomas Dallamano and family; Antonio Semeraro and family; Pierrette Pressing; la Marie de Didenheim.

PAGES 60-61, 78-79, 90-91, 122-123, 127, 128, 146, 156-157, 176-177, 180-181: Photographer's Assistant, Clement Duquenne. Set Designer, Christelle Goudin. Special thanks to Jean François Aloisi (www.studio-aloisi.com)

ADDITIONAL RETOUCHING, BILEL BOUCHOUIT.
THANKS TO ORANGE DIGITAL, LONDON
WWW.ORANGE.UK.COM

ABOUT THE BOOK

Swarovski especially commissioned world-renowned designers to create the one-of-a-kind wedding designs featured in this book. They represent the beautiful fusion of design skills and creative spirit, illuminated by the brilliance of CRYSTALLIZED™ – *Swarovski Elements*. These unique pieces took more than a year to bring to their full-blown, glittering perfection and will fire the imagination and bring delight to any woman contemplating that very special day. These are designs that would make any bride's dreams come true…

ABOUT THE BRAND

CRYSTALLIZED™ – *Swarovski Elements* is the product brand of Swarovski.

Back in 1895, Daniel Swarovski had a dream of creating a crystal so perfect that it captured both the eye and the heart. Now CRYSTALLIZED™ – *Swarovski Elements* makes that dream come true, symbolizing beauty in the eye of the beholder and the technological excellence and innovation that is Swarovski. CRYSTALLIZED™ – *Swarovski Elements* are not only found at international galas like the Academy Awards and the Cannes Film Festival, but also crack the code of conformity in everyday life.

The "Made with CRYSTALLIZED™ – *Swarovski Elements*" tag can be found on fashion, jewellery and interior pieces that use the ultimate crystal, the product of more than a century of dedication to perfection.